Study Guide

T0369598

Geography
for CSEC®

Simon Ross
Alison Rae
Michael Clarke
Henderson Nurse
Judy Rocke

OXFORD
UNIVERSITY PRESS

Great Clarendon Street, Oxford, OX2 6DP, United Kingdom

Oxford University Press is a department of the University of Oxford. It furthers the University's objective of excellence in research, scholarship, and education by publishing worldwide. Oxford is a registered trade mark of Oxford University Press in the UK and in certain other countries

British Library Cataloguing in Publication Data
Data available

978-0-19-841386-8

11

Printed by CPI Group (UK) Ltd, Croydon CR0 4YY

Acknowledgements
Cover photograph: Mark Lyndersay, Lyndersay Digital, Trinidad www.lyndersaydigital.com
Illustrations: David Russell Illustration
Page make-up: Pantek Media, Maidstone

The author and the publisher would also like to thank the following for permission to reproduce material:

p14(t): from 'Geography in Place: Homework Copymasters' by Michael Raw and Sue Shaw, published by Collins Educational an imprint of Harper Collins (1999); **p14(b):** adapted from Earth and Man by B.J. Knapp; **p22:** from 'Landslide Hazard Geo Factsheet' by Simon Ross, published by Curriculum Press (2001). Reproduced with permission; **p55:** Nutrients Cycling in an Ecosystem Copyright © 2009 Field Studies Council; **pp116-117:** © World Trade Press; **p123:** Demographic Transition Model from www.coolgeography.co.uk Copyright © Robert Gamesby; **p124:** Adapted from Demographic Statistics (various years) © 2012 Statistical Institute of Jamaica; **p128:** Copyright © United Nations 2012; **p135(t):** Copyright © 2012, Government of Barbados; **p156:** from Philip's Certificate Atlas for the Caribbean (6th Edition); **p164:** from Caribbean Lands by J. MacPherson, published by Longman an imprint of Pearson Education (1980); **p100:** US Geological Survey, Department of Interiors/USGS; **p102:** Copyright © 2006 AOML. All rights reserved; **p103:** Bureau of Meteorology Copyright 2012; **p107:** Lindsay, J. M., Robertson, R.E.A., Shepherd, J.B. & Ali, S. (eds) 2005. Volcanic Hazard Atlas of the Lesser Antilles. Seismic Research Unit, The University of the West Indies, Trinidad & Tobago, W.I; **p109:** © National Oceanic and Atmospheric Administration/ National Weather Service (2004).

Photographs
Cover: Marc Lyndersay; **p7:** Kevin West/AP/Press Association Images; **p13:** Vladimir Melnik/Fotolia; **p15:** Ulrich Doering/ Alamy Stock Photo; **p16:** Island Images/Alamy Stock Photo; **p17:** Shutterstock; **p19:** © Brandon J. Vogt, University of Colorado, Colorado Springs; **p21:** Dr. Marli Miller, VISUALS UNLIMITED/ SCIENCE PHOTO LIBRARY; **p22:** VANDERLEI ALMEIDA/Getty Images; **p24:** Maher/iStockphoto; **p25:** christian-colista/Fotolia;

p27: Annie Griffiths Belt/Getty Images; **p28:** Dave Saunders/Art Directors & Trip; **p29(t):** Orietta Gaspari/iStockphoto; **p29(b):** © Barbados Tourism Authority; **p35:** Danita Delimont/Alamy Stock Photo; **p42:** NOAA/Science Photo Library; **p45:** Sipa Press/ Rex Features; **p46:** Arctic-Images/Getty Images; **p49:** Alexander/ Fotolia; **p50:** Helene Rogers/Art Directors and Trip; **p51(t):** Wigton Windfarm; **p51(b):** Karen Austen; **p52:** Fenton/Fotolia; **p53(t):** SteveStone/iStockphoto; **p53(b):** Sam Toren/Alamy Stock Photo; **p58:** blickwinkel/Alamy Stock Photo; **p57:** geogphotos/Alamy Stock Photo; **p60:** Trees That Feed; **p61(t):** Iwokrama Canopy Walkway; **p61(b):** Pete Oxford/Getty Images; **p62:** REUTERS/Eduardo Munoz; **p63:** sweetlifephotos/iStockphoto; **p64:** Shutterstock; **p70:** Tom Bean/Corbis; **p71(l):** mediacolor's/Alamy Stock Photo; **p71(r):** Birgit Prentner/iStockphoto; **p73:** Phil Degginger/Alamy Stock Photo; **p74:** Michael Snell/Getty Images; **p78:** Alphotographic/Alan Hewitt/ iStockphoto; **p79:** Shutterstock; **p80:** Olivier Staples/Alamy Stock Photo; **p81:** Chris Warren/Getty Images; **p84:** RIEGER Bertrand/ hemis.fr/Getty Images; **p85:** © Garrett Nagle; **p88:** Shutterstock; **p91:** Mika Specta/Fotolia; **p94:** Sergio Pitamitz/robertharding/ Getty Images; **p95:** Nelly Boyd / Alamy Stock Photo; **p96:** THONY BELIZAIRE/AFP/Getty Images; **p99:** Westend61 GmbH/Alamy Stock Photo; **p101:** Federico Gambarini/DPA/Press Association Images; **p103:** Glen Hinkson/Reuters/Corbis; **p104:** Joe Raedle/Getty Images; **p105:** Carlyle Noel/AP/Press Association Images; **p106:** © Garrett Nagle; **p107:** © Garrett Nagle; **p108:** © Matthew Kyte/ Alamy Stock Photo; **p114(t):** Shutterstock; **p114(b):** Frank van den Bergh/iStockphoto; **p114(t):** wrangel/iStockphoto; **p114(bl):** Jacques Descloitres, MODIS Land Rapid Response Team, NASA/GSFC; **p114(br):** Shutterstock; **p120(t):** Fotos593/Shutterstock; **p120(b):** Paul Harris/Getty Images; **p121(t):** Shutterstock; **p121(m):** Steve Mason/Getty Images; **p121(b):** Shutterstock; **p126:** Barry Lewis/ Alamy Stock Photo; **p128:** John Brown/Alamy Stock Photo; **p131:** photosite/Fotolia; **p133(t):** Robert Ulrich/Destination Jamaica; **p133(b):** © Katherine James; **p135(b):** MARKA/Alamy Stock Photo; **p139(t):** Shutterstock; **p139(b):** Jim West/Alamy Stock Photo; **p140:** The Nature Conservancy; **p141(t):** Shutterstock; **p131(b):** Vadim Demianovich/123rf; **p142:** Wesley Bocxe/SCIENCE PHOTO LIBRARY; **p143:** Tony Arruza/Getty Images; **p144:** Lefteris Papaulakis/ Shutterstock; **p150:** Prisma Bildagentur AG/Alamy Stock Photo; **p151:** REUTERS/Alamy Stock Photo; **p153:** VisualField/iStockphoto; **p157(t):** Shutterstock; **p157(m):** Andrey Lobachev/Shutterstock; **p157(b):** Copyright © 2012, www.blackrocklodge.com; **p159(t):** Zak Waters/Alamy Stock Photo; **p159(b):** Shutterstock; **p160:** © Garrett Nagle; **p161(t):** © Garrett Nagle; **p161(b):** dbimages/ Alamy Stock Photo; **p167:** Shutterstock; **p172:** John Larson/Fotolia; **p174:** © Simon Ross; **p176(t):** dbimages/Alamy Stock Photo; **p179:** robertharding/Alamy Stock Photo; **p180:** SIMON FRASER/SCIENCE PHOTO LIBRARY; **p181:** Ruslan Bustamante/Alamy Stock Photo.

Artwork by Cenveo and Dave Russell (**p23**, **p46**).

Every effort has been made to trace the copyright holders but if any have been inadvertently overlooked the publisher will be pleased to make the necessary arrangements at the first opportunity.

Although we have made every effort to trace and contact all copyright holders before publication this has not been possible in all cases. If notified, the publisher will rectify any errors or omissions at the earliest opportunity

Links to third party websites are provided by Oxford in good faith and for information only. Oxford disclaims any responsibility for the materials contained in any third party website referenced in this work

Contents

Contents

Access your support website for additional content and activities here:
www.oxfordsecondary.com/9780198413868

Introduction

This Study Guide has been developed exclusively with the Caribbean Examinations Council (CXC®) to be used as an additional resource by candidates, both in and out of school, following the Caribbean Secondary Education Certificate (CSEC®) programme.

It has been prepared by a team with expertise in the CSEC® syllabus, teaching and examination. The contents are designed to support learning by providing tools to help you achieve your best in Geography and the features included make it easier for you to master the key concepts and requirements of the syllabus. Do remember to refer to your syllabus for full guidance on the course requirements and examination format!

This Study Guide is supported by a website which includes electronic activities to assist you in developing good examination techniques:

• **On Your Marks** activities provide sample examination-style short answer and essay-type questions, with example candidate answers and feedback from an examiner to show where answers could be improved. These activities will build your understanding, skill level and confidence in answering examination questions.

• **Test Yourself** activities are specifically designed to provide experience of multiple-choice examination questions and helpful feedback will refer you to sections inside the Study Guide so that you can revise problem areas.

This unique combination of focused syllabus content and interactive examination practice will provide you with invaluable support to help you reach your full potential in CSEC® Geography.

Theory of plate tectonics

The structure of the Earth

If you slice an apple in half you will see three layers. The thin apple skin is the outer layer. Beneath this is the thick fleshy layer and at the centre is the apple core. The structure of the Earth is a bit like this (see Figure 1.1.1):

• **Crust** – the thin solid outer layer up to a thickness of about 70 km. Notice on Figure 1.1.1 that there are two types of crust, **oceanic** and **continental**.

• **Mantle** – this is a very thick layer extending to about 2,900 km. It is mostly dense and solid, although there is a thin semi-liquid layer in the upper mantle.

• **Core** – this can be divided into a liquid outer core and an iron-rich solid inner core. Temperatures here are extremely hot (5,500°C). The centre of the Earth is 6,400 km below the surface.

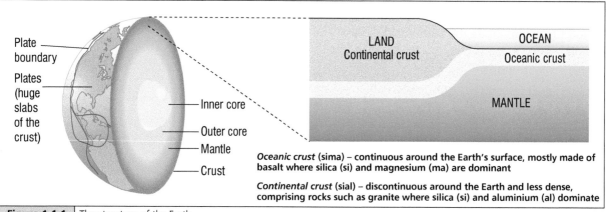

Oceanic crust (sima) – continuous around the Earth's surface, mostly made of basalt where silica (si) and magnesium (ma) are dominant

Continental crust (sial) – discontinuous around the Earth and less dense, comprising rocks such as granite where silica (si) and aluminium (al) dominate

Labels: Plate boundary; Plates (huge slabs of the crust); Inner core; Outer core; Mantle; Crust; LAND Continental crust; OCEAN Oceanic crust; MANTLE

Figure 1.1.1 The structure of the Earth

The theory of plate tectonics

Unlike the skin of an apple the Earth's crust is not a continuous layer. Instead it is broken into several large sections called **plates**. Each plate is about 100 km thick and is made up of the crust and the upper part of the mantle. The solid plates rest on a semi-liquid layer in the upper mantle and this enables them to move in relation to each other.

Look at Figure 1.1.2. Notice the following features:

• The Earth is split into several large plates, such as the Pacific and North American, and a number of much smaller plates, such as the Cocos plate and the Caribbean plate.

• The arrows indicate the direction of movement of the plates – on average they move just a few centimetres each year, roughly the same speed as the growth of your fingernails!

• Earthquakes are concentrated at the edges (boundaries) of the plates. This is where pressure builds up and is then suddenly released, resulting in an earthquake.

- There are four main types of plate margins: divergent, convergent, collision and transform.

What causes the plates to move?

Deep within the Earth the temperatures are extremely high. As the heat spreads out and flows towards the surface it forms a number of large convection (heat) cells (see Figure 1.1.3). These heat flows, called **convection currents**, rise from deep in the mantle and move towards the surface. They then spread below the crustal plates, cool and finally descend back down into the mantle.

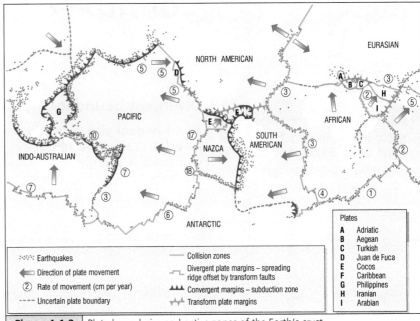

Plates	
A	Adriatic
B	Aegean
C	Turkish
D	Juan de Fuca
E	Cocos
F	Caribbean
G	Philippines
H	Iranian
I	Arabian

Earthquakes
Direction of plate movement
② Rate of movement (cm per year)
Uncertain plate boundary
Collision zones
Divergent plate margins – spreading ridge offset by transform faults
Convergent margins – subduction zone
Transform plate margins

Figure 1.1.2 Plate boundaries and active zones of the Earth's crust

What is the evidence for plate tectonics?

Some 250 million years ago the continents of the world were joined together to form one enormous continent called Pangaea. Since then the continents have drifted apart to their current position. They are still moving today as part of the world's giant plates.

The scientific evidence to support 'continental drift' includes:

- Identical rocks in South America and West Africa.
- When two continents, such as South America and Africa, are placed together they join up to form a perfect fit, rather like two pieces of a jigsaw puzzle.

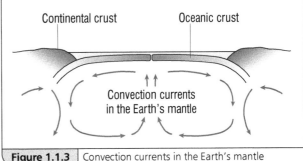

Figure 1.1.3 Convection currents in the Earth's mantle

- Identical species of land-based fossils (creatures that could not fly or swim) have been found in continents that are today separated by wide oceans.
- The rocks on the ocean floor (oceanic plate) become steadily older the further they are from the middle of the ocean. As fresh volcanic rocks form at a mid-oceanic ridge (divergent margin) a conveyor-like movement pushes the rocks outwards from the centre.

During the 1960s and 1970s further scientific evidence led to a greater understanding of convection currents and of the mechanisms involved in plate tectonics. Patterns of earthquakes, volcanoes, mountain ranges and deep ocean trenches provided evidence of the precise location of the active plate boundaries.

Even today, scientists are still developing their understanding of the theory of plate tectonics in the light of recent earthquakes and volcanic activity.

EXAM TIP

In order to start preparing for your examination you must first obtain a copy of the current syllabus. Remember to practise drawing diagrams that you may need to use to answer questions in the examination.

1.2 Types of plate boundary

LEARNING OUTCOME

- Understand the processes and landforms at divergent, convergent, collision and transform plate margins.

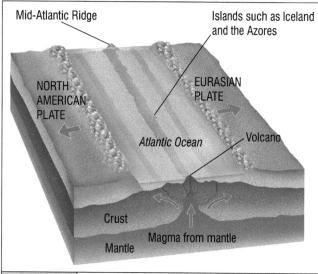

Figure 1.2.1 Divergent plate margin: the mid-Atlantic Ridge

Figure 1.2.2 Convergent plate margin: the Andes, South America

Divergent boundary

At a **divergent** plate boundary (margin) two plates are moving away from each other. This type of boundary is sometimes called a **constructive margin**. This is because new crust is being formed, effectively 'constructing' new plate.

Look at Figure 1.2.1. Notice the following features:

- A rising convection current is causing the crust to crack, allowing molten rock (**magma**) to pass through it on its way towards the surface.
- Some magma escapes to the surface as **lava** erupted from underwater volcanoes. The volcanoes at this boundary form a mountain range called a **mid-oceanic ridge**. In places this rises above the surface to form islands, such as Iceland in the North Atlantic.
- Over millions of years, as new plate material forms at the mid-oceanic ridge, the plates extend outwards and diverge.

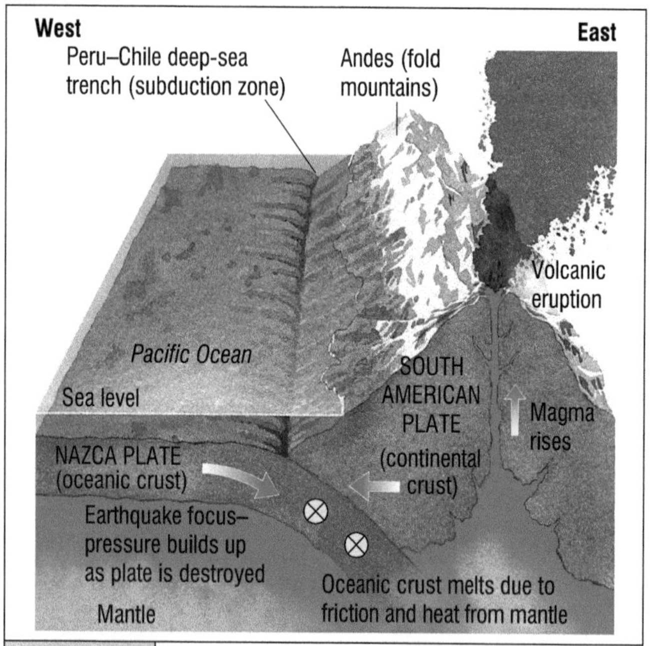

Convergent boundary

At a **convergent** (or **destructive**) plate boundary two plates are moving towards one another. If one of the plates is made of dense oceanic crust it will dive down beneath the other plate to form a **subduction zone**. Here, immense heat melts and destroys the subducting plate.

Look at Figure 1.2.2. Notice the following features:

- The Nazca plate to the west is diving beneath the less dense continental crust that forms part of the South American plate.
- As the Nazca plate descends, friction along the plate margin triggers earthquakes.
- The oceanic crust is melting and magma is forcing its way to the surface to form volcanoes.
- The crumpling of sea-floor sediments at this boundary creates fold mountains which, together with the newly formed volcanoes, form the Andes.

Collision margin

When two plates of continental crust converge they form a **collision margin**. Here, there is no subduction since both are of the same density. Instead the layers in the seabed between them crumple to form fold mountain ranges such as the Himalayas (see Figure 1.2.3):

- The enormous pressures and sudden cracking of rocks often triggers powerful earthquakes in these regions.
- There is no magma at these plate boundaries owing to the lack of subduction. This means that there are no volcanoes.

Transform boundary

At a **transform** plate boundary two plates are sliding alongside each other (see Figure 1.2.4a). The two plates may be moving in opposite directions or they may be moving at different speeds in the same direction. There is no subduction taking place at this margin and no creation of magma. This explains why there are no volcanoes along the San Andreas Fault (see Figure 1.2.4b).

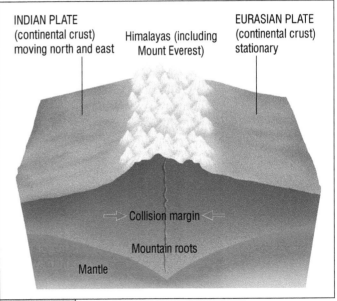

| **Figure 1.2.3** | Collision boundary: the Himalayas |

EXAM TIP

Practise drawing cross-sections of the three types of plate boundaries because you may be asked to do so in the examination.

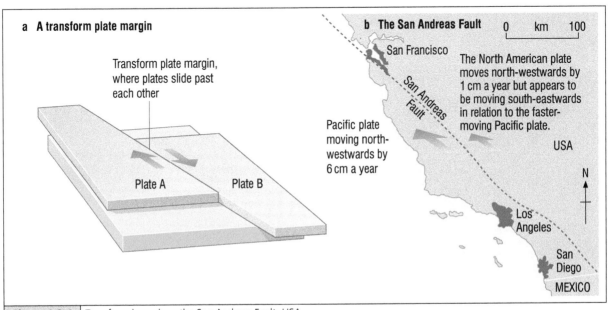

| **Figure 1.2.4** | Transform boundary: the San Andreas Fault, USA |

LEARNING OUTCOME

- Understand the types of plate margins and landforms associated with the Caribbean plate.

The Caribbean plate

Much of the Caribbean region lies on the Caribbean plate (see Figure 1.3.1). The boundaries of the Caribbean plate are extremely active as it is being squeezed by converging plates on either side. Notice the following features:

- On the northern edge there is a transform boundary between the Caribbean plate and the North American plate. Sideways movement occurring along this boundary has been responsible for several major earthquakes, the most recent being the 2010 Haiti earthquake, which killed over 230,000 persons.

- At the western boundary, oceanic crust making up the Cocos plate is subducting beneath the Caribbean plate, forming a zone of volcanoes, earthquakes and fold mountains in Central America.

- The southern boundary is highly complex, being part convergent and part transform. While earthquakes do occur here, it is not as active as the other Caribbean plate boundaries.

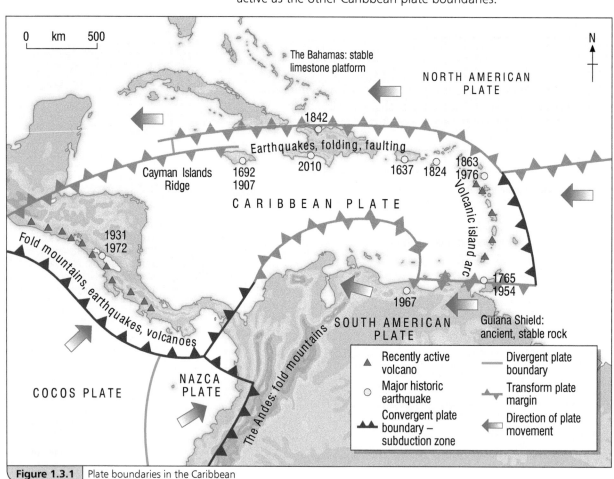

Figure 1.3.1 Plate boundaries in the Caribbean

- To the east an active convergent boundary exists between the South American plate and the Caribbean plate. The subducting South American plate is responsible for the formation of a chain of mostly volcanic islands called the Lesser Antilles.

Formation of the Lesser Antilles volcanic arc

Most of the islands that form the Lesser Antilles in the eastern Caribbean are volcanic. They have been formed at a convergent plate boundary where the South American plate is subducting beneath the Caribbean plate (see Figure 1.3.2).

Lines of weakness develop in the overlying continental crust and magma rising from deep underground reaches the surface to form a chain of volcanoes called an island arc. Many of the volcanoes have erupted violently in the past, such as Mt Pelée on Martinique, which killed 30,000 persons in 1902. In recent years, Soufrière Hills on Montserrat has been erupting, leading to the evacuation of many villagers from the south of the island (see Figure 1.3.3).

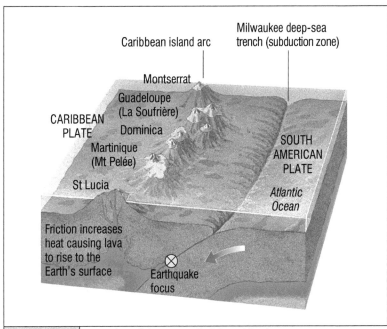

Figure 1.3.2 | Formation of the eastern Caribbean island arc

Figure 1.3.3 | The eruption of the Soufrière Hills volcano, Montserrat, in 1997

Occurrence and distribution of earthquakes and volcanoes

Earthquakes

An **earthquake** is a sudden violent shaking of the ground. Look at Figure 1.4.1 and notice the following features of an earthquake:

• The point within the crust where an earthquake originates is called the **focus**.

• The point on the ground surface immediately above the focus is called the **epicentre**.

• The shockwaves that radiate out from the focus are **seismic waves**. These are responsible for the shaking that is felt on the ground.

• An earthquake usually triggers movement along a crack called a **fault**.

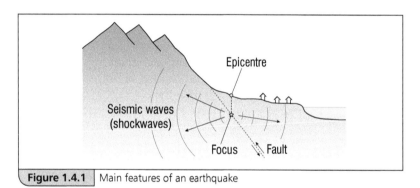

| Figure 1.4.1 | Main features of an earthquake |

Each year there are thousands of earthquakes across the world, the majority of which are not strong enough to be felt. When earthquakes are plotted on a world map they form an interesting pattern (see Figure 1.4.2).

Notice that earthquakes tend to be concentrated in clear linear belts, for example around the edges of the Pacific Ocean and through the middle of the Atlantic Ocean. This is because the majority of earthquakes are found at the plate boundaries (see also Figure 1.3.1, page 6). Here enormous pressures build up before suddenly being released. It is this sudden breaking or snapping, deep within the Earth's crust, that creates an earthquake.

Volcanoes

Volcanoes are often tall conical landforms resulting from the emission of lava, rocks, ash, steam and poisonous gases such as sulphur dioxide and chlorine. Figure 1.4.3 shows the typical features of a volcano. Notice how it

| Figure 1.4.2 | Major earthquakes zones around the world |

has become larger with every eruption and how it is made of alternate layers of lava and ash.

Volcanoes do vary enormously in their size and shape owing to the chemical composition of the magma (see page 13).

Look at Figure 1.4.4, which shows the distribution of volcanoes.

- As with earthquakes the majority of volcanoes are found along plate margins. It is here where there is molten rock or magma to supply the volcanoes.

- Can you identify the famous **'Ring of Fire'** stretching around the edge of the Pacific Ocean? This is where the greatest concentration of volcanoes lies.

- Notice that there are no volcanoes at collision margins (such as the Himalayas) or transform margins (such as the northern part of the Caribbean plate). This is because there is no supply of magma.

- Some isolated volcanoes exist a long way from plate margins, such as Mauna Loa on Hawaii. These locations are known as **'hot spots'** and are formed where the crust is particularly weak, allowing the underlying magma to break through along cracks and fractures.

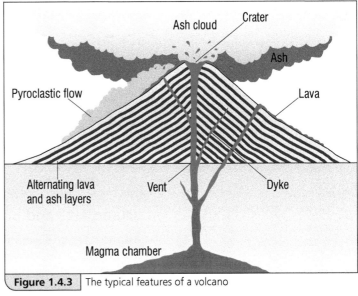

Figure 1.4.3 | The typical features of a volcano

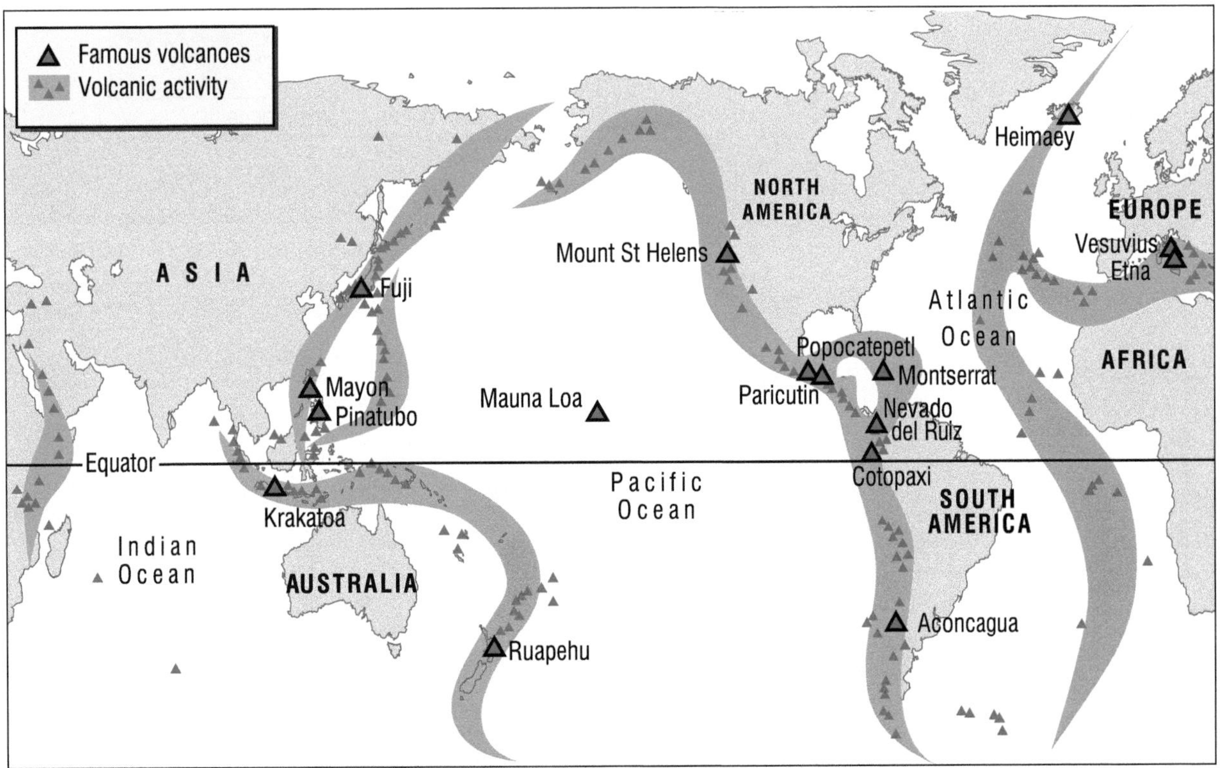

Figure 1.4.4 | Global distribution of volcanoes

1.5

Occurrence and distribution of island arcs, ocean trenches, fold mountains and major faults

Island arcs and ocean trenches

Island arcs and **ocean trenches** are landforms associated with mid-oceanic convergent plate margins. As one oceanic plate dives beneath another a deep ocean trench is formed. As the plate subducts, melting occurs forming magma. This rises to the surface to form volcanoes which eventually break the water surface to form islands. A series of volcanoes along a length of the plate margin creates an island arc (see Figure 1.5.1).

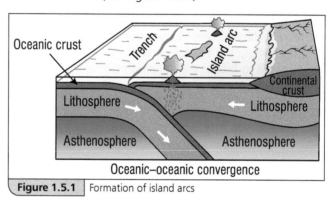

Figure 1.5.1 Formation of island arcs

Figure 1.5.2 shows the distribution of island arcs and ocean trenches. Notice that the majority are located around the Pacific 'Ring of Fire'.

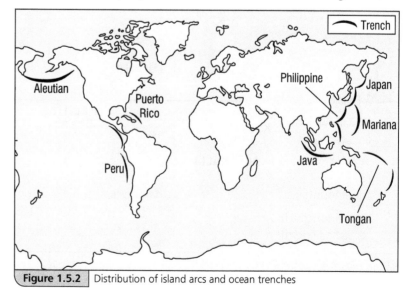

Figure 1.5.2 Distribution of island arcs and ocean trenches

Fold mountains

At convergent and collision margins, ocean sediments and continental crust can buckle and fold (bend) as a result of the enormous pressures squeezing the rocks together. Huge **fold mountain** ranges such as the Andes and Himalayas can form as these folded rocks are thrust upwards by the converging plates at these plate margins (see Figure 1.5.3).

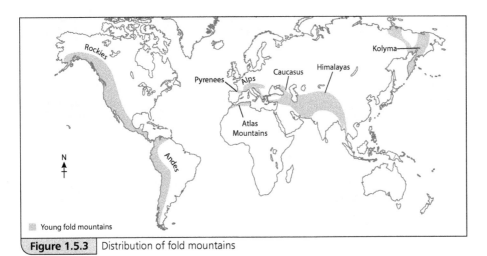

Figure 1.5.3 | Distribution of fold mountains

Major faults

The enormous pressures generated by tectonic activity can cause extensive fracturing or faulting of the crust. **Major faults** are often associated with transform plate margins where opposing forces tear the rocks apart, for example the San Andreas Fault. Figure 1.5.4 shows the distribution of these major faults.

The Mariana Trench is the world's deepest trench, with a depth of 11,000 m. This distance below sea level is equivalent to the cruising altitude above the ground of most aeroplanes!

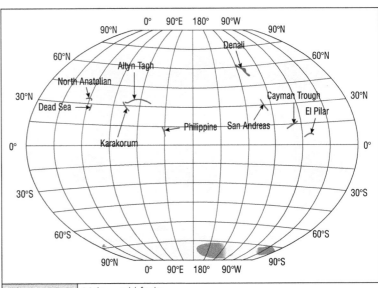

Figure 1.5.4 | Major world faults

SUMMARY QUESTIONS

1 Explain why ocean trenches and island arcs occur together in the oceans.

2 Describe the distribution of fold mountains.

3 Why do major faults form at tectonic plate margins?

Intrusive and extrusive volcanic features

- Understand the difference between intrusive and extrusive features.
- Understand the features associated with intrusive and extrusive activity.

DID YOU KNOW?

Off the north coast of Grenada, near Sauteurs, a dyke rose in the sea overnight (during the early part of the last century), forming a natural breakwater and producing a safe area for bathing on the normally rough north coast.

What is the difference between intrusive and extrusive features?

Magma is a mixture of molten rock, gases and liquids and is formed in the mantle. As it passes through the crust most of it cools before it reaches the surface. This cooling and solidifying of magma in cracks and joints forms **intrusive** volcanic features.

If magma reaches the Earth's surface, it will form **extrusive** volcanic features, the most obvious one being a volcano. So, try to remember that **in**trusive means 'in' the crust and **ex**trusive means on the surface.

Types of intrusive volcanic features

Look at Figure 1.6.1. Notice that there are several types of intrusive volcanic features:

- **Batholith** – this is an enormous mass of igneous rock, often hundreds of kilometres across, which forms when magma cools deep inside the crust. In the Caribbean the best-known example is the Tobago batholith, which extends from west to east and is about half the size of the island.

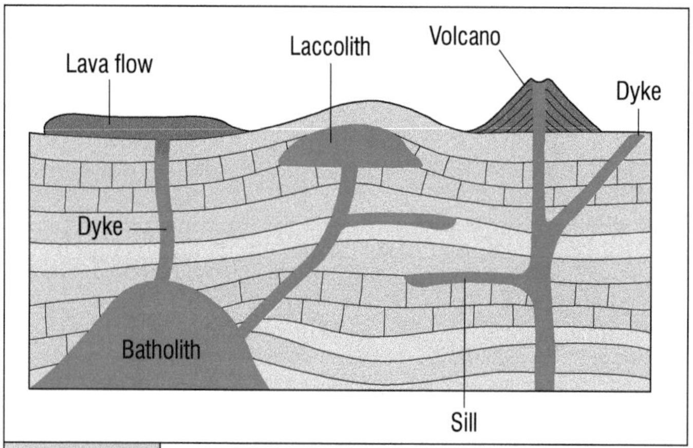

- **Dyke** – this is formed when magma passes through cracks or joints that cut across beds (layers) of rock. Dykes often occur in groups called **swarms**, for example at the southern tip of St Lucia.

- **Sill** – when magma forces its way between beds of rock it may solidify to form a sill.

- **Laccolith** – this is rather like a blister that has been formed between two layers of sedimentary rock, causing overlying rocks to arch upwards.

Figure 1.6.1 | Volcanic features

EXAM TIP

When answering questions about volcanoes you should be able to draw and label the distinctive features of the type of volcano you are describing.

Types of extrusive volcanic features

Look again at Figure 1.6.1 and notice that some of the volcanic features have been formed on the surface. These are extrusive volcanic features. They are formed when magma breaks through the crust to reach the surface. Once on the surface, the magma loses its gases. The liquid remaining is called **lava**.

- **Volcano** – most volcanoes are formed over many thousands of years by a series of eruptions through a central **vent** or opening. With each successive eruption the volcano grows a little higher. It is possible to identify two broad types of volcano: **shield** and **composite**. Figure 1.6.2 describes the differences between them.

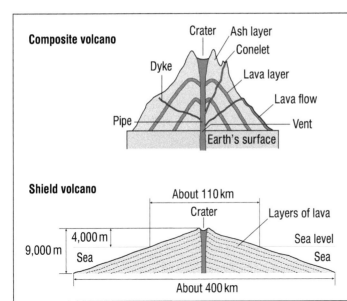

Composite volcano

Crater | Ash layer
Conelet
Dyke
Lava layer
Lava flow
Pipe
Vent
Earth's surface

Shield volcano

About 110 km
Crater
Layers of lava
4,000 m
Sea level
9,000 m
Sea
Sea
About 400 km

Composite

- Steep, conical volcano
- Typically formed at destructive plate margins
- Acidic magma (lava)
- Explosive eruptions

Shield

- Flat and broad volcano
- Typically formed at constructive margins
- Basic magma (lava)
- Gentle eruptions

Figure 1.6.2 Extrusive volcanic features

Occasionally a violent eruption may cause a volcano to blow its top off leaving behind a huge crater called a **caldera** (see Figure 1.6.3). If the underlying magma chamber has been emptied by the eruption, the surface may collapse to form a deep basin, which may in time contain a lake.

- **Lava plateau** – in some places, for example on Iceland on the Mid-Atlantic Ridge, fluid (basic) lava spreads out from linear cracks to cover large areas of the ground surface. These eruptions are called **fissure eruptions** (*fissure*=crack). One of the most extensive lava plateaus in the world is the Deccan Plateau in India, which covers nearly 650,000 km^2 (for comparison, the size of Jamaica is 10,991 km^2!).

Types of lava

It is possible to identify two broad types of lava (and magma):

- **Basic lava** – this is rich in iron and magnesium but has a low silica content. It is very hot, often reaching temperatures of 1,000–1,200°C. It is very 'runny' (fluid) and will flow on the surface for considerable distances to form broad, gently sloping cones. When it cools it forms an igneous rock called basalt. Basic lava is associated with constructive plate margins and with the formation of shield volcanoes.

- **Acid lava** – this low-temperature magma (800–1,000°C) is rich in silica, which makes it more viscous (thicker, less fluid) than basic lava. It does not flow far on the surface before it solidifies and results in high steep cones. Acid lava is associated with the formation of composite volcanoes at destructive plate margins. Eruptions tend to be more violent than at basic (shield) volcanoes.

DID YOU KNOW?

The Yellowstone Caldera in Wyoming, USA measures 55 × 72 km^2 in size and is the site of one of the world's 'supervolcanoes'. The caldera formed when the underlying magma chamber emptied during an eruption and the surface collapsed to form a huge basin. Yellowstone last erupted some 17,000 years ago.

Figure 1.6.3 The water-filled Quilotoa caldera in Chile

Intrusive volcanic landscapes

Intrusive volcanic features are often formed many hundreds of metres below ground. It is only when the overlying rocks have been removed by erosion that they become exposed on the surface to form landscape features.

Intrusive igneous rocks are usually tough and resistant to erosion. When exposed at the surface they are often eroded more slowly than the surrounding rocks and form ridges or upland areas.

• Vast batholiths may be exposed to form uplands, such as Dartmoor and Bodmin Moor in south-west England (see Figure 1.6.4).

| Figure 1.6.4 | Exposed granite batholith in south-west England |

• Sills and dykes are much smaller than batholiths and, when exposed, tend to form dips or ridges in the landscape (see Figure 1.6.5).

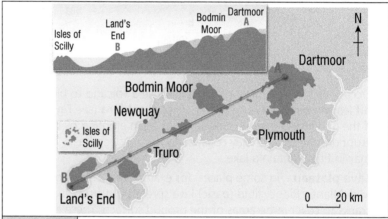

| Figure 1.6.5 | Landscape features formed by sills and dykes |

Extrusive volcanic landscapes

Extrusive volcanic features create immediate landscapes, either in the form of spectacular volcanoes or as extensive lava plateaus. On the surface these landforms are affected by weathering processes, such as oxidation (volcanic rocks are often rich in iron) and freeze-thaw.

Rivers and glaciers will sculpt these landscapes, forming valleys and gorges.

• Lava plateaus tend to form relatively flat landscapes. Rivers will carve broad valleys and the channels themselves will often be meandering (see Figure 1.6.6).

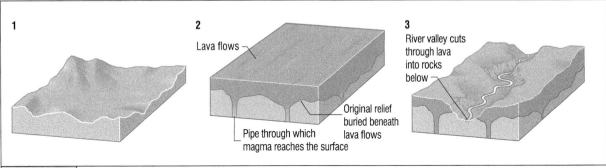

1

2

Lava flows

Original relief
buried beneath
lava flows

Pipe through which
magma reaches the surface

3

River valley cuts
through lava
into rocks
below

Figure 1.6.6 Formation and erosion of a lava plateau

Figure 1.6.7 The eroded volcano of Ol Doinyo Lengai in Tanzania

• Steep-sided volcanoes will be subjected to severe river erosion as the steep gradient leads to fast-flowing rivers. Deep gullies and valleys will radiate out from the centre of the volcano and large deposits of sediment (alluvial fans) will spread out at its base. Over a very long period of time all that will be left is the volcanic plug in the centre of the volcano (see Figure 1.6.8).

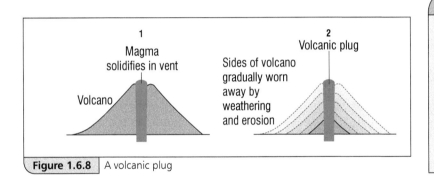

1

Magma
solidifies in vent

Volcano

2

Volcanic plug

Sides of volcano
gradually worn
away by
weathering
and erosion

Figure 1.6.8 A volcanic plug

The rock cycle

The rock cycle

The rocks that make up the Earth's crust are in a constant state of change due to processes such as weathering, erosion, transportation and deposition. It is this recycling of the Earth's rocks that is termed the rock cycle (see Figure 1.7.1).

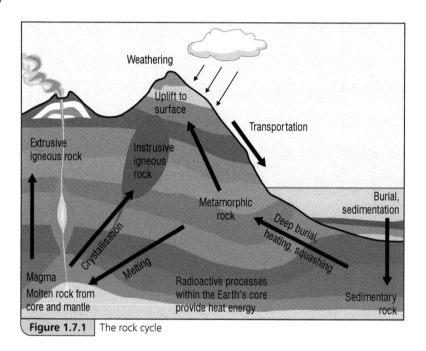

Figure 1.7.1 | The rock cycle

Figure 1.7.1 shows that the Earth's crust is made of three types of rock:

• **Igneous rocks** – these are rocks that have formed from the cooling of magma (*ignis* is the Latin word for 'fire') either below the surface (intrusive) or above the surface (extrusive). Igneous rocks are crystalline and are usually hard and resistant to erosion. Examples include granite (intrusive) and basalt (extrusive).

• **Sedimentary rocks** – these rocks form from the accumulation of sediment, most commonly in the oceans. They include sandstones, shales and limestones and they often contain signs of life (fossils). Sedimentary rocks usually form layers or beds. They tend to be weaker than igneous rocks and are more easily eroded.

• **Metamorphic rocks** – these rocks have undergone change as a result of intense heat or pressure. They are extremely strong and resistant to erosion, forming mountain ranges in many parts of the world. Examples of metamorphic rocks include slate (formed from shale and used as roofing), quartzite (from sandstone) and marble (from limestone).

Figure 1.7.2 | Limestone rock on Bathsheba beach in Barbados

There are examples of all three types of rock in the Caribbean, with the sedimentary rock limestone being one of the most common (see Figure 1.7.2).

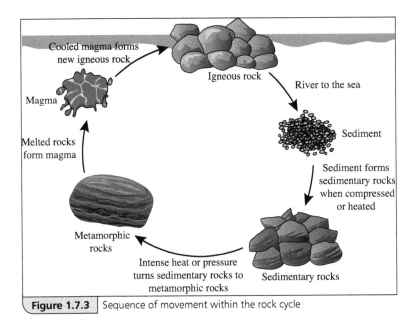

Figure 1.7.3 | Sequence of movement within the rock cycle

As Figure 1.7.3 shows, rocks are constantly 'on the move' within the rock cycle.

For example, igneous rocks at ground surface will be weathered and eroded by the wind and rain. The broken pieces of rock will then be transported by rivers or glaciers to be deposited in the sea. The layers of sediment that build up on the seabed will then be compressed and heated to form sedimentary rocks. These rocks may then be subjected to intense heat or pressure causing them to turn into metamorphic rocks. If the rocks are melted, magma will be formed which, when cooled, will form new igneous rock – and so the cycle is complete!

Figure 1.7.4 | Granite rocks on a beach

SUMMARY QUESTION

Draw a flow diagram to show how a grain of sand in the mountains can eventually be turned into the metamorphic rock quartzite.

Weathering

Weathering is the gradual breakdown or decay of rocks in their original place (in situ) at or close to the ground surface. As the name suggests it usually results from the weather such as rainfall and changes in temperature.

When rocks have been weakened they are easily picked up and carried away by wind, water (rivers and the sea) and ice (glaciers). This is called **erosion**. The combination of weathering and erosion in lowering a landscape is called **denudation**.

It is possible to identify three types of weathering:

1 **Physical weathering**. This involves rocks breaking apart but without any chemical change taking place.

2 **Chemical weathering**. This is where a chemical change causes rocks to dissolve or decay.

3 **Biotic (biological) weathering**. This involves living organisms, such as plants and animals (for example rabbits), or acids from rotting vegetation.

Several factors influence the type of weathering that occurs at any one place, such as the climate, the type of rock and the amount and type of vegetation. Often more than one type of weathering occurs at any one place.

Physical weathering

You need to understand three types of physical weathering: frost action, pressure release and temperature changes.

Frost action

Frost action, sometimes called freeze-thaw or frost shattering, is one of the most effective processes of physical weathering, although it is not very widespread in the Caribbean. Look at Figure 1.8.1 to see how it operates.

In order for frost action to be effective, there needs to be:

- plenty of rainfall
- frequently fluctuating temperatures above and below freezing
- rocks with cracks or holes.

This explains why frost action is severe in sub-Arctic regions, such as northern Canada, and mountains, such as the Rockies and the Andes. Much of the Caribbean is too warm for frost action to occur and, at the other extreme, Antarctica is too cold!

When frost action affects rocks on an exposed cliff or mountainside, angular rock fragments collect at the base to form scree. The jagged rock fragments may be carried by rivers and ice, where they become important 'tools' of erosion.

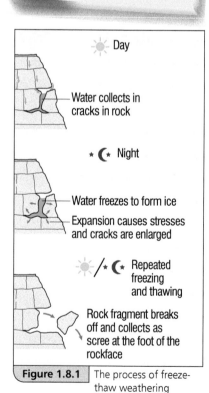

Day

Water collects in cracks in rock

Night

Water freezes to form ice

Expansion causes stresses and cracks are enlarged

Repeated freezing and thawing

Rock fragment breaks off and collects as scree at the foot of the rockface

Figure 1.8.1 The process of freeze-thaw weathering

Figure 1.8.2 | Crack caused by pressure release

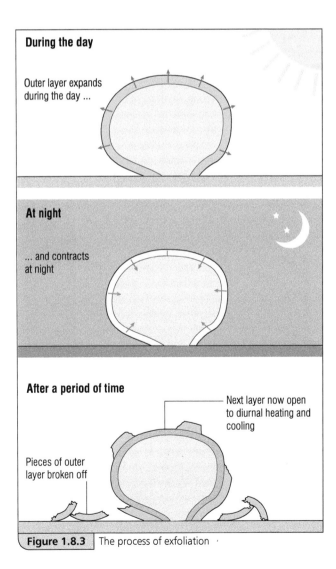

DID YOU KNOW?

Temperatures in hot deserts can reach over 45°C during the day and plummet below freezing at night. This is because the lack of cloud cover maximises daytime temperatures but allows heat to escape at night. The highest recorded temperature was 56.7°C in Death Valley, California, USA, in 1913.

Pressure release

Rocks deep underground are compressed by the immense weight of the rocks on top of them. When these overlying rocks are eroded, the pressure is released and the rocks below expand upwards, rather as if they were breathing out! This is **pressure release**.

Pressure release causes cracks to form parallel to the surface (see Figure 1.8.2).

Pressure release is responsible for causing large-scale rounded landforms, such as Half Dome in Yosemite National Park, USA. In the Caribbean, pressure release has been partly responsible for some of the granite landforms on Tobago.

Exfoliation

Extreme changes in temperature, such as those experienced in hot deserts, can also lead to exfoliation in rocks. High temperatures can cause the outer layer of rocks to expand whereas very cold temperatures lead to contraction. Regular temperature fluctuations will weaken the outer skin, eventually causing it to flake away (see Figure 1.8.3).

Some rocks, such as granite, are made up of different minerals. These minerals expand and contract at different rates causing the rock to break apart into granules. This is called granular disintegration.

During the day

Outer layer expands during the day ...

At night

... and contracts at night

After a period of time

Next layer now open to diurnal heating and cooling

Pieces of outer layer broken off

Figure 1.8.3 | The process of exfoliation

- Understand the processes of chemical and biotic (biological) weathering.

Carbon dioxide is more soluble in water at low temperatures. This means that the process of carbonation is more effective in cold climates than warm, tropical climates.

In some parts of the world, for example in Cheshire, UK, salt deposits underground are deliberately dissolved using pumped water. Once dissolved, the salty water (called brine) is pumped back to the surface and the water is evaporated to leave behind the solid salt. Salt is commonly used in the chemical industry.

Chemical weathering

Chemical weathering involves chemical changes taking place within a rock. It most commonly occurs when rocks are in contact with water. This explains why it is most active in tropical environments that experience high rainfall totals. Chemical weathering may cause minerals to be dissolved or cause them to turn into weak and easily eroded clay.

Carbonation

Carbonation is a process of chemical weathering that affects calcareous (calcite-rich) rocks such as limestone. Limestone is a common rock in the Caribbean. Look at Figure 1.8.4 to see how carbonation operates.

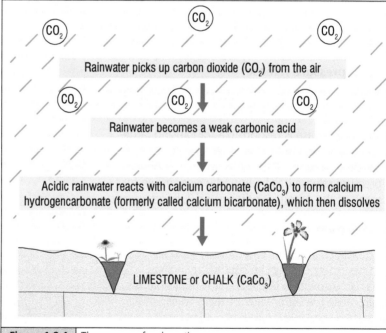

Rainwater picks up carbon dioxide (CO_2) from the air

Rainwater becomes a weak carbonic acid

Acidic rainwater reacts with calcium carbonate ($CaCo_3$) to form calcium hydrogencarbonate (formerly called calcium bicarbonate), which then dissolves

LIMESTONE or CHALK ($CaCo_3$)

Figure 1.8.4 The process of carbonation

Carbonation is responsible for a number of landforms associated with limestone (karst) scenery, such as limestone pavements and swallow holes (see pages 26–7).

Hydrolysis

Hydrolysis involves chemical change due to reaction with water. When mildly acidic rainwater falls on granite, a common igneous rock, the mineral feldspar reacts and turns into a white clay called

Figure 1.8.5 | Granite weathered by hydrolysis

kaolin (or china clay). This process weakens the granite, causing it to disintegrate (see Figure 1.8.5).

Biological weathering

Biological weathering results from the physical and chemical effects of living organisms. One of the most effective processes involves the growth of tree roots, which can prise apart joints in rocks (see Figure 1.8.6). Tree roots are amazingly strong and can penetrate several metres into underlying bedrock. Water may flow along these roots causing chemical weathering too.

Animals such as earthworms, coneys, rabbits and insects burrow into soil and weak rocks. This not only further weakens the rock but also enables water to soak into the ground where it may carry out chemical weathering.

Rotting vegetation will increase the acidity of rainwater as it collects on the ground and then soaks into the soil and rock. By increasing its acidity, the water becomes more effective in weathering the bedrock.

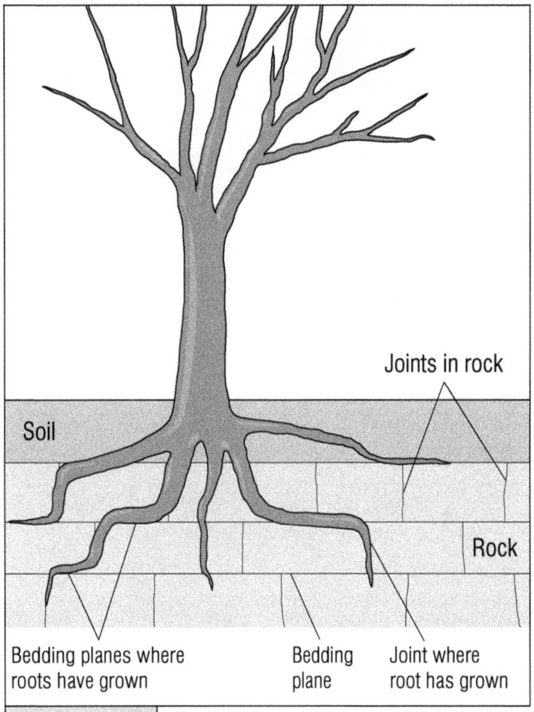

Joints in rock

Soil

Rock

Bedding planes where roots have grown

Bedding plane

Joint where root has grown

Figure 1.8.6 | Tree root action

SUMMARY QUESTIONS

Look at Figure 1.8.5.

1 What is the evidence that the rock is being affected by processes of chemical weathering?

2 Do you think biological weathering is happening?

3 Do you think frost action is likely to affect the rocks here?

Mass movement

- Understand the processes associated with mass movement.

Mass movement is the downhill movement of soil and rock under the influence of gravity. Landslides are an example of a fast movement whereas soil creep is an example of a slow movement.

Landslides

A **landslide** is a sudden downslope movement of part of a hillside. Landslides can involve large blocks of rock sliding downhill very rapidly. Alternatively, saturated soil and rock can 'flow' downhill and travel some distance. These are **mudflows**.

Several factors make a slope unstable and likely to collapse (see Figure 1.9.1). Notice that there are both physical and human factors.

There is usually a sudden event that triggers a landslide on an unstable slope, such as heavy rain, an earthquake or a volcanic eruption, as follows:

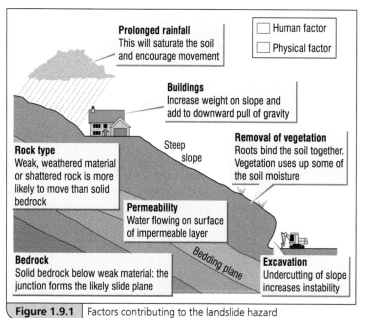

Prolonged rainfall
This will saturate the soil and encourage movement

☐ Human factor
☐ Physical factor

Buildings
Increase weight on slope and add to downward pull of gravity

Rock type
Weak, weathered material or shattered rock is more likely to move than solid bedrock

Steep slope

Removal of vegetation
Roots bind the soil together. Vegetation uses up some of the soil moisture

Permeability
Water flowing on surface of impermeable layer

Bedding plane

Bedrock
Solid bedrock below weak material: the junction forms the likely slide plane

Excavation
Undercutting of slope increases instability

Figure 1.9.1 Factors contributing to the landslide hazard

- **Heavy rain**. Water lubricates and adds weight to a slope. Water pressure often increases within the slope and this can trigger a landslide. Extreme rainfall events, such as hurricanes in the Caribbean or monsoon rains in India, frequently trigger landslides and mudflows. In 1999, torrential rain in Caracas, Venezuela triggered mudflows that killed over 30,000 persons and left over 200,000 persons homeless. In 2010, heavy rain triggered a massive landslide in the Brazilian city of Niterói, close to Rio de Janeiro. A wall of mud and rock slammed into an area of slum housing causing about 200 deaths.

- **Earthquakes**. Sudden ground shaking may cause an unstable slope to collapse. In 1970, a powerful earthquake caused the partial collapse of Huascarán mountain in Peru. The avalanche of rock and ice, travelling at speeds in excess of 300 km/h destroyed the town of Yungay in the Rio Santa Valley and killed some 20,000 persons.

- **Volcanic eruptions**. Volcanic eruptions are extremely violent events. Melting ice and snow can combine with ash to form a devastating mudflow called a lahar. In 1985, the volcano Nevado del Ruiz in Colombia erupted. An immense and fast-moving wall of mud slammed into the town of Armero, killing an estimated 22,000 persons.

Figure 1.9.2 Destruction caused by landslides after heavy rain in Brazil

Mameyes, Puerto Rico (1985)

Following a period of torrential rainfall associated with Tropical Storm Isabel, a huge slab of hillside collapsed in Mameyes, part of the sprawling city of Ponce. The landslide destroyed about 120 houses and killed over 100 persons, possibly as many as 300. This is the greatest number of casualties from a single landslide event in the Caribbean. Scientists believe that sewage discharged directly into the ground, together with a leaking pipe, may have contributed to the disaster.

Tobago (2004)

In November 2004, two individuals were killed and five wounded in a landslide that followed six hours of torrential rain. The clearing and burning of land on hillsides has been a contributory factor in landslides on the island.

- **Mining.** Coal mining can occasionally trigger landslides. In 1903, 76 persons were killed when a 30 million cubic metre chunk of Turtle Mountain collapsed on the small mining settlement of Frank in Alberta, Canada. In 1966, one of the UK's worst natural disasters involved the collapse of a coal spoil (waste) tip at Aberfan in Wales: 116 children and 5 teachers died when the landslide smashed into the primary school.

DID YOU KNOW?

The biggest landslide ever recorded occurred in 1980 when a huge section of the north face of Mt St Helens volcano collapsed unleashing a devastating volcanic eruption.

Soil creep

Soil creep is an extremely slow downhill movement of soil. While it is too slow to be able to see it happening, you can see evidence of the process on hillsides (see Figure 1.9.3).

Wet soil is more likely to move downhill, which is why the process is quite active during the wet season in tropical climates, such as the Caribbean. Movement often involves the alternate expansion and contraction associated with wetting and drying or freezing and thawing. This process is called heave.

EXAM TIP

Make sure that you understand the instructions in an examination. If you are asked to describe a landslide *do not* explain how it occurs.

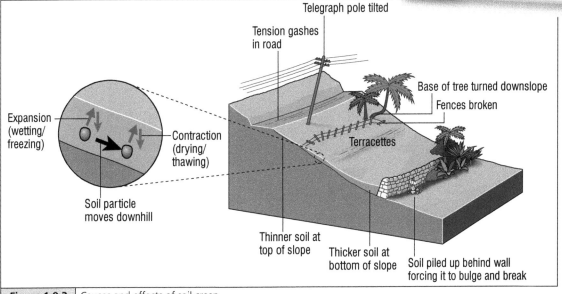

Figure 1.9.3 | Causes and effects of soil creep

Limestone – formation, characteristics and processes

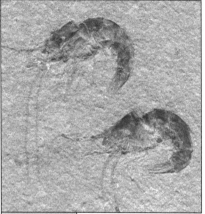

Figure 1.10.1 A pair of fossilised shrimp

Formation

Limestone is one of the world's most common types of rock. It is a sedimentary rock that forms in shallow seas under tropical conditions. In fact, new limestone is being formed at the present time in calm waters close to the Bahamas and in coral reefs throughout the Caribbean.

- Limestone is very rich in the chemical **calcium carbonate** ($CaCO_3$) and is known as a **calcareous** rock.
- Most limestone is formed from the remains of organic matter, such as shells, corals and plants. This accounts for its high concentration of calcium carbonate and explains why limestone is often full of interesting fossils (see Figure 1.10.1).

There are several different types of limestone:

- **Carboniferous limestone**. This grey limestone forms upland areas in the UK, such as the Pennine Hills. It was formed some 340 million years ago in tropical seas that were rich in shellfish and corals.
- **Jurassic limestone**. This type of limestone is found throughout the Caribbean. Formed 120–150 million years ago it is widespread in Cuba, Jamaica and Puerto Rico.
- **Oolitic limestone**. Ooliths are tiny balls of limestone, usually smaller than a pea. When a small fragment of shell or rock is rolled on the seabed, calcium carbonate dissolved in the water may be precipitated to form limestone. Over time, as more and more limestone forms on the shell or rock fragment, it grows in size to form an oolith. The ooliths eventually form great thicknesses and become compressed to form oolitic limestone. In the Caribbean, oolitic limestone can be found on the Turks and Caicos Islands. It is currently being formed on the Bahamas Platform.
- **Chalk**. Chalk is a white type of limestone that was formed in the Cretaceous geological period (145–65 million years ago). It is very rich in calcium carbonate (97 per cent) and is commonly found in the UK. Have you heard of the 'white cliffs of Dover'?

Characteristics of limestone

Limestone has a number of important characteristics that affect the processes acting on it and the landforms it produces. These are described in Figure 1.10.2.

Processes

The physical and chemical characteristics of limestone (see Figure 1.10.2) affect the types of processes that operate on it.

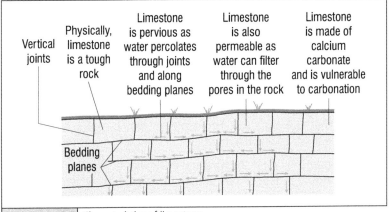

| | | Limestone is pervious as water percolates through joints and along bedding planes | Limestone is also permeable as water can filter through the pores in the rock | Limestone is made of calcium carbonate and is vulnerable to carbonation |

Vertical joints — Physically, limestone is a tough rock

Bedding planes

Figure 1.10.2 Characteristics of limestone

- **Carbonation**. This type of chemical weathering is very effective because limestone is so rich in calcium carbonate. Rainwater that has absorbed carbon dioxide from the air becomes mildly acidic (carbonic acid). This reacts with the calcium carbonate and causes it to slowly dissolve (see page 20). Carbon dioxide is more soluble in colder conditions. This explains why carbonation in the Caribbean is more likely to be effective during cooler nights rather than during the day. Chemical weathering is responsible for producing the extraordinary jagged limestone outcrop at Hell on Grand Cayman (see Figure 1.10.3).

The formula for carbonation is:

$$CaCO_3 \quad + \quad CO_2 \quad + \quad H_2O \quad \rightarrow \quad Ca(HCO_3)_2$$

Calcium carbonate   Carbon dioxide   Water   Calcium hydrogencarbonate (calcium bicarbonate)

- **Frost action**. This is common in temperate regions of the world. Water can collect in joints and cracks in the limestone. When it freezes, it expands, forcing the crack apart. Repeated cycles of freezing and thawing will eventually cause fragments of rock to break away (see Figure 1.8.1, page 18).
- **Mass movement**. Occasionally blocks of limestone may become detached resulting in landslides. Frost action may be responsible for rockfalls, when individual rock fragments fall from cliffs.
- **River erosion**. Limestone is pervious and water will readily flow through the joints and along bedding planes, sometimes forming fast-flowing underground rivers. These rivers are capable of carrying out intensive erosion to form features such as caverns. On the surface, however, there will be few rivers. This lack of surface river erosion partly explains why limestone tends to form upland areas.

Figure 1.10.3 Severely weathered limestone surface, Hell, Grand Cayman

Limestone landforms

Limestone landscapes

Limestone is a physically tough and resistant rock that usually forms upland areas. Its permeability results in few surface rivers unless the water table (the upper level of underground water) is particularly high. Chemical weathering causes it to dissolve, leaving behind very little rock material to form a soil. This explains why limestone areas are often bare and rocky, with few trees.

Look at Figure 1.11.1. It shows some of the landforms that can be found in limestone areas. Notice that some of the features are underground.

Surface landforms

Limestone pavements

- **Limestone pavements** are large and generally flat, exposed areas of limestone.
- The joints are often enlarged by weathering to form deep cracks called **grykes**. The blocks of rock between the grykes are called **clints**.
- Limestone pavements are very common in the Pennines in the UK. This is because, in the past, advancing glaciers stripped away the pre-existing soil and vegetation, exposing the limestone to weathering. They are also present around St Lucy and Barbados, and on Antigua.

Gorges and dry valleys

- In the past, when water tables were higher or when limestone was frozen during an ice age (for example in the UK some 12,000 years ago), water would have been able to flow over the surface of the limestone.

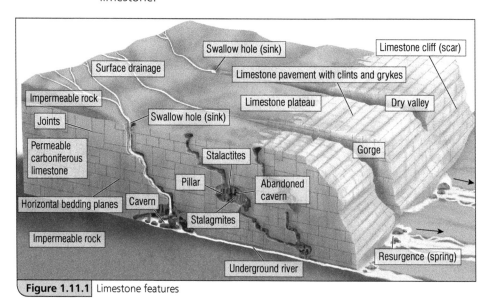

Figure 1.11.1 Limestone features

- **Valleys** and steep-sided **gorges** were eroded by fast-flowing rivers or glacial meltwater (Fern Gully is an example of a limestone gorge in Jamaica).
- Since water tables have fallen, these valleys and gorges have become 'dry'.

Swallow holes and surface depressions

- A **swallow hole** or sink is an enlarged joint down which water plunges as it flows off an impermeable rock onto limestone.
- Erosion and weathering processes often lead to the swallow hole becoming wide enough for potholers to enter underground cave systems (see Figure 1.11.2).
- Large surface depressions called dolines are formed by extensive chemical weathering or the collapse of limestone. These can be up to 30 m in diameter.

Underground landforms

Caverns and caves

- As water flows along joints and bedding planes it is often confined into small spaces. This increases water pressure and can enable the water to be a powerful erosive force, carving passages and enlarging them to form underground **caverns** (see Figure 1.12.4, page 29). In the formation of caverns, processes of carbonation and solution also aid in enlarging joints.
- When the water eventually reappears at the surface as a **resurgence** (spring) it often forms a **cave**. (A cave has an opening to the outside whereas a cavern is totally enclosed underground.) An example of this is the One Eye river near Balaclava in Jamaica.

Stalactites, stalagmites and pillars

- Water seeping through limestone is very rich in dissolved calcium carbonate. When the water evaporates, for example inside a large abandoned cavern, it leaves behind a tiny deposit of calcite.
- If water is dripping down from the ceiling, the calcite deposits slowly form an icicle-like feature called a **stalactite**.
- Immediately below the stalactite, where water has dripped onto the floor of the cavern, calcite may also be deposited to form a stumpy **stalagmite**.
- Over thousands of years a stalactite might become joined to the stalagmite below to form a **pillar** or column.
- **Underground rivers** may flow through limestone to emerge as resurgences on the ground surface.

Figure 1.11.2 Cavers explore a huge cavern

Limestone landforms in the Caribbean

- Understand the characteristics and formation of surface karst landforms in the Caribbean, including cockpit karst and tower karst.
- Understand the characteristics and formation of Harrison's Cave in Barbados, an example of an underground limestone feature.

Limestone is widespread throughout the Caribbean, for example in Cuba, Jamaica, Barbados, the Bahamas and the Cayman Islands. There are many excellent examples of surface and underground landforms.

Tropical karst landscapes

The term 'karst' is sometimes used to describe the barren dry landscapes associated with limestone. The term itself comes from southern Europe, from the Kras region in Slovenia.

Two distinctive types of tropical karst have been identified, both of which exist in the Caribbean. They are cockpit karst and tower karst.

Cockpit karst

- **Cockpit karst** is characterised by rounded conical hills rising up to about 150 m in height, separated by depressions called cockpits (see Figure 1.12.1).

EXAM TIP

Don't confuse cockpits with clints and grykes. Remember that clints and grykes are small features on limestone pavements while cockpits are circular depressions bordered by hills.

Figure 1.12.1 Cockpit Country in Jamaica

- The conical hills usually rise up to a uniform height.
- This landscape is thought to result from intensive chemical weathering (carbonation) that is focused on widened joints and solution holes, creating the cockpits.
- Cockpit karst may be part of a sequence of landscape development (see Figure 1.12.2) in tropical regions where limestone outcrops are roughly horizontal and there is a regular pattern of joints.
- River erosion during times of higher water tables may have contributed to the formation of the cockpits as well as the collapse of roofs of underground caverns.

Tower karst

- **Tower karst** has a much more variable relief, with the hills rising to a range of different heights (see Figure 1.12.3). The hills (towers) are often steep-sided and may have caves and solution notches at their base. Examples of tower karst can be seen in China, Malaysia and Cuba.
- Tower karst may represent a landscape that has developed from cockpit karst (see Figure 1.12.2). The tropical conditions lead to active weathering and erosion, eventually causing the towers to break apart and collapse. The land between the towers becomes flat as the cockpits are in-filled with sediment.

Harrison's Cave, Barbados

Harrison's Cave in Barbados exhibits many spectacular features, including stalactites, stalagmites and pillars (see Figure 1.12.4). The cave system was first identified 200 years ago but was only opened to tourists from 1981. It is now Barbados' top tourist attraction. There are several caves and caverns open to the public and accessed by tram. The largest cavern is the 'Great Hall', which reaches a height of over 30 m.

Figure 1.12.3 Tower karst emerging from the wide Valle de Viñales in Cuba

Figure 1.12.4 Harrison's Cave in Barbados

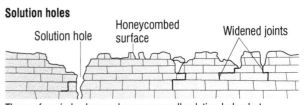

Solution holes

Solution hole · Honeycombed surface · Widened joints

The surface is broken up by many small solution holes but the overall surface remains generally level.

Cockpit karst

Cockpit · Water table

Cockpit karst is usually a hilly area in which many deep solution holes have developed to give it an 'eggbox' appearance.

Tower karst

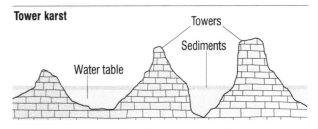

Towers · Sediments · Water table

The widening and deepening of the cockpits has destroyed much of the limestone above the water table. Only a few limestone towers remain, sticking up from a flat plain of sediments that have filled in the cockpits at a level just above the water table. Eventually the towers will be entirely eroded, and disappear.

Figure 1.12.2 Features of tropical karst

Weather and climate in the Caribbean

- Understand the difference between weather and climate.
- Understand how weather is recorded in the Caribbean.
- Understand the characteristics of the Caribbean's tropical marine climate.
- Understand the effect of relief on climate.

What is the difference between weather and climate?

- **Weather** – the short-term day-to-day condition of the atmosphere, relating to rainfall, humidity, pressure, temperature, cloud cover and winds.
- **Climate** – the long-term average weather, usually calculated over a period of 30 years.

While the weather may change from day to day the climate remains the same. Any changes to the climate take place over several decades. Scientists have found evidence of a slight warming of the world's climate, which has led to the current issue of **global warming**.

The weather varies from day to day and from place to place. A coastal location may be cloudy and a bit cooler than a place inland, and rain on the coast may fall as snow on the top of a mountain.

Some places have climatic conditions that are slightly different from neighbouring areas. This is known as a **microclimate**.

- Large towns and cities have slightly warmer climatic conditions than nearby rural areas. This is because urban areas generate heat (buildings, transport and industries) and absorb and re-radiate heat from the Sun. This is called the **heat island effect**.
- Woodlands experience less variation in diurnal (daily) temperatures because the tree canopy provides shade during the day but prevents heat escaping at night.

Weather in the Caribbean

Look at Figure 1.13.1. It describes the weather forecast for Antigua for five consecutive days. Notice that it includes details of the temperature, rainfall, humidity, cloud cover and winds. The current weather described at the top tells us that it is:

- partly cloudy with a temperature of 75°F (23°C)
- the winds are blowing from the north-east at 26 kph
- it is humid (78 per cent) but not raining
- the atmospheric pressure is 76.3 cm.

The weather forecast for the next few days is not so good.

temperature: 75 °F (23 °C)
air/sky: partly cloudy

wind: from the north-east at 26 kph
relative humidity: 78%
barometer: 76.3 cm

5-Day Forecast
weather station: Antigua
last updated: 5:14 am CT

TUE	WED	THU	FRI	SAT
rainy	rainy	rainy	rainy	rainy
82 °F (27 °C) to 73 °F (22 °C)	82 °F (27 °C) to 71 °F (21 °C)	82 °F (27 °C) to 71 °F (21 °C)	80 °F (26 °C) to 73 °F (22 °C)	82 °F (27 °C) to 73 °F (22 °C)

Figure 1.13.1 Weather forecast for Antigua

Climate in the Caribbean

The Caribbean experiences a tropical maritime climate.

Average daily temperature (°C)

Location	J	F	M	A	M	J	J	A	S	O	N	D
Kingston, Jamaica	30 (19)	30 (19)	30 (20)	31 (21)	31 (22)	32 (23)	32 (23)	32 (23)	32 (23)	31 (23)	31 (22)	31 (21)
Castries, St Lucia	28 (21)	28 (21)	29 (21)	31 (22)	31 (23)	31 (23)	31 (23)	31 (23)	31 (23)	21 (22)	29 (22)	28 (21)
Bridgetown, Barbados	28 (21)	28 (21)	29 (21)	30 (22)	31 (23)	31 (23)	30 (23)	31 (23)	31 (23)	30 (23)	29 (23)	28 (22)
St Clair, Trinidad and Tobago	31 (21)	31 (20)	32 (20)	32 (21)	32 (22)	31 (22)	31 (22)	31 (22)	32 (22)	32 (22)	32 (22)	31 (21)

Average daily maximum (minimum in brackets)

Average monthly rainfall (mm)

Location	J	F	M	A	M	J	J	A	S	O	N	D	Annual average total
Kingston, Jamaica	23	15	23	31	102	89	89	91	99	180	74	36	852
Castries, St Lucia	135	91	97	86	150	218	236	269	252	236	231	198	2,199
Bridgetown, Barbados	66	28	33	36	58	112	147	147	170	178	206	97	1,278
St Clair, Trinidad and Tobago	69	41	46	53	94	193	218	246	193	170	183	125	1,631

Figure 1.13.2 Climate data for a selection of locations in the Caribbean

- Temperatures vary little throughout the year (21–27°C), although in the wet season (May–November) temperatures tend to be a little higher than in the dry season.
- Rainfall totals are quite high (generally over 1,000 mm a year) with most of it falling as tropical storms during the hurricane season from June to November.

Look at Figure 1.13.2. It describes the climatic characteristics of a selection of places in the Caribbean. Notice that climatic conditions are broadly similar across the Caribbean.

Figure 1.13.3 is a climate graph that shows the climate for Bridgetown, Barbados. Notice that temperatures are shown as line graphs whereas rainfall is shown using bars. This is a standard type of diagram that you may be asked to interpret in an examination.

DID YOU KNOW?

In 2009–2010 the Caribbean countries of Guyana, Grenada, St Lucia and Barbados experienced a record drought. It began in October 2009 – typically the region's wettest month of the year.

Each of these countries recorded their lowest rainfall totals for October to March since records began, according to the Caribbean Institute for Meteorology and Hydrology.

In Barbados as of 8 April 2010, there were more than 1,000 brush fires for the year to date, compared with 361 during the same period in 2009.

For more information, go to http://www.ncdc.noaa.gov/sotc/hazards/2010/4#drought.

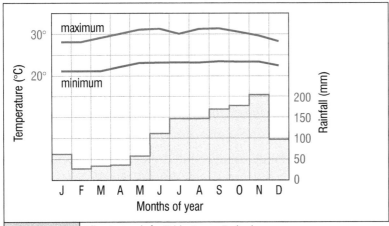

Figure 1.13.3 Climate graph for Bridgetown, Barbados

Factors affecting weather and climate

Several factors affect the weather and climate of a place. They include latitude, altitude, relief, distance from the sea and winds.

Latitude

Latitude is the main factor affecting temperature. At the Equator, the Sun is directly overhead for much of the year. This results in a high intensity (concentration) of insolation (see Figure 1.14.1), leading to high temperatures. In contrast, at the Poles, the Sun is lower in the sky. This causes the radiation from the Sun to be spread out over a larger surface area and therefore the temperatures are lower.

Notice also on Figure 1.14.1 that the radiation from the Sun has to pass through a greater thickness of atmosphere at the Poles compared with the Equator. This accentuates the temperature differences.

The higher temperatures at the Equator result in rising air, the formation of clouds and periods of heavy rain. This accounts for the equatorial climate being warm and wet.

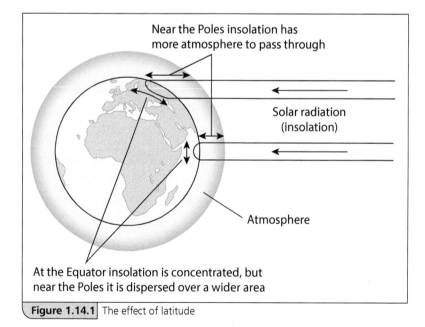

Figure 1.14.1 The effect of latitude

Altitude and relief

The altitude or relief of an area can affect both temperatures and rainfall:

- Temperature – temperature decreases with altitude, roughly 10°C every 1 km (1,000 metres). This is because as altitude increases, air pressure is reduced and this causes a drop in temperature (see Figure 1.14.2).
- Rainfall – if air is forced to rise up and over a mountain range it is forced to cool. This will lead to condensation and rain formation. This type of rainfall is called relief rainfall and it is common in the Caribbean, as the St Lucia example on page 34 demonstrates.

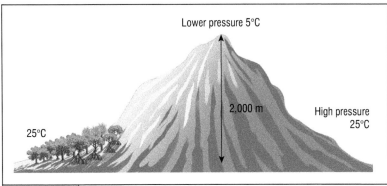

Figure 1.14.2 The effect of altitude or relief

Distance from the sea (continentality)

Coastal areas tend to experience high levels of humidity and rainfall and more moderate (less extreme) temperatures than areas inland. Such areas are said to experience a maritime climate. In contrast, areas further inland, away from the influence of the sea, tend to experience a more continental climate, with less rainfall and greater extremes of temperature.

This factor is of little importance on most of the Caribbean islands as they are too small to experience any degree of continentality. However, elsewhere in the world (such as the USA and Europe), this is an extremely important factor, accounting for very cold winters and hot summers in the interiors.

Winds

Winds are important in transferring moisture and heat. The dominant wind direction is called the prevailing wind. The Caribbean is mostly affected by prevailing winds from the north-east – the trade winds. This explains why north- and east-facing coastlines may receive more rainfall and experience more moderate temperatures than further west and south.

DID YOU KNOW?

Water has a higher specific heat capacity than land. It takes five times as much heat to raise the temperature of water by 1°C than it does to raise the temperature of land. This explains why land warms up and cools down much more quickly than water. Can you think why water has a higher specific heat capacity?

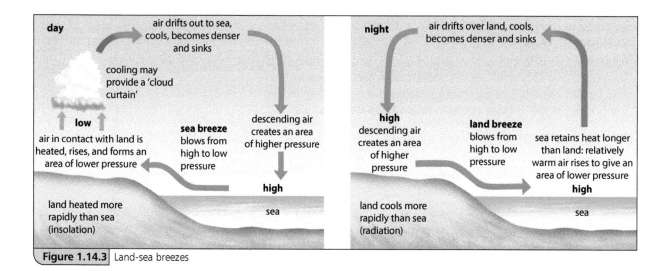

Figure 1.14.3 Land-sea breezes

Land and sea breezes

Coastal areas can be affected by local land and sea breezes, which introduce cooler air, lowering temperatures (see Figure 1.14.3).

Factors affecting weather and climate in St Lucia

Look at Figure 1.14.4. Notice that the relief (variations in height) of St Lucia has an impact on the pattern of rainfall in the island. The highest rainfall totals are over the mountains towards the south.

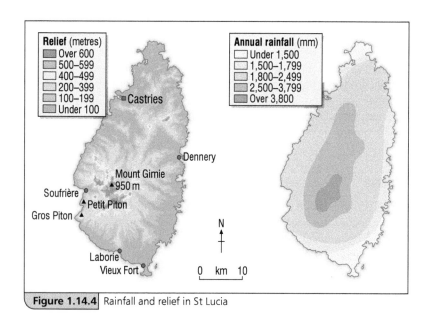

Figure 1.14.4 Rainfall and relief in St Lucia

Study Figure 1.14.5 to see why the highest rainfall is over the mountains.

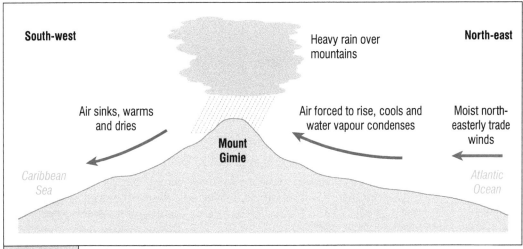

South-west

Heavy rain over mountains

North-east

Air sinks, warms and dries

Air forced to rise, cools and water vapour condenses

Moist north-easterly trade winds

Mount Gimie

Caribbean Sea

Atlantic Ocean

Figure 1.14.5 Relief rainfall over Mt Gimie, St Lucia

- The prevailing (most frequent) winds are the north-easterly trade winds. They bring warm, moist air to St Lucia from the Atlantic Ocean.
- As this air reaches the mountains, it is forced to rise. It cools and water vapour in the air condenses to form thick clouds and heavy rain.
- High amounts of rain falls over the mountains.
- When the air descends, it warms and becomes drier. This drier, sheltered down-slope region is sometimes called a **rainshadow**.

Mountains tend to experience lower temperatures than lowland areas, decreasing by 1°C for every 100 m of ascent. This is caused by a reduction in air pressure with increasing altitude.

SUMMARY QUESTIONS

1 Use a labelled diagram to explain why equatorial regions experience higher temperatures than polar regions.

2 How and why might the east coast of a Caribbean island experience weather that is different from that in the west?

3 Explain the formation of a sea breeze.

Figure 1.14.6 Mount Gimie, St Lucia

1.15 Equatorial and tropical maritime climates

LEARNING OUTCOME

- Understand the main characteristics of equatorial and tropical maritime climates.

Equatorial climate

Figure 1.15.1 shows the global distribution of the equatorial climate. It broadly corresponds with the distribution of the tropical rainforest biome. The main characteristics of the equatorial climate are:

- hot conditions – generally 26°C or higher throughout the year
- high rainfall totals, in excess of 2,000 mm per year
- lack of distinctive seasons (summer/winter) but there is a wet/dry season – for example, in Manaus, the wet season lasts from November to May whereas in June–October it is relatively dry
- greater diurnal (daily) range in temperature than seasonal differences (see the climate data for Manaus, Brazil in Figure 1.15.2).

Rainfall usually takes the form of torrential downpours in the afternoon as clouds build due to the high humidity and rising temperature. Cloud cover restricts temperatures during the day so that it never becomes excessively hot.

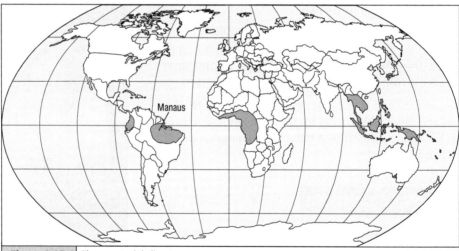

Figure 1.15.1 The equatorial climate

	J	F	M	A	M	J	J	A	S	O	N	D
Average monthly temperature (°C)	28	28	28	27	28	28	28	29	29	29	29	28
Monthly total rainfall (mm)	278	278	300	287	193	99	61	41	62	112	165	220

Figure 1.15.2 Climate data for Manaus, Brazil

Tropical marine climate

Figure 1.15.3 shows the distribution of the tropical marine climate. It is focused on eastern coasts of tropical lands, exposed to the trade winds throughout the year. It is the climate experienced across most of the Caribbean. The main characteristics of the climate are:

- high temperatures, usually in excess of 26°C

- high rainfall, between 1,200 mm and 2,000 mm per year

- distinctive wet and dry season, with the highest rainfall totals being in the late summer and autumn (see the climate data for Montego Bay in Figure 1.15.4).

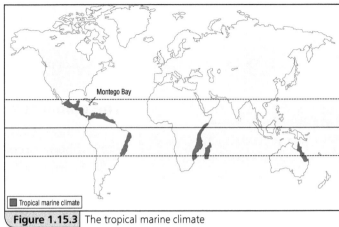

Figure 1.15.3 The tropical marine climate

In the Caribbean, the north-east trade winds blow all year round, bringing moisture from the Atlantic Ocean. Rain can take the form of relief rainfall, where the air is forced to rise over mountains, or convectional rainfall triggered by high temperatures during the afternoon.

Places with tropical marine climates may also experience tropical waves (see page 41). These are belts of low pressure which generate a heavier burst of rainfall.

DID YOU KNOW?

Some tropical waves develop into tropical depressions or even hurricanes.

	J	F	M	A	M	J	J	A	S	O	N	D
Average monthly temperature (°C)	25	25	26	26	27	28	29	29	28	27	26	26
Monthly total rainfall (mm)	70	30	30	60	80	80	60	80	110	130	120	100

Figure 1.15.4 Climate data for Montego Bay, Jamaica

SUMMARY QUESTIONS

1 Study Figure 1.15.2. Draw a climate graph for Manaus and add labels to describe the main characteristics of the equatorial climate.

2 How does the tropical marine climate differ from the equatorial climate?

1.16   Caribbean weather systems

LEARNING OUTCOMES

- Understand the global atmospheric circulation.
- Understand the formation of the ITCZ.
- Understand the formation of common weather systems in the Caribbean (anticyclones, cold fronts and tropical waves).

The global atmospheric circulation

The weather systems affecting the Caribbean are part of the **global atmospheric circulation**. Look at Figure 1.16.1. Notice that there are three large circulation cells in each hemisphere. These cells are a major influence on the weather experienced on the ground.

Notice that the Caribbean lies beneath the Hadley Cell in the northern hemisphere. It is this part of the global atmospheric circulation that is responsible for much of the weather experienced in the Caribbean.

- At the boundary of the two **Hadley Cells**, close to the Equator, air converging at the ground is forced to rise. This creates an unstable zone of cloud and rain called the **Inter Tropical Convergence Zone** (ITCZ). The position of the ITCZ is largely determined by the position of the overhead Sun.

- At about 30° N air is sinking towards the surface. This forms a large area of high pressure called an **anticyclone**. This is responsible for creating the prevailing north-easterly winds – the trade winds – that blow towards the Caribbean for much of the year.

- As the overhead Sun moves between the Tropic of Cancer and the Tropic of Capricorn, so the circulation cells shift slightly north and south of the Equator. This explains the changes in weather experienced in the Caribbean during the course of a year.

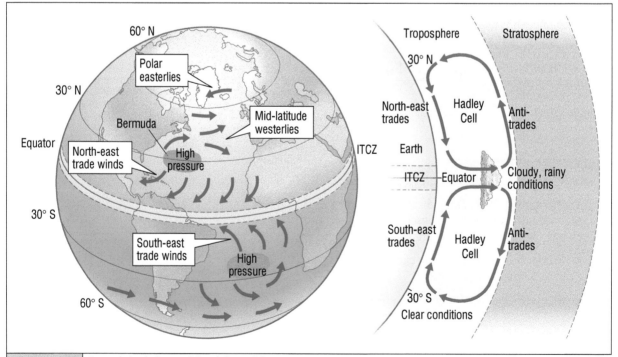

Figure 1.16.1 General circulation model and the Caribbean

38

The Inter Tropical Convergence Zone (ITCZ)

The ITCZ is a broad zone of very unstable weather that forms at the boundary of the two Hadley Cells (see Figure 1.16.1).

- At the ground surface, warm moist air converges and is forced to rise.
- This results in rapid cooling and the formation of towering thunderstorm clouds (see Figure 1.16.2).

In **winter** (in the northern hemisphere) the ITCZ moves south to lie close to the Equator. The weather in much of the Caribbean is affected by the large anticyclone to the north and is generally settled with more sunshine and less rainfall.

In **summer** (in the northern hemisphere), as the overhead Sun moves north of the Equator, the ITCZ shifts northwards to affect much of the southern Caribbean. This accounts for the heavy rainfall and more unsettled conditions experienced in the region.

The ITCZ brings periods of very heavy rainfall to countries in the southern Caribbean, such as Trinidad, St Lucia, Guyana and Barbados. It is responsible for the marked wet season that occurs in these regions between June and November (see Figure 1.13.2, page 31).

The ITCZ is also an important factor in the formation of hurricanes (see pages 42–5), which explains why the Caribbean is most affected by hurricanes in the period between August and November.

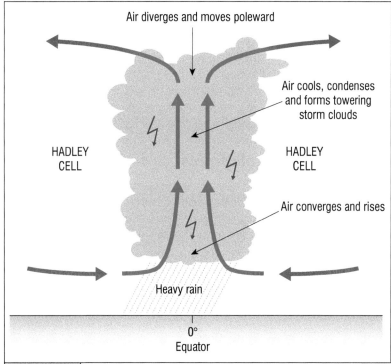

Figure 1.16.2 Formation of the ITCZ

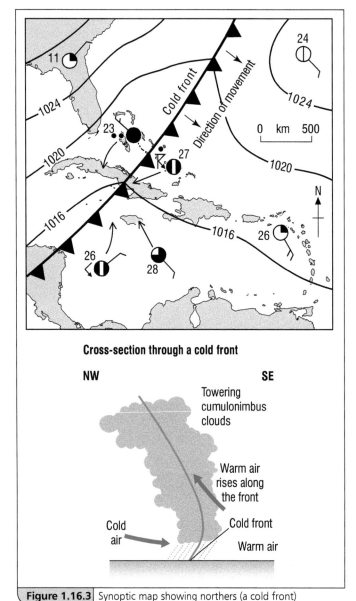

Cross-section through a cold front

NW

SE

Towering cumulonimbus clouds

Warm air rises along the front

Cold air

Cold front

Warm air

Figure 1.16.3 Synoptic map showing northers (a cold front)

Anticyclones

An anticyclone is an area of relatively high atmospheric pressure that causes settled weather conditions. The weather associated with an anticyclone is often sunny and there will be little rainfall.

Look at Figure 1.16.1. Notice that a large anticyclone, which is known as the Azores High Pressure Cell, has formed at a latitude of about 30° N, to the north of the Hadley Cell. This is because air is sinking in this region leading to the high pressure on the ground. This anticyclone is responsible for the dry season months experienced throughout much of the Caribbean.

As winds circulate around this area of high pressure they blow towards the Caribbean from the north-east. These are the **north-east trade winds** and they form the prevailing winds in the region.

The sinking air reduces the likelihood of surface air rising, cooling and condensing to form cloud and rain. With an absence of clouds, long hours of sunshine will be experienced. At night, temperatures can fall sharply as surface heat escapes to space.

Cold fronts

Occasionally in the winter, cold air sweeps across parts of the northern Caribbean from North America. The boundary of this colder air on the ground is called a **cold front**.

Figure 1.16.3 shows a cold front on a weather map. Notice that the warmer air ahead of the cold front is forced to rise. This forms cloud and heavy rain, which can be damaging to crops on north-facing slopes. The northerly winds behind the cold front are locally known as **northers**.

Some Northers have reached as far south as Trinidad, bringing periods of heavy rain and a drop in temperature. The cold air from the USA is warmed as it moves south and travels over the Caribbean Sea. This means that the temperature drop is less significant in the far south of the region.

Tropical waves

Tropical waves are belts of relatively low pressure that travel across the Atlantic Ocean along the edge of the ITCZ. They bring periods of unsettled weather with heavy rain, most commonly between May and November.

As Figure 1.16.4 shows, the trade winds have a relatively moist lower layer and a drier upper layer. If a wave develops (rather like a wave at sea), the moist surface layer rises to a height of 7,000 m or more. At this altitude, air becomes sufficiently cool to condense and form cloud and rain.

Tropical waves are generated by heat, which forces the air to rise, creating an area of relatively low pressure. They are large features, often extending over 1,000 km. This means that unsettled weather could last for several days in any one place. Once a tropical wave has passed, the weather will tend to be cloudy for a few days.

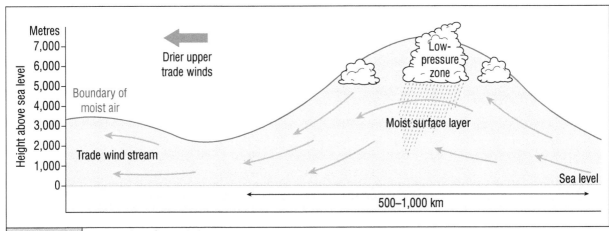

Figure 1.16.4 Cross-section of a tropical wave

Hurricanes

- Understand the definition of a hurricane.
- Understand how hurricanes form and develop.

What is a hurricane?

Look at Figure 1.17.1. It is a satellite photo of a hurricane in the Caribbean. Can you see the 'eye' of the hurricane, right in the centre of the swirling mass of cloud?

A **hurricane** is a massive and very powerful tropical storm that can cause widespread destruction and loss of life. The Caribbean is often affected by hurricanes that form over the Atlantic Ocean off the coast of West Africa and then move westwards. They usually occur between July and November. The official hurricane season is from June to November.

What forms a hurricane?

While scientists are not certain what triggers a hurricane, they tend to form in the following conditions:

- over warm water (over 26.5°C), which explains why they occur in the tropics
- when sea temperatures are at their highest
- at a latitude greater than 5 degrees North or South. Closer to the Equator the air is calm in the 'doldrums' and there is not enough 'spin' resulting from the rotation of the Earth
- in tropical regions of severe air instability (ITCZ) where air is converging on the surface and rising rapidly.

When these conditions occur a hurricane can form. Figure 1.17.2 shows the main hurricane-forming regions of the world and the common tracks taken by hurricanes.

How do hurricanes develop?

Look at Figure 1.17.3, which shows a cross-section through a hurricane. This is how a hurricane forms and develops.

- Air rises rapidly over a warm ocean where huge quantities of water are evaporated very quickly. As the air rises it cools and the vapour condenses to form cloud.
- The rotation of the Earth sets up a spinning motion and the storm assumes its characteristic Catherine-wheel shape, spinning in an anti-clockwise direction (in the northern hemisphere) (see Figure 1.17.1).
- The area of disturbed weather that forms is first described as a tropical depression and is given a number. If the winds intensify then a tropical storm forms and the weather system is given a name.
- When surface winds reach an average of 120 kph the storm officially becomes a named hurricane.
- Once formed, the hurricane is carried across the ocean by the prevailing winds from east to west.
- On reaching land, the supply of warm water (the hurricane's fuel) is cut off and the storm begins to weaken.

Figure 1.17.1 The distinctive shape of a hurricane in the Caribbean

Notice on Figure 1.17:3 the narrow tube of cold dense air sinking towards the surface in the centre of the storm. This is the **eye** of the hurricane that you can see clearly in Figure 1.17.1. The edge of the eye is a towering bank of cloud called the eye wall. It is here that the strongest winds will be experienced.

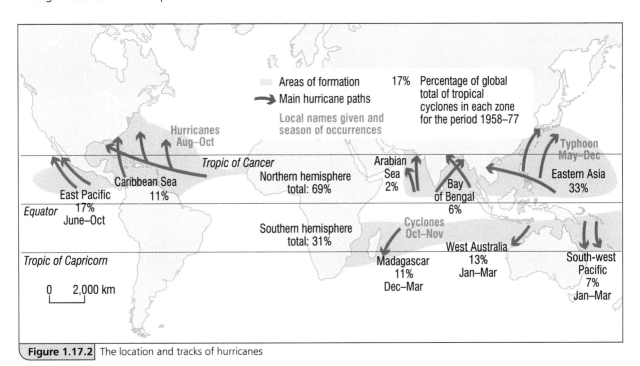

Figure 1.17.2 The location and tracks of hurricanes

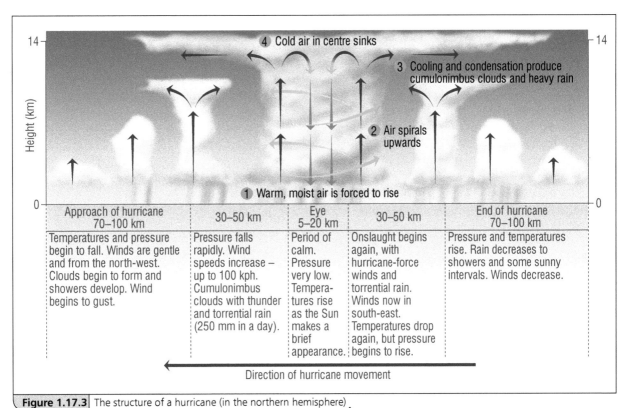

Figure 1.17.3 The structure of a hurricane (in the northern hemisphere)

What are the effects of hurricanes?

Hurricanes can have a number of effects on islands and coastal regions.

- *Strong winds*. With wind speeds in excess of 120 kph and gusts of over 200 kph, hurricanes can cause a great deal of damage. Roofs will be blown off houses, power lines torn down and crops flattened.
- *Heavy rainfall*. The torrential rainfall (often over 200 mm) associated with hurricanes can bring widespread flooding and landslides, damaging roads, bridges, crops and buildings.
- *Storm surge*. Driven onshore by the strong winds, high seas (often 3–5 m in height) surge inland over low-lying areas and up river valleys. Storm surges caused by hurricanes are the biggest killers. A storm surge will flatten everything in its path rather like a tidal wave. It will destroy crops and inundate vast areas with salty water.

CASE STUDIES

1 Hurricane Omar 2008

Hurricane Omar developed in the eastern Caribbean Sea in October 2008. It took an unusual track south-westwards and then turned to the north-east, intensifying to become a category 4 hurricane with a wind speed up to 215 kph.

Hurricane Omar struck the Caribbean islands of Antigua and Barbuda causing over US$50 million damage, destroying several homes and devastating farmland. Large areas were inundated by floodwater and services such as electricity were cut off. Puerto Rico was also badly affected.

Despite the widespread and costly damage nobody was killed by the hurricane. This was thanks to careful forecasting and prediction by scientists who were able to use satellites and radar to track the storm. Warnings were given and many locals were moved to higher ground and to the safety of hurricane shelters. On Anguilla tourists were told to leave the island ahead of the storm.

2 Hurricane Ivan 2004

In September 2004, Grenada was devastated by a powerful category 4 hurricane that caused immense damage to the island and killed 39 persons. The total damage was estimated at over US$1 billion.

- Over 14,000 homes were destroyed as the island was lashed by 200 kph winds and 18,000 persons were left homeless.
- Almost every building in the capital, St George's, was damaged or destroyed by the hurricane.
- 75 out of the 77 schools on the island were damaged or destroyed.
- Services such as water and electricity were cut off.
- There was widespread damage to crops, resulting in losses of up to 90 per cent.

How can the hurricane hazard be reduced?

Satellite and radar enable scientists to view and to track hurricanes, and computers can be used to predict their likely course. Warnings are then issued to areas at risk.

Hurricane Watch – Be prepared! Hurricane conditions are likely in the next 36 hours. Batten the windows, collect water and emergency supplies.

Hurricane Warning – Time to act! Hurricane conditions are expected in 12–24 hours. Evacuate low-lying areas or seek shelter.

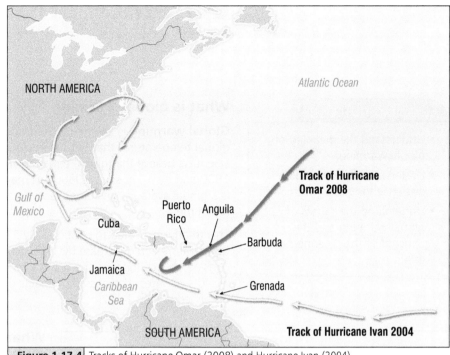

Figure 1.17.4 Tracks of Hurricane Omar (2008) and Hurricane Ivan (2004)

Those living in the Caribbean are aware of the dangers of hurricanes and know how to respond when warnings are issued. Many areas have hurricane shelters, which are strong and secure buildings constructed to withstand the full fury of the storms. Despite these preparations, hurricanes continue to be a major threat to the residents and economies of the Caribbean.

Figure 1.17.5 A demolished building front after Hurricane Ivan

DID YOU KNOW?

Caribbean hurricanes

The Abaco Islands have been struck by 18 severe hurricanes since 1851. They are the hurricane 'capital' of the Caribbean. Since 1944, Cuba, Key West and Nevis have been struck by 7 major storms (roughly one every 8–9 years). Bonaire and Curaçao have been struck the least.

1.18

Global warming – evidence and causes

LEARNING OUTCOMES

- Understand the meaning of global warming.
- Understand the scientific evidence for global warming.
- Understand the causes of global warming and the concept of the greenhouse effect.

What is global warming?

Global warming is the term used to describe the increase in average global temperatures that has taken place in the last few decades. Scientists believe that global temperatures have risen by 0.74°C since 1900 and by 0.5°C since 1980. This may not sound very much but it is a global average – in some places temperatures have increased by much more.

This trend is expected to continue. By 2100, the average global temperature could increase by 1.8°C to 4.0°C. This would lead to considerable changes to the world's natural ecosystems and the world's climates. The possible impacts of global warming will be discussed in Unit 1.19.

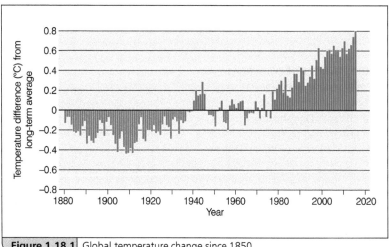

Figure 1.18.1 | Global temperature change since 1850

What is the evidence for global warming?

Evidence comes from direct temperature readings, together with the study of historic records.

Instrument readings

Direct measurements of temperature using thermometers have been taken since about 1850. However, it is only in the last few decades that thermometers have provided accurate information across the world. Since 1980, direct measurements have recorded a clear upward trend, providing very strong evidence for global warming.

Ice cores

When snow falls and turns to ice, water molecules and air bubbles become trapped and provide a frozen record of the Earth's climate at the time when the snow fell. Scientists have taken deep ice cores in Antarctica and Greenland and have analysed the water and trapped air. Their results suggest a steady rise in temperature over the last few decades.

Figure 1.18.2 | An ice core being examined in the Antarctic

Arctic ice cover

Over the last 30 years, the Arctic ice has thinned to almost half its earlier thickness. In the future, scientists believe that parts of the Arctic may become completely ice-free during the summer. By the end of the century, there may no longer be any Arctic ice.

Glacier retreat

The World Glacier Monitoring Service estimates that up to 25 per cent of global mountain glaciers could have disappeared by 2050. There is considerable photographic evidence of rapid glacier retreat across the world, supporting the belief that the world is becoming warmer.

What are the natural causes of global warming?

To understand the causes of global warming, you first need to understand an important natural feature of the atmosphere called the **greenhouse effect**.

Look at Figure 1.18.3 and notice how it works:

- Incoming **short-wave radiation** (visible light) from the Sun passes largely uninterrupted through the atmosphere to reach the Earth.
- The incoming solar radiation that heats the Earth is called **insolation**.
- This energy heats up the Earth's surface, which in turn gives off heat in the form of **long-wave radiation**.
- Some of this heat from the Earth escapes to space but some is trapped and absorbed by greenhouse gases in the atmosphere.
- This warms the atmosphere, creating a kind of insulating blanket around the Earth. This is the greenhouse effect. Without it, the temperature would be too cold and life would not exist on Earth.

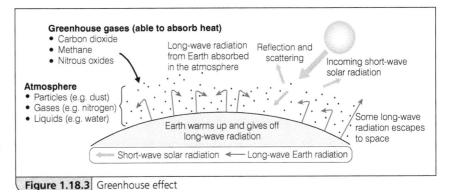

Figure 1.18.3 Greenhouse effect

How have human activities affected global warming?

Scientists believe that, in recent decades, there has been an increase in the emissions of greenhouse gases, for example carbon dioxide released by burning fossil fuels in power stations (see Figure 1.18.4). The increased concentration of greenhouse gases in the atmosphere has resulted in more heat from the Earth being absorbed, thereby increasing the greenhouse effect.

Many scientists believe that this **enhanced greenhouse effect** resulting from human activities accounts for the recent rise in global temperatures.

Greenhouse gas	Human contributions
Carbon dioxide: accounts for an estimated 60 per cent of the 'enhanced' greenhouse effect. Global concentration of carbon dioxide has increased by 30 per cent since 1850	Burning fossil fuels (e.g. oil, gas, coal) in industry and power stations to produce electricity, car exhausts, deforestation and burning wood
Methane: very effective in absorbing heat. Accounts for 20 per cent of the 'enhanced' greenhouse effect	Decaying organic matter in landfill sites and compost tips, rice farming, farm livestock, burning biomass for energy
Nitrous oxides: very small concentrates in the atmosphere are up to 300 times more effective at capturing heat than carbon dioxide	Car exhausts, power stations producing electricity, agricultural fertilisers, sewage treatment

Figure 1.18.4 Greenhouse gases

The effects of global warming

LEARNING OUTCOMES

- Describe and explain the possible impacts of global warming.
- Understand that global warming may bring both advantages and disadvantages.
- Understand the possible impacts on the Caribbean.

The effects of global warming worldwide

Most scientists agree that global warming is happening and that it is likely to have an impact on the world's natural systems. It is, however, uncertain what those effects will be and which parts of the world will be affected most.

Any effects of global warming will take place over a long time period, probably decades. Only through looking at long-term trends will scientists be able to conclude with any certainty that global warming is having an impact. Any single event, for example a powerful hurricane, cannot be blamed on global warming.

Predictions about the likely impacts of global warming are made using computer models. Some of the possible impacts, both advantages and disadvantages, are described below and shown in Figure 1.19.1.

Advantages

- Current cold environments will become warmer and will be able to grow food crops.
- Areas where cereal crops, such as wheat, are grown may become more extensive owing to a longer growing season, increasing the production of food.
- Canada's Northwest Passage may become ice-free, allowing it to be used for shipping.

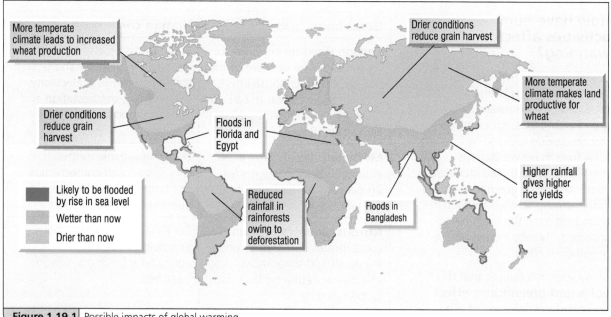

Figure 1.19.1 Possible impacts of global warming

- As temperatures increase in densely populated areas, demand for energy for heating may fall.
- There may be fewer deaths or injuries caused by cold weather.

Disadvantages

- Global sea levels are expected to rise by 18–59 cm by 2100, putting low-lying islands and deltas at risk from flooding. Such areas include the Netherlands, Bangladesh, the Maldives, the Cayman Islands, the Bahamas, and Turks and Caicos in the Caribbean.
- Parts of Africa may become drier, leading to droughts, migration and possibly increased famines.
- Cereal yields may fall in parts of India, Africa and the Middle East.
- Melting glaciers in the Himalayas may increase flooding in Nepal, India and China.
- Hurricanes may become more violent in the North Atlantic.
- An additional 220–400 million people may be at risk from malaria in China and central Asia.
- Climate change will affect ecosystems and some species; for example polar bears in the Arctic may be threatened by the melting of the floating ice that they need for hunting and survival (see Figure 1.19.2).

Figure 1.19.2 Are polar bears likely to become extinct in the future?

CASE STUDY	Impacts of climate change in the Caribbean and USA

Caribbean

- Rising sea levels could flood low-level islands such as the Bahamas and the Cayman Islands.
- Increased rates of coastal erosion could threaten beaches and coastal ecosystems. This in turn could have a negative impact on tourism.
- The warming of tropical seas can cause harmful bleaching of corals. Between 2005 and 2015, an estimated 300 km of Belize's barrier reef was bleached and it could die. With global warming, this could become more extensive, threatening the fishing industry and tourism.
- Warmer ocean temperatures could result in more intense hurricane activity, which could prove very costly to the Caribbean.
- Erratic rainfall could affect crop yields, water supply and irrigation, leading to poverty and migration.

USA

- Weather patterns could change significantly, bringing floods to some areas and drought to others.
- Moderate warming may lead to increased crop production.
- Fragile mountain and arctic ecosystems may suffer habitat loss and some species may become extinct.
- Sea-level rise could flood low-lying coastal areas, e.g. the Gulf of Mexico and parts of Florida's coastal wetlands.
- Tropical diseases could spread more widely, threatening human health.
- Warming will increase electricity demand, e.g. for air conditioning.

Reducing the impact of global warming

How can greenhouse gas emissions be reduced?

Individual actions

Individuals and local communities have a very important part to play in reducing greenhouse gas emissions. Ways to achieve this include the following:

- Conserving energy at home by using low-energy light bulbs, switching off electrical appliances when not in use and wearing an extra sweater rather than turning on the heating (in colder regions).
- Walking, cycling or using public transport rather than private cars to reduce vehicle emissions.
- Reducing waste by recycling materials.
- Becoming involved in campaigns to put pressure on governments to reduce emissions.

National actions

Governments can adopt policies to reduce emissions. These might include the following:

- Setting targets for reduction in emissions.
- Encouraging renewable energy production, such as wind, solar and hydroelectricity, by providing grants and tax incentives.
- Using technology and introducing strict regulations to reduce emissions from power stations and car exhausts.
- Encouraging the development of public transport systems, particularly in towns and cities.
- Encouraging people to recycle and to reduce waste.
- Providing grants for people to insulate their homes to reduce energy consumption.

International actions

Global warming is an international problem that spreads beyond national borders. In the long term, the solution to the problem has to be through international action.

In 2005, the Kyoto Protocol became international law. It states that:

Over 170 countries agreed to reduce carbon emissions by an average of 5.2 per cent below their 1990 levels by 2012. Of the major greenhouse gas emitters, only Australia and the USA refused to sign the treaty.

In 2015, 195 countries adopted the Paris Agreement, the first ever universal and legally binding global climate deal. The major target is to keep the global temperature increase below 2°C and limit it to 1.5°C above pre-industrial levels. Progress will be reviewed every five years.

Figure 1.20.1 A recycle bin for coloured glass in Trinidad

Carbon trading and climate protection payments

Carbon trading

If a country or organisation within a country has cut its carbon emissions to a level that is below its target, it has 'spare' carbon credits. These carbon credits can then be traded (**carbon trading**) with a country or organisation that has not been able to cut its emissions. Overall, a balance is maintained through international cooperation and trade.

Tree-planting programmes can also be used to 'buy' carbon credits. Trees absorb carbon dioxide and therefore remove it from the atmosphere.

Climate protection payments

In many tropical regions, burning is used as a method to clear rainforest land for agriculture. This releases huge quantities of carbon dioxide into the atmosphere. A recent approach to reducing emissions has involved the international community through **climate protection payments**, which establishes a value for an area of forest and pays governments not to carry out deforestation. In this way emissions can be reduced and important natural habitats protected.

Figure 1.20.2 Wigton wind farm in Jamaica

Renewable energy in the Caribbean

In an attempt to reduce carbon emissions, several countries in the Caribbean have introduced renewable energy projects:

- Jamaica – supported by the Netherlands, Wigton wind farm has 23 wind turbines and already meets Jamaica's renewable energy targets.
- Barbados – there are over 32,000 solar water heaters on the roofs of houses, businesses and hotels. They save around US$6.5 million in fuel that would otherwise have been imported.
- Barbados is considering the use of offshore wind turbines to generate electricity.
- St Lucia, Dominica and Grenada – these countries are seeking to become the world's first non-carbon-fuelled economies by developing wind, wave and solar power to meet all their energy needs.
- Nevis, St Lucia and Dominica – here there are opportunities for exploiting geothermal energy.

Figure 1.20.3 Solar heater to provide hot water in Barbados

- Understand the individual and government responses to global warming in a developed country, the UK.

In some parts of the UK, parents and their children are encouraged to join together with other parents and children to form a 'walking bus' to travel between home and school. This cuts down on the use of vehicles and provides children (and parents!) with useful exercise.

Responses to global warming in the UK

The growth of the 'green' movement

In common with many countries, the UK has seen a growing public awareness and concern about environmental, or 'green', issues. All the political parties in the UK have policies aimed at conserving the environment and reducing the impact of global warming. Actions are taken by individuals, local authorities and the government to try to reduce the emissions of greenhouse gases.

Individual responses

Energy conservation

Individual households conserve energy by using low-energy appliances and double glazing to retain heat during the winter. Government grants are available to encourage people to use solar panels to generate electricity that can be fed into the national grid. In some areas, grants are also available for home insulation.

Recycling

Waste recycling is widespread, with products such as paper, cardboard, glass and plastics being sorted in homes before being collected to be recycled. Households are encouraged to compost kitchen waste.

Carbon offset payments

Some people choose to pay a carbon offset fee when making bookings for airline flights. Air travel is a highly polluting form of transport and is responsible for emitting greenhouse gases into the atmosphere. These payments can be used to plant trees.

Figure 1.20.4 Solar panels on the roof of a house in the UK

Government responses

Developing renewable energy

The UK government is committed to reducing carbon emissions by 80 per cent by 2050. Much of this saving will come from the development of renewable energy. By 2020, the UK aims to meet 15 per cent of its energy requirements from renewable sources.

The UK is fortunate in having a variety of options for renewable energy, including wind, wave, hydroelectric and geothermal. Much of the focus in recent years has been on the construction of wind farms. Wind power contributed 11 per cent of the UK's electricity generation in 2015. The UK is the sixth largest producer of wind energy in the world, with around 7,000 wind turbines in operation.

Figure 1.20.5 An offshore wind farm

Reducing vehicle emissions

The UK has introduced stricter MOT (Ministry of Transport) tests on vehicle exhausts and it has set higher taxes for vehicles that require a large amount of petrol. Computer technology is used to make vehicle exhausts more efficient and less polluting.

Additionally, the government supports transport initiatives such as bus lanes and cycle ways to encourage people to use alternative forms of transport. In some cities, such as London, congestion charges are used to try to reduce the number of vehicles travelling into the city centre. In London, the charge in 2016 was £11.50 a day.

Many UK cities have 'park and ride' schemes. Cars are left in huge car parks on the outskirts of cities and a frequent cheap bus service transports people to and from the city centre.

Figure 1.20.6 Cyclists do not have to pay the congestion charge in London

1.21

Ecosystems

LEARNING OUTCOMES

- Understand the definition of an ecosystem.
- Understand how nutrients are recycled in an ecosystem.
- Understand the importance of climate and soils in the development of ecosystems.

What is an ecosystem?

An **ecosystem** is a community of plants and wildlife together with the environment in which they live. This includes the soil and the atmosphere. All the different aspects (**components**) of an ecosystem interact with each other and often depend on each other for their survival.

It is possible to identify **living** (biotic) and **non-living** (abiotic) components of an ecosystem. Living components include plants and animals, whereas non-living components include rainfall, temperature, rocks and soil.

Ecosystems can be small scale, such as a freshwater pond (see Figure 1.21.1) or coral reef, or they can be large scale, such as a tropical rainforest or desert. Large-scale global ecosystems are called **biomes**.

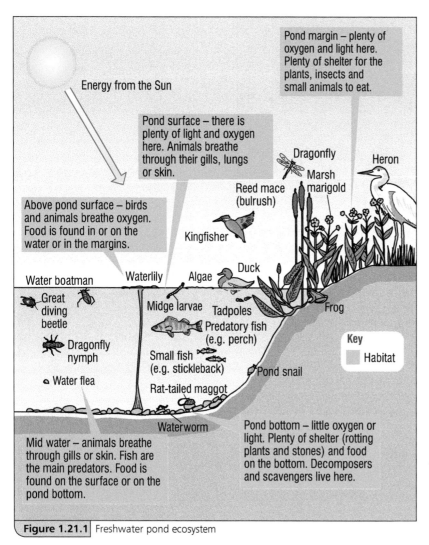

Energy from the Sun

Pond margin – plenty of oxygen and light here. Plenty of shelter for the plants, insects and small animals to eat.

Pond surface – there is plenty of light and oxygen here. Animals breathe through their gills, lungs or skin.

Above pond surface – birds and animals breathe oxygen. Food is found in or on the water or in the margins.

Dragonfly

Heron

Marsh marigold

Reed mace (bulrush)

Kingfisher

Waterlily   Algae

Duck

Water boatman

Great diving beetle

Midge larvae   Tadpoles

Predatory fish (e.g. perch)

Frog

Key

☐ Habitat

Dragonfly nymph

Small fish (e.g. stickleback)

Pond snail

Water flea

Rat-tailed maggot

Waterworm

Mid water – animals breathe through gills or skin. Fish are the main predators. Food is found on the surface or on the pond bottom.

Pond bottom – little oxygen or light. Plenty of shelter (rotting plants and stones) and food on the bottom. Decomposers and scavengers live here.

Figure 1.21.1 Freshwater pond ecosystem

How are nutrients recycled in an ecosystem?

One of the most important features of an ecosystem is the constant recycling of **nutrients** (plant foods). Look at Figure 1.21.2 and notice the following features:

- The Sun is the source of energy.
- Energy from the Sun is converted into usable energy (carbonates) by producers (plants) through the process of photosynthesis.
- Energy is then passed on through being eaten by consumers.
- When the producers and consumers die, they decompose and fungi and bacteria return the nutrients to the soil.
- Plants (producers) make use of nutrients in the soil to help them to grow.

The importance of climate

Rainfall and temperature affect the types of ecosystems that exist in a particular region. For example, tropical rainforests are well suited to hot and wet climates. Rainfall is a source of nutrients for plants, and water is essential for plant growth and animal life.

Temperatures affect plant growth too. The minimum temperature for plant growth is 6°C. In the Caribbean this means that there is continuous growth of plants as they are not limited by low temperatures. High temperatures together with moisture speed up decomposition, which explains why fallen leaves decompose rapidly in tropical environments.

The importance of soils

Soil provides material in which plants can anchor their roots, as well as important nutrients to help them grow. Soil is formed from two sources:

1 **Mineral** matter derived from the weathering of bedrock. In the tropics, chemical weathering is very effective in breaking down rock, which explains why some soils may reach a depth of 30 m.

2 **Organic** material from rotting vegetation. Organic material decomposes to form material called humus, which in the Caribbean often appears colourless.

Look at Figure 1.21.3. Notice that soils contain water and/or air, together with mineral and organic material. It is also an important habitat for earthworms and small insects. The characteristics of a soil – its fertility (the ease with which nutrients are available to plants), thickness, colour and texture – depend on several factors such as climate, vegetation, rock type and human activities. It can take thousands of years to form, yet can be washed away by a flash flood in a few minutes. Such a precious resource needs very careful management.

The importance of biotic conditions

Living organisms play an important role in the development of ecosystems. Figure 1.21.1 shows the important relationships that exist between the species. Figure 1.21.2 shows the role of organisms in nutrient cycling without which an ecosystem would collapse.

Humans also play an important part. Those that live nearby often form an important part of natural ecosystems, managing them to supply useful products. Many natural ecosystems are fragile and can easily be harmed. For example, a coral reef can be severely damaged by oil pollution or agricultural chemicals. For this reason ecosystems need to be managed carefully to preserve them for future generations.

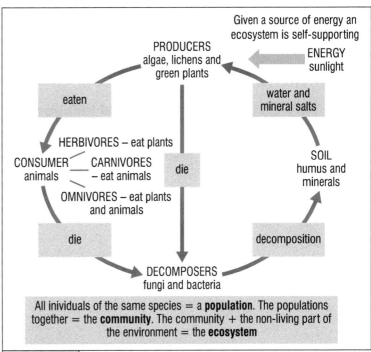

Figure 1.21.2 Nutrient cycling in an ecosystem

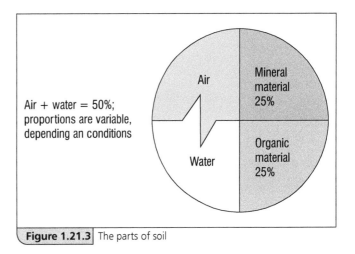

Figure 1.21.3 The parts of soil

DID YOU KNOW?

The tallest trees on Earth, reaching heights in excess of 115 m, are the sequoias or Californian redwoods. They are evergreen trees and are very long living – some are thought to be 1,200–1,800 years old! Before logging and widespread deforestation, they used to be widespread along the coast of California, USA.

Tropical rainforest biome

Global location

The **tropical rainforest** is the most productive natural ecosystem in the world. An estimated 40 per cent of the world's species of plants and animals live in the rainforest. It covers an area of some 375 million hectares and 5 per cent of the world's land surface.

Look at Figure 1.22.1. Notice that tropical rainforest stretches across the world from South America, through parts of Africa and into South East Asia. The densest areas of rainforest lie between 10 degrees north and 10 degrees south of the Equator.

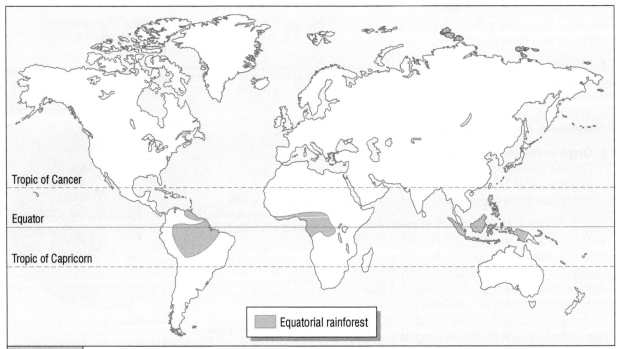

Tropic of Cancer

Equator

Tropic of Capricorn

Equatorial rainforest

Figure 1.22.1 Location of the tropical rainforest biome

Currently there is a great deal of concern about the threat of deforestation. Deforestation is causing many natural habitats to be wiped out and may be having an impact on the world's climate and on global warming.

Climate

The climate in a tropical rainforest is, as the name suggests, warm and wet. Throughout the year the temperature averages about 27°C and it changes little from month to month. Rainfall totals are high, usually 1,000–2,000 mm per year, and rainfall occurs throughout the year.

Figure 1.22.2 shows the climate graph for Zamboanga, Philippines.

- Temperature remains high throughout the year, hardly changing from month to month.
- Rainfall is also high throughout the year, although there is a wetter period from May to December. October is the wettest month with an average of 142 mm of rain.

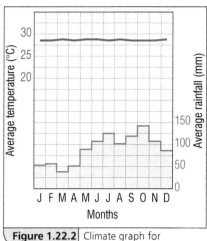

Figure 1.22.2 Climate graph for Zamboanga, Philippines

Soils

The soils in tropical rainforests are surprisingly low in nutrients considering the lush vegetation they support. There are several reasons for this:

- Most of the nutrients are found at the surface where dead leaves decompose quickly in the warm and wet conditions. Once released they are quickly absorbed by the plant roots so do not enrich the soil.
- The plants are well adapted to absorb these surface nutrients quickly through their shallow roots.
- Fungi growing on roots also help to transfer nutrients directly to the growing plants.
- Heavy tropical downpours quickly dissolve and wash away nutrients through the soil – this is called **leaching** (see Figure 1.22.3).

Figure 1.22.3 Shallow roots exposed by soil erosion

DID YOU KNOW?

There is great competition for light in the canopy. It is survival of the fittest! Some trees have leaves with flexible stems so that they can twist and turn to follow the movement of the Sun during the day. In this way they are able to maximise photosynthesis and grow at a more rapid rate than other trees.

Vegetation

The climatic conditions (warm and wet) are ideal for plant growth, which explains the lush vegetation found in equatorial regions. One of the main features of a tropical rainforest is the layering (**stratification**) of the plants and trees.

Top canopy

Here the very tallest trees (called **emergents**) can be found, often reaching heights in excess of 40 m. These fast-growing trees outcompete other trees to reach maximum sunlight. Many birds and insects live in this unique habitat.

Middle canopy

This is the main canopy of the rainforest, forming a dense green cloud-like 'top' to the rainforest. Some 90% of the wildlife lives in this layer, including most birds, mammals like sloths and many species of monkeys. Specialist plants such as **epiphytes** (plants that can absorb nutrients directly from water and air) and **lianas** (vigorous creepers rooted to the ground far below) are found here. The canopy intercepts up to 80 per cent of the rain falling on the rainforest and 70 per cent of the light.

Lower canopy

This extends between 5 m–10 m from the forest floor and mostly comprises small trees and saplings. With limited sunlight, the vegetation is more open.

Shrub and ground layer

Conditions here are very shaded, apart from where fallen trees have enabled shafts of sunlight to penetrate through the dense canopy above. Shade-loving plants such as small rubber and Swiss cheese plants are found here, along with some ground cover plants. Wildlife here eats fruit and seeds from the litter.

Rainforest plants have become well adapted to living in an equatorial climate (see Figure 1.22.5).

* Trees have smooth bark on their trunks – the lack of frost and fire means that they do not need thick protective bark.
* Taller trees, typically the emergent species, have wide buttress roots to provide extra stability.
* The warm and wet climate means that there is no seasonal leaf fall, so trees grow and shed leaves throughout the year.
* Tree leaves tend to be leathery in texture to resist the strong sunshine. They have a drip tip to help them shed water quickly after a tropical downpour.

Figure 1.22.4 An example of cauliflorous tree, the cacao tree

- To promote productivity, flowers and fruit grow directly from trunks and branches of trees – this is known as **cauliflory** (see Figure 1.22.4). The seeds of emergent trees are light and fluffy, enabling them to be readily dispersed by the wind that blows above the main canopy.

Nutrient recycling is very important in tropical rainforests. The warm and wet conditions promote very rapid decomposition by fungi and bacteria, and the rapid take up by fast-growing plants. This accounts for the relative low levels of nutrients in the soil. Heavy rainfall can remove nutrients from the soil (leaching). The vast majority of nutrients are stored in the biomass (living matter, particularly plants).

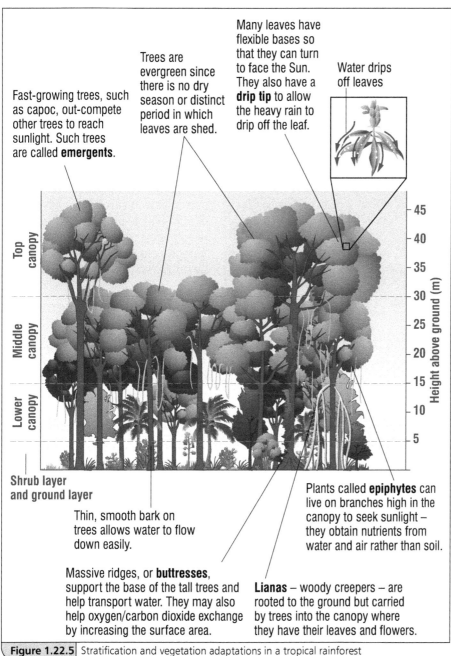

Figure 1.22.5 Stratification and vegetation adaptations in a tropical rainforest

Positive and negative impacts of human activities in tropical rainforest biomes

Human activities can have positive and negative impacts on tropical rainforest biomes.

Positive impacts

Many people believe that deforestation should be stopped. Indeed, there are many good reasons to support this point of view. However, the economies of countries in the tropics, including the Caribbean, often depend to some extent on forest products and gain some benefits from deforestation.

If the solution is to avoid placing a ban on deforestation, then it has to involve **sustainable management** so that forests are utilised but protected for future generations. This involves the protection of virgin rainforest and careful management of commercial operations. Trees need to be replanted and illegal and unregulated deforestation needs to be outlawed (see Figure 1.23.1).

Sustainable management in Guyana

Forestry is extremely important in Guyana. Timber products account for 5 per cent of Guyana's gross domestic product (GDP) and the industry employs around 20,000 persons. While Guyana still has almost 75 per cent of its land area covered by forest, it has seen significant deforestation since the late 1990s. This is largely the result of demands for commercial agriculture, mining, logging, road building and fuelwood collection.

Figure 1.23.1 Haitian children planting breadfruit with the Trees That Feed Foundation

Reafforestation

Reafforestation involves replanting trees. The Guyanese government has set up a number of projects using money from aid agencies such as the Worldwide Fund for Nature and the World Conservation Union. These have involved replanting local species of trees that have been cut down.

One example is in the Barima region where local communities are growing *Euterpe oleracea*, a type of manicole palm, to be replanted in local forests. Palm hearts from *Euterpe oleracea* palms supply a

US$2 million export canning industry. It is the most important non-forest product in north-west Guyana.

Iwokrama Project

The Iwokrama Project is a conservation and research project in central Guyana, set up in 1996 to promote the sustainable use of tropical rainforests. It has become a living natural laboratory for sustainable tropical forest management and research into global warming.

There are also opportunities for ecotourism in the forest, which enable tourists to learn about the forest ecosystem. The rainforest here is incredibly rich in wildlife, with over 1,500 species of flowers and 400 mammals. The region's waterways are home to the world's highest recorded diversity of fish species. Aerial walkways have been constructed (see Figure 1.23.2) to take visitors high into the canopy where the bulk of the plants and animals live.

In addition to research and tourism, forest products such as timber, honey and tropical fish for aquariums are being exploited sustainably to earn money to support the local communities.

Forest Stewardship

The Forest Stewardship Council (FSC) is leading the way in promoting sustainable management of tropical rainforests. It awards a certificate to companies that have demonstrated environmentally friendly practices, such as low-impact logging and reafforestation programmes. Consumers of timber are, increasingly, only buying wood that has the FSC stamp.

In 2006, the Barima company's forests in the west of Guyana received the FSC certificate. However, just nine months later, in 2007, the certificate was suspended when a number of irregularities were discovered. This is a major blow to both the company and to Guyana.

Satellite monitoring

In 2008, the Guyana Forestry Commission announced that it would be using satellite technology to monitor its tropical rainforests and check for signs of illegal logging. Using satellite images, it will be possible to digitally tag timber and track its movements. The project is part funded by the Japanese-based International Tropical Timber Organisation.

Negative impacts

Deforestation can lead to economic benefits as resources are exploited

Figure 1.23.2 Aerial walkway in the Iwokrama Forest, Guyana

Figure 1.23.3 Low impact logging in Iwokrama

CASE STUDY | Flooding in Haiti (2004)

In 2004, Hurricane Jeanne caused devastating floods, killing over 3,000 persons. Over 330 mm of rain fell in just a few hours.

The scale of the floods was blamed on many years of deforestation. The lack of tree cover and the very thin topsoils were unable to store water, resulting in rapid surface run-off and flooding.

In the past, 98 per cent of Haiti was forested. Much of this was cleared to make way for sugar plantations and to provide fuel for the sugar mills. Valuable mahogany was shipped to Europe to be made into furniture.

Recently, rapid population growth and increased poverty have led to people chopping down trees to make and sell charcoal. The loss of trees has also caused water tables to fall, creating water shortages for farmers.

Figure 1.23.4 | Haitians try to fix their homes after a flood destroyed their houses during a storm

and land is used for commercial farming. However, the long-term negative impacts of deforestation tend to outweigh the positives.

Impacts of deforestation in the Caribbean

Increased flood risk

The removal of forest exposes the soil to the full force of the tropical storms that hit the Caribbean. Without the umbrella effect of the trees, water flows quickly over the ground surface into rivers, and floods often result.

Soil erosion

No longer protected by forest, the thin topsoil is easily eroded during heavy rainstorms. Deep gullies form and the land becomes useless for farming. Rivers become choked with sediment, increasing the flood risk downstream.

Soil exhaustion

Tropical rainforest soils leak nutrients and they can quickly become exhausted if used intensively for farming. They are then even more likely to be eroded by wind and rain.

Damage to coral reefs

Sediment washed out to sea following heavy rainfall can lead to sedimentation, causing coral to die. The clouding of the normally clear tropical waters reduces sunlight and increases stress on the organisms of the coral reef. Scientists believe that reefs in Jamaica, the Dominican Republic and Puerto Rico are all at risk from sedimentation caused by deforestation.

Decline in aquifers

Water stored in rocks below the surface forms underground reservoirs called **aquifers**. These are extremely important sources of water in the Caribbean and many farmers draw water from wells to irrigate their crops.

Figure 1.23.5 Hawksbill turtle

The presence of trees retains water on the land and enables it to soak slowly into the soil and the rocks. When trees are cut down, the water tends to flow quickly over the surface and less filters downwards. This causes the water table to fall. Rivers and wells dry up as a result and water shortages are caused.

Ecological damage

The loss of habitats and subsequent reduction in biodiversity is a major concern in the Caribbean's rainforests. A number of endangered species, such as the Puerto Rican parrot, are under threat. Coastal forests are important breeding grounds for Hawksbill turtles (see Figure 1.23.5), and these are under threat from deforestation in Guadeloupe.

Tourism

Tourism is an important source of income as many people are attracted by tropical rainforests. Damage and destruction will have a negative effect, with tourists deciding to visit rainforests elsewhere in the world.

Global impacts

Tropical rainforests act as huge **carbon sinks**. That is, they absorb carbon from the atmosphere and help to reduce the build up of greenhouse gases. If rainforests are destroyed, less carbon will be absorbed and the greenhouse gases will become more concentrated and effective. This could lead to increased global warming.

An additional problem is that when trees are cut down and burned, carbon is released back into the atmosphere.

CASE STUDY | Deforestation in Jamaica

Causes of deforestation

In the past, most of Jamaica was covered by rainforest. Today, there are only fragments of forest in Jamaica's remote and mountainous interior. Over 75 per cent of original rainforest has been lost. The main causes of deforestation have been:

- bauxite mining and the construction of access roads
- commercial agriculture, particularly coffee plantations
- tourist developments around the coast
- logging
- charcoal burning.

Impacts of deforestation

Deforestation has had several impacts:

- Exposed soil is now much more vulnerable to soil erosion and landslides following heavy rain. In 1988, torrential rain associated with Hurricane Gilbert caused widespread flooding and loss of life, much of which was blamed on deforestation.
- Sedimentation is a major cause of damage to coral reefs. This is caused by loose soil being swept out to sea following heavy rainfall.
- Rainforests help to retain water during dry periods. Deforestation has led to water shortages and some rivers have dried up.
- Species diversity has decreased as forests have been cut down.
- Traditional lifestyles and knowledge about local plants and their medicinal uses is being lost.

Soil

LEARNING OUTCOMES

- Understand the main constituents of soil.
- Understand the factors affecting the development of latosols.

Soil can be defined as a mixture of minerals, organic matter, gases, liquids and organisms that together support life on Earth. Put another way, soil is 'the stuff that plants grow in'! (See Figure 1.24.1.)

There are five main constituents of soil:

- **Inorganic (mineral) matter** – this is derived from weathered rock or sediment (the parent material). It provides the physical bulk of most soils, providing an anchor for plant roots. Weathered minerals release important nutrients or plant foods. This process occurs rapidly in tropical regions such as the Caribbean, promoted by the high temperatures and rainfall.

- **Organic matter** – this is rotted (decomposed) vegetation that adds bulk and cohesion to the loose rock material. It provides important nutrients for plant growth and also helps to retain moisture in the soil.

- **Gases** and **liquids** – soil contains air pockets which may contain gases or water, both of which are important in soil formation and in maintaining healthy growing conditions for plants.

- **Organisms** – biota such as earthworms are very important in mixing a soil, particularly in drawing down surface litter into the topsoil. Fungi and bacteria are also important in soil formation, especially in the decomposition of dead vegetation.

Figure 1.21.3 page 55 shows the main constituents of soil. Notice that air/water accounts for 50 per cent of soil.

Latosols

Latosols are deep soils that typically form in tropical rainforest environments. They are characterised by being red in colour due to high concentrations of iron and aluminium. They are generally not very fertile.

Figure 1.24.2 shows a typical latosol soil profile. It describes the main characteristics of the soil and identifies some factors affecting its development.

- Climate – the warm and wet climate causes rapid chemical weathering of the parent material, accounting for the great depth of the soil. The high rainfall leads to water draining through the soil, dissolving minerals such as iron and redepositing them further down. As we have seen, this is called leaching (see Figure 1.22.3, page 57). It accounts for the low levels of fertility and the reddish colour of the lower soil horizons (layers). The climate also promotes decomposition as fungi and bacteria thrive in these conditions.

Figure 1.24.1 Soil crumb structure

- Vegetation – the lush rainforest vegetation provides plenty of dead organic matter to be decomposed. Although this adds large quantities of nutrients to the soil, the plants quickly absorb them and leave the soil impoverished and relatively infertile.
- Biota – many organisms thrive in the soil's warm and wet conditions. They help to mix up the nutrients, making them available to the plants. These conditions are ideal for decomposers such as fungi and bacteria, which release nutrients from rotting vegetation.
- Water – water drains rapidly through soils, dissolving and carrying away nutrients (leaching), and causing the soils to be relatively infertile.

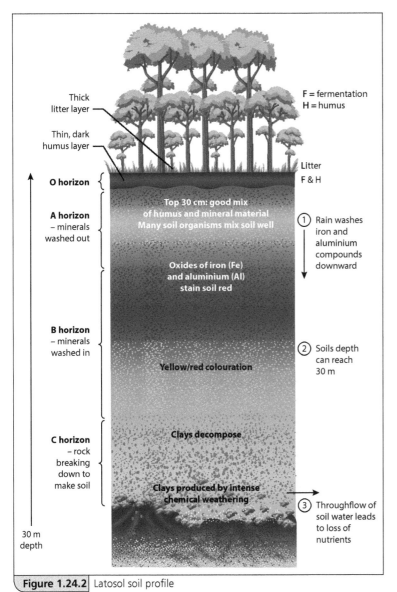

Figure 1.24.2 | Latosol soil profile

Adapted from D. Waugh (2009) *Geography: An Integrated Approach*, 4th edition, Nelson Thornes p. 318

SUMMARY QUESTIONS

1 What is soil and how does it form?

2 Draw a simple diagram to describe the main characteristics and processes responsible for the formation of latosols.

The hydrological cycle

Water is the most precious resource on Earth. Without water the Earth would be a dead planet. Water is constantly on the move, being recycled between the ocean, the land and the atmosphere. This is called the **hydrological cycle** (see Figure 1.25.1).

Notice that the hydrological cycle involves **stores** (e.g. oceans and ice) and **flows** (e.g. groundwater flow and rivers). There are three important processes in the hydrological cycle that convert water into different states: evaporation, condensation and precipitation.

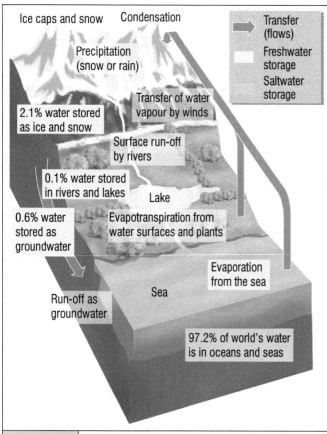

Figure 1.25.1 The hydrological cycle

- **Evaporation** – the conversion of water liquid into water vapour. Evaporation is most effective in sunny conditions when the air is warm and dry and when it is moving over the surface (windy). Under these conditions water is absorbed by the air and converted from a liquid to a gas – **water vapour**. Evaporation requires energy, commonly in the form of heat from the Sun. Most evaporation occurs over the oceans.

- **Condensation** – the conversion of water vapour (gas) into water liquid. When air is forced to cool, either by travelling over a cold ground surface (e.g. ice) or when it rises, the air contracts and is no longer able to hold so much water vapour. When a critical temperature (**dew point**) is reached, the air becomes **saturated** and the water vapour begins to be converted to water droplets. This is condensation. The water droplets suspended in the air form clouds or, if close to the ground, mist and fog. Condensation can be seen in homes on glass windows, on the outside of a glass of ice water or other cold liquids, or inside cars if warm moist air is in contact with a cold surface.

- **Precipitation** – the transfer of water from the air to the ground. When water droplets can no longer remain suspended in the air they usually fall to the ground as rain. Other forms of precipitation include hail, snow and sleet (a mixture of rain and snow).

Drainage basin hydrological cycle

A **drainage basin** is an area of land drained by a river and its tributaries (see Figure 1.25.2).

The movement of water through a drainage basin is shown in Figure 1.25.3. This is called the **drainage basin hydrological system**. Notice that there are several stores, transfers and outputs within the system.

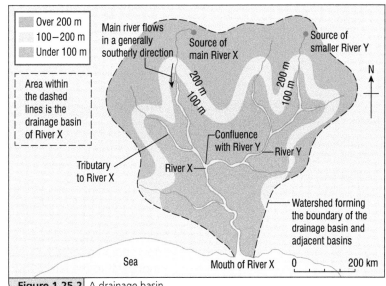

Figure 1.25.2 A drainage basin

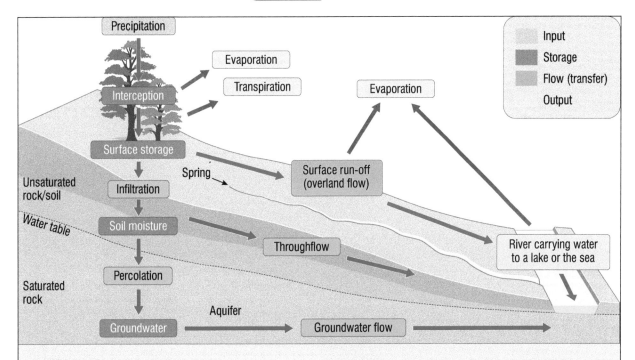

Precipitation: any source of moisture reaching the ground, e.g. rain, snow, frost

Interception: water being prevented from reaching the surface by trees or grass

Surface storage: water held on the ground surface, e.g. puddles

Infiltration: water sinking into soil/rock from the ground surface

Soil moisture: water held in the soil layer

Percolation: water seeping deeper below the surface

Groundwater: water stored in the rock

Evaporation: water lost from ground/vegetation surface

Transpiration: water lost through pores in vegetation

Surface run-off (overland flow): water flowing on top of the ground

Throughflow: water flowing through the soil layer parallel to the surface

Groundwater flow: water flowing through the rock layer parallel to the surface

Water table: current upper level of saturated rock/soil where no more water can be absorbed

Aquifer: saturated rock forming an underground water reservoir

Spring: water emerging onto the ground surface from underground

Figure 1.25.3 Drainage basin hydrological system

Drainage system – fluvial processes

- Understand the fluvial processes of transportation, erosion and deposition.

Fluvial processes

Most of a river's energy is used to overcome friction. Only about 5 per cent is used to transport sediment downstream or erode the river's banks and bed.

One of the most important factors affecting river processes is velocity – the speed of flow. While velocity increases slightly downstream, it does vary considerably within the river channel itself. It also varies from day to day and between the different seasons. A torrential downpour can lead to a sudden increase in river velocity, as can snowmelt in the late spring or early summer in countries that experience winter.

Transportation

There are four processes by which a river's sediment, or **load**, can be transported downstream. Notice in Figure 1.26.1 that the larger particles tend to be rolled along the river bed whereas the smaller (lighter) particles are more easily picked up and suspended. You can see how important velocity is in affecting which particles are transported by which process.

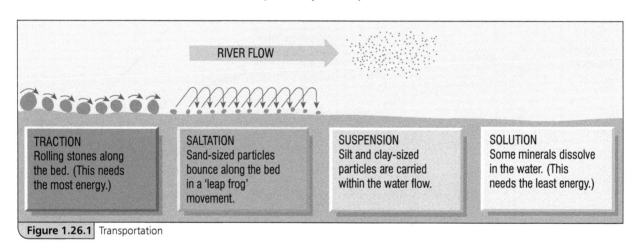

RIVER FLOW

TRACTION
Rolling stones along the bed. (This needs the most energy.)

SALTATION
Sand-sized particles bounce along the bed in a 'leap frog' movement.

SUSPENSION
Silt and clay-sized particles are carried within the water flow.

SOLUTION
Some minerals dissolve in the water. (This needs the least energy.)

Figure 1.26.1 Transportation

Erosion

There are four processes of river erosion:

- **Hydraulic action** – the sheer force of flowing water.
- **Corrasion** – the scouring action as rocks carried in the river are scraped along the bed and banks.
- **Attrition** – as rocks are bashed against each other and are dragged along the bed, they gradually become smaller and more rounded. This explains why river sediment tends to decrease in size and become less angular with distance downstream (see Figure 1.26.2).

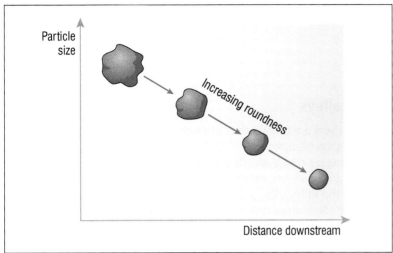

Figure 1.26.2 Erosion by attrition

EXAM TIP

In an examination you are often asked to describe and give examples of specific features in a river's course. Make sure you can illustrate the features with a well-labelled diagram.

- **Solution** – the dissolving of rocks, such as limestone, owing to the mildly acidic effects of carbon dioxide being dissolved in the water.

Deposition

Deposition takes place when velocity decreases and the river is unable to transport its load. This happens when a river enters the sea or a lake, which explains the extensive deposits of mud in river estuaries and river mouths. Deposition will also occur on the inside bend of a meander where velocity is lower (see Figure 1.27.5, page 72).

In most rivers there is an order of deposition, with coarser sediment being deposited near the source and very fine grained sediment – silt and clay – being deposited towards the river mouth (see Figure 1.26.3).

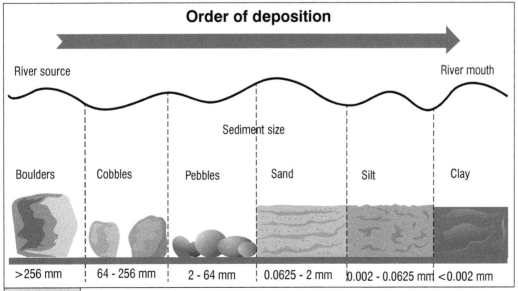

Figure 1.26.3 Order of deposition in a river

River valleys

While all rivers are unique they often display similar characteristics and landforms from source to mouth. In the upper course a river often carves a steep-sided **V-shaped valley** (see Figure 1.27.1). Notice that mass wasting is an important process affecting the shape of the upper slopes of the valley. Harder outcrops of rock jut into the valley forcing the river to flow around them. These are called interlocking spurs. The river itself, which is usually narrow and shallow, tumbles over the rocky river bed to form swirling eddies and whirlpools.

Potholes

The swirling action of the water in a river's upper course often forms hollows or depressions in the river bed called **potholes**. They are formed mainly by the process of corrasion, when one or more pebbles grind out a hollow as the water swirls round and round, rather like the action of a drill!

Rapids

If the river bed is uneven, possibly owing to alternating bands of hard and soft rock, a series of small steps called **rapids** may form.

Figure 1.27.1 A V-shaped valley in Dominica

These are rather like mini-waterfalls and they often provide exciting challenges for canoeists. There are many examples of rapids in the Caribbean, for example at Kurupukari on the Essequibo River in Guyana.

Waterfalls and gorges

A **waterfall** is a sudden 'step' in the long profile of a river. It often forms when a river crosses a relatively hard band of rock (see Figure 1.27.2). It may also form where a river flows over a cliff or escarpment.

- Erosion of the weaker rock beyond leads to the formation of a step over which the water plunges.
- Over a period of thousands of years the water erodes a deep plunge pool beneath the waterfall.
- Corrasion and hydraulic action slowly undercut the waterfall, resulting in the formation of an overhang.
- Unable to hold its own weight, the overhang collapses and the waterfall retreats upstream forming a steep-sided **gorge**.

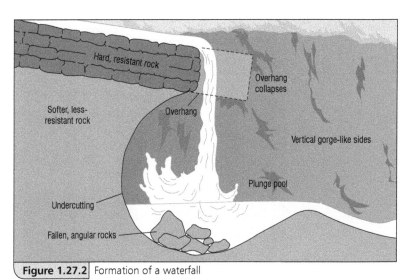

Figure 1.27.2 Formation of a waterfall

Figure 1.27.3 Kaieteur Falls, Guyana

Figure 1.27.4 Angel Falls, Venezuela

- Understand the characteristics and formation of meanders, oxbow lakes and braiding.
- Understand the characteristics and formation of floodplains, levees and deltas.

Meanders

A meander is a sweeping bend in a river. It is a common feature of a river in its middle and lower course. The land on either side of a meandering river is usually flat and forms the river's floodplain.

Look at Figure 1.27.5, which shows the main features of a meander.

- Highest velocity occurs around the outside bend of the meander.
- Erosion occurs on the outside bend, where velocity is high, to form a **river cliff**.
- Deposition occurs on the inside bend, where velocity is low, to form a **point bar** (slip-off slope).

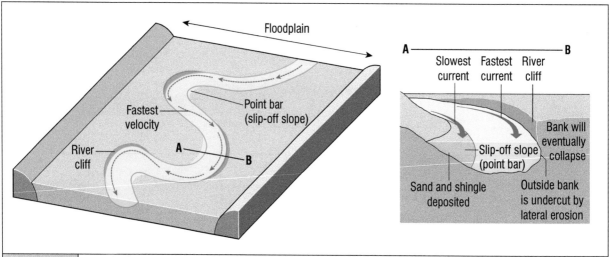

Figure 1.27.5 Meander features

Over a long period of time the lateral (sideways) erosion on the outside bend, together with deposition on the inside bend, causes the meander to move across the floodplain. This is called **meander migration**.

Oxbow lakes

Oxbow lakes are horseshoe-shaped lakes that are found on river floodplains close to a meandering river. They are former meander bends that have been cut off by the river during a period of high discharge or flooding.

Look at Figure 1.27.6.

- Figure 1.27.6a. Notice that the meander is almost doubling back on itself.
- Figure 1.27.6b. As erosion takes place on either side of the meander the meander 'neck' gets narrower.
- Figure 1.27.6c. During a flood the water breaks through the meander neck, cutting off the old meander. Deposition at the side of the new channel gradually seals off the old meander, which now becomes an oxbow lake.

Once formed, the oxbow lake will slowly become silted up and it will eventually dry up altogether.

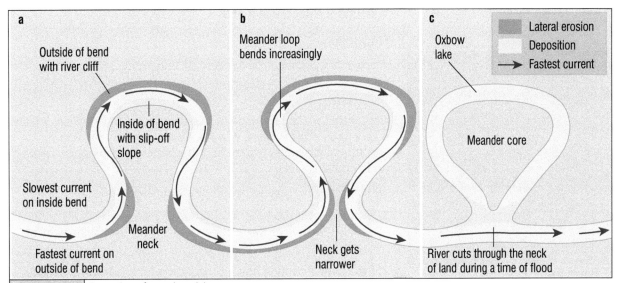

Figure 1.27.6 Formation of an oxbow lake

Braiding

A braided river is one that is divided into several smaller channels, separated by islands of deposited sediment (see Figure 1.27.7). Braiding occurs most commonly in rivers that have variable rates of discharge and carry large amounts of sediment. Seasonal changes in river discharge occur as there is limited rainfall in the dry season and greater rainfall in the wet season. During intense and prolonged rainfall in the wet season the river is able to transport larger gravels and boulders. After the intense rainfall, the discharge is reduced and the heavier bedload is deposited on the river bed. These gravels and boulders form obstacles in the path of the sluggish river and cause more sediments to be deposited. The river often splits into several separate channels and flows around the objects. After some time this deposited sediment forms river islands, aits or eyots.

Water is taken (abstracted) from several rivers in the Caribbean, which can reduce their discharge and also cause the braiding to occur.

Figure 1.27.7 A braided river in Iceland

In Canada and Iceland, many of the rivers are fed by glacial meltwater.

• The high volume of discharge during the spring and early summer (when ice and snow is melting) transports a great deal of sediment, particularly sand and gravel.

• However, during periods of lower discharge (at night and during the autumn and winter), heavier sediment is deposited rapidly, causing the river to split into several separate channels that weave around the deposited islands.

Floodplain

A floodplain is an area of flat land on either side of a river. It is most extensive in the lower course of a river and is usually found where the river is meandering.

Floodplains are largely made of fine river sediment called silt, which is very fertile. This explains why floodplains are very productive agricultural areas (see Figure 1.27.8). Oxbow lakes may also be found on floodplains.

Two important processes operate to form floodplains:

1 Meander migration over thousands of years slowly widens the valley as erosion at the outside meander-bends nibbles away at the valley sides.

2 Extensive deposition of silt occurs every time the river bursts its banks during a flood. This may happen several times a year.

Figure 1.27.8 Aerial view of a floodplain

Levees

A levee is a raised river bank. It is formed when the water in the river channel overtops its banks during a flood (see Figure 1.27.9).

• As the water overflows, velocity falls and coarse sediment such as gravel and sand are deposited on the river bank.

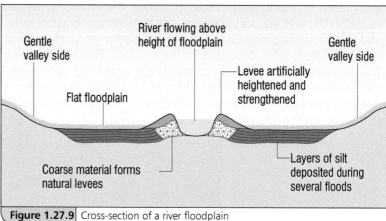
Figure 1.27.9 Cross-section of a river floodplain

- Repeated flooding, over many years, results in the gradual raising of the river banks above the level of the floodplain to form distinct levees.

River banks can be raised artificially to protect floodplains from flooding. In some parts of the world, for example the USA, these artificial embankments are also called levees.

Deltas

A delta is an extensive area of sediment formed by deposition at the mouth of a river or where a river flows into a lake. Look at Figure 1.27.10 which shows how a delta is formed.

- A river carries a vast amount of sediment in its lower course.
- When it meets the sea or flows into a lake, the velocity decreases rapidly, leading to deposition of the sediment.
- Heavier sediment (sand) is deposited first, followed by finer silt and clay as the velocity continues to fall.
- Over time, the layers of sediment build up to form new land. Gradually the coast extends out into the sea or the lake.
- Rivers flowing over deltas are often forced to split into separate channels called **distributaries**. This is because the reduction in the river's velocity leads to increasing amounts of deposition.

The River Nile in Egypt forms an excellent example of a delta as it flows into the Mediterranean Sea (see Figure 1.27.11). This triangular-shaped delta is called an **arcuate delta**. The other main type of delta is a **bird's foot delta**, where the distributaries extend into the sea, flanked by deposits of sediment. The Mississippi is an excellent example of this type of delta.

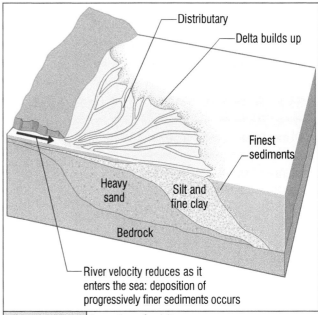

Figure 1.27.10 | Formation of a delta

EXAM TIP

When studying for your examination, try to learn the name of a specific example for each type of delta. Marks are usually allocated for examples.

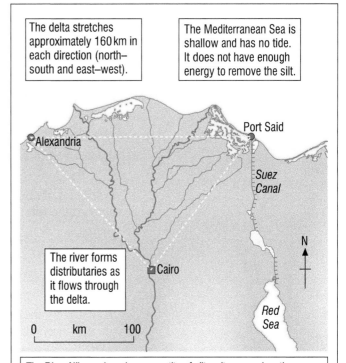

The delta stretches approximately 160 km in each direction (north–south and east–west).

The Mediterranean Sea is shallow and has no tide. It does not have enough energy to remove the silt.

The river forms distributaries as it flows through the delta.

The River Nile carries a huge quantity of silt as it approaches the sea. The silt contains many nutrients, so makes good farmland, and fish thrive in the nutrient-rich water. The silt, which has accumulated over centuries, forms a flat, fertile delta, which is now a densely settled area.

Figure 1.27.11 | The Nile delta

Coastal system – wave processes

What causes waves?

Waves are most commonly formed by **friction** as the wind blows over the surface of the sea. They can also be formed by earthquakes, volcanic eruptions or underwater landslides. These events are rare but can lead to the formation of devastating **tsunami**.

In 2004, a massive earthquake triggered giant tsunami waves that swept across the Indian Ocean killing some 240,000 persons. In 2011, a massive earthquake in north-east Japan triggered tsunami waves that killed over 16,000 persons and disrupted the supply of nuclear energy to the economy.

What causes waves to break?

Look at Figure 1.28.1. Notice that in deep water the surface waves form part of a circular movement of water. This explains why there is actually very little horizontal movement of water in the oceans. However, look what happens as the waves get nearer to the coast:

- As the sea near the shore is shallow the circular motion of the waves is interrupted by friction with the seabed.
- The water motion becomes more elliptical (shaped like a rugby ball).
- The wave grows in height and begins to topple forward.
- Eventually the wave breaks on the shore. Water moves up the beach as the swash and then drains back down the beach as backwash.

The power of the waves when they reach the coast depends on three factors:

1 *Distance of open water over which the wind has blown*. This is called the **fetch**. The longer the fetch the more powerful the waves.

2 *Strength of the wind*. The stronger the wind, the more powerful the waves.

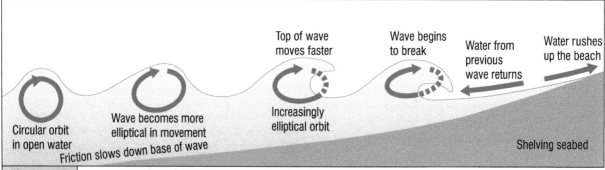

Figure 1.28.1 Waves approaching the coast

3 *Duration of the wind.* If strong winds have blown over a long period of time, this will result in powerful waves.

Constructive and destructive waves

It is possible to identify two types of waves.

1 Constructive waves

Constructive waves are low but powerful waves that surge up the beach when they break (see Figure 1.28.2). Their swash is much more powerful than their backwash, much of which percolates through the beach as the water flows back to the sea. Constructive waves are created by storms many miles away from the coast and they travel fast across the ocean. They are called 'constructive' waves because they transport beach material to the top of the beach, thereby 'constructing' it.

2 Destructive waves

Destructive waves are essentially the opposite to constructive waves (see Figure 1.28.3). They are taller and tend to crash down onto a beach rather than surging up the beach. There is little swash but the backwash is powerful. This leads to the erosion of the lower beach, hence the term 'destructive'. Destructive waves are usually formed during local storms that are centred close to the coast.

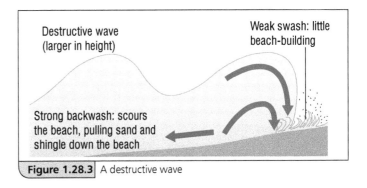

Figure 1.28.2 A constructive wave

Figure 1.28.3 A destructive wave

Winds and waves in the Caribbean

Look at Figure 1.28.4. It shows the winds and waves affecting the coast of Barbados. Notice the following features:

- The **prevailing** (most common) winds (the **trade winds**) blow from the north-east.
- East-facing coastlines tend to be affected by high-energy waves. This explains why surfing is popular along these exposed coastlines. It also accounts for the features of erosion that are formed by these powerful waves.
- West-facing coastlines are sheltered from the trade winds and experience less powerful waves. Deposition dominates, forming wide sandy beaches. Tourism is popular along these sheltered coastlines.

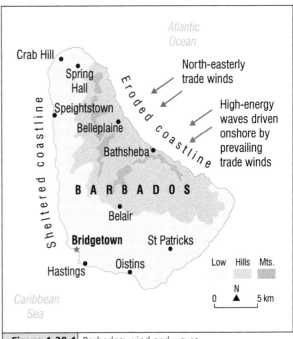

Figure 1.28.4 Barbados: wind and waves

Processes of coastal erosion

There are four processes of coastal erosion:

- **Hydraulic action** – the sheer force of the waves as they break against a cliff, causing broken rock fragments to be dislodged (see Figure 1.28.5).
- **Corrasion** (or **abrasion**) – pebbles are picked up by the sea and flung against a cliff. The constant sandpapering effect of pebbles pushed up and down a rocky platform by wave action is called abrasion.
- **Solution** – the dissolving of soluble rock, such as limestone.
- **Attrition** – as rocks rub against each other they gradually become smaller and more rounded. This process relates purely to rocks coming into contact with one another, and is not about the erosion of cliffs.

Figure 1.28.5 Waves break against the rocks near Devil's Bridge in Antigua

Coastal erosion is most effective when the waves are powerful and contain a lot of energy. These waves need to break at or close to the foot of a cliff if they are to carry out erosion. This explains why erosion is active on coasts that have narrow beaches, steeper underwater gradients and face the prevailing winds, such as the east coast of Barbados.

Sediment transport and deposition

There are many different types of sediment at the coast, including beautiful white coral sand, the more common yellow sand, pebbles (shingle) and mud. The waves, tides and offshore currents constantly move this sediment up and down the beach and along the coastline. This is coastal **transportation**.

Look at Figure 1.28.6. It shows the common processes of sediment transportation. These processes will usually operate at the same time, moving particles of different sizes. Small particles will be picked up and suspended in the water whereas larger particles will be rolled or bounced along the seabed.

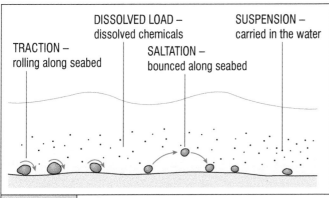

Figure 1.28.6 Sediment movement

One important factor affecting the movement of sediment at the coast is the direction of the approaching waves:

- If waves approach the coast head on, sediment will simply be moved up and down the beach.
- If the waves approach the coast at an angle, sediment will move in a zig-zag pattern along the beach. This is called **longshore drift** (see Figure 1.29.7, page 83). It will often result in a build-up of sediment at one end of the beach.

Deposition of sediment occurs when the velocity (speed of flow) of the water is reduced and the sediment can no longer be carried or moved by the sea. This occurs most commonly in sheltered areas, for example in a bay (see Figure 1.28.7).

Figure 1.28.7 Parlatuvier Bay, Tobago

Landforms of coastal erosion

Cliffs and wave-cut platforms

Figure 1.29.1 Little Bay, Barbados

Look at Figure 1.29.1. It shows the main features associated with a cliffed coastline. Over hundreds of years the cliff gradually retreats and the **wave-cut platform** at its foot becomes wider. Figure 1.29.2 describes what happens.

- Repeated erosion (hydraulic action and corrosion) at the foot of the cliff results in a **wave-cut notch**.
- The wave-cut notch becomes enlarged, creating an overhang of rock above it.

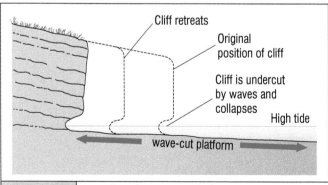

Figure 1.29.2 Formation of a wave-cut platform

- The overhang of rock collapses, perhaps following a period of stormy weather, to form a pile of rocks at the foot of the cliff.
- The sea erodes away the loose pile of rocks.
- Abrasion smoothes and extends the underlying wave-cut platform.
- The sequence repeats itself so that the cliff face retreats and the wave-cut platform becomes more extensive.

In parts of the Caribbean where limestone is exposed at the coast, solution (chemical dissolving) and wave action can create a **low-tide platform**. Unlike a wave-cut platform, it is not exposed at low tide (see Figure 1.29.3).

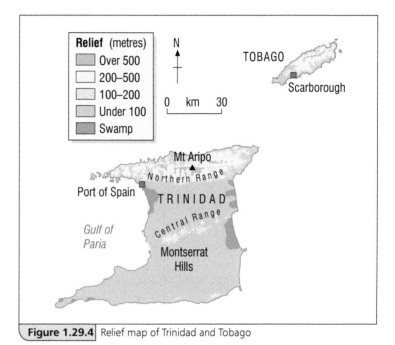

Figure 1.29.3 A low-tide platform

Headlands and bays

Headlands and bays are common coastal features in the Caribbean and elsewhere in the world.

- **Headland** – a section of rocky coastline that protrudes into the sea.
- **Bay** – a pronounced indentation in the coastline usually found between two headlands.

Headlands and bays most commonly form when rocks of different strengths are exposed at the coast or where alternating bands of high and low land reach the coast. Look at Figure 1.29.4 which shows the relief of Trinidad. Notice how the headlands (points) and bays on the east and west coast match the high and low land. On the north coast, the headlands and bays are carved in the tough metamorphic rocks with bays at the mouths of the river valleys formed along areas of lower resistance.

Figure 1.29.4 Relief map of Trinidad and Tobago

Caves, arches and stacks

Exposed headlands are affected by powerful erosive waves. There are several distinctive landforms associated with the erosion of a headland, such as sea caves, arches and stacks (see Figure 1.29.5). A sequence of events explains the formation of these landforms (see Figure 1.29.6).

Figure 1.29.5 Erosion on an exposed headland

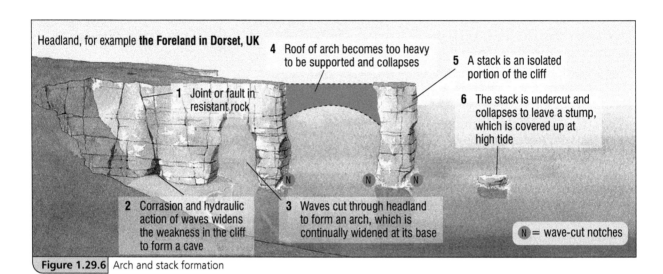

Headland, for example **the Foreland in Dorset, UK**

4 Roof of arch becomes too heavy to be supported and collapses

5 A stack is an isolated portion of the cliff

1 Joint or fault in resistant rock

6 The stack is undercut and collapses to leave a stump, which is covered up at high tide

2 Corrasion and hydraulic action of waves widens the weakness in the cliff to form a cave

3 Waves cut through headland to form an arch, which is continually widened at its base

N = wave-cut notches

Figure 1.29.6 Arch and stack formation

- Weaknesses in the cliffs, such as joints (vertical cracks) and faults will be exploited by the processes of hydraulic action and corrosion to form **sea caves** on opposite sides of a headland.
- Over time the sea caves become enlarged and eventually join to form an **arch**.
- Weathering and erosion processes enlarge the arch, and the roof gradually becomes thinner.
- Eventually the roof of the arch collapses under its own weight, leaving behind an isolated pillar of rock called a **stack**.
- Gradually the stack is eroded until all that is left is a low rock outcrop exposed only at low tide. This is called a **stump**.

Landforms of coastal deposition

Beaches

A **beach** is a deposit of sand and/or pebbles found at the coast. **Beaches** are the most common and widespread landforms of coastal deposition. Sandy beaches are most likely to be formed in sheltered stretches of coast, where the gentle waves are only capable of carrying finer sediment. Beaches made of pebbles (shingle) tend to form along high-energy coastlines where the more powerful waves can transport larger particles onshore.

Look at Figure 1.29.8. Notice how a beach has formed in the bay. This is called a **bayhead beach**. Deposition has occurred here because the waves in the bay have less energy than at the headlands. This is caused by the waves being distorted by the shape of the coastline – a process called **wave refraction**.

- In the open water, wave energy is spread out evenly along the wave fronts.
- As the waves approach the shore they become distorted by the shape of the coast.
- This causes energy (shown by lines called orthogonals) to become concentrated at the headlands to form features of erosion such as cliffs.
- In the bays, energy is reduced (notice that the orthogonals spread apart) and sediment is deposited to form a beach.

Wooden groynes slow down movement and widen the beach

Backwash carries material directly down the beach under gravity

Swash carries material obliquely up the beach

Depletion of sand

Accumulation of sand

C Third position

B Second position

A First position of pebble

Direction of longshore drift

Waves approach beach at an angle – often determined by the prevailing wind

Figure 1.29.7 Longshore drift

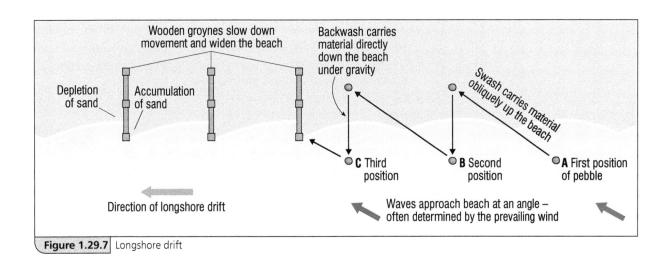

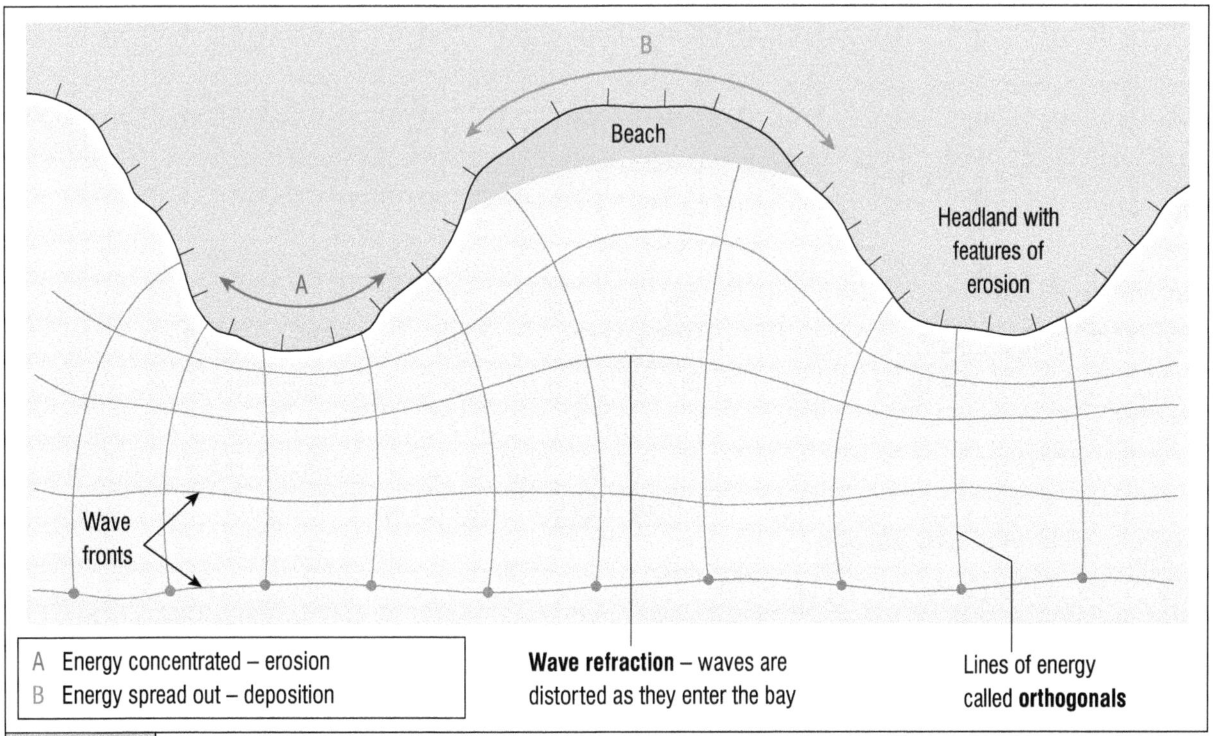

B

Beach

Headland with features of erosion

A

Wave fronts

A Energy concentrated – erosion
B Energy spread out – deposition

Wave refraction – waves are distorted as they enter the bay

Lines of energy called **orthogonals**

Figure 1.29.8 Wave refraction

- Understand the characteristics and formation of spits, tombolos and bars.

Spits

A **spit** is a narrow finger of sand or pebbles that juts out into the sea from the land. It is formed when sediment transported along the coast by longshore drift is deposited at a bend in the coastline.

Look at Figure 1.29.9 to see the development of a spit.

- Over time the sediment gradually extends into the sea at the point where the coastline changes its shape.
- Fine muds are deposited in the very calm sheltered waters behind a spit to form **mudflats** and **saltmarshes**.
- The tip of the spit becomes curved to form a **recurved tip** or **hook** owing to changes in the wind and wave direction.

The important thing to remember about a spit is that it is actual land. It does not become submerged by the sea at high tide.

DID YOU KNOW?

The longest spit in the world is the 110 km long Arabat spit in the Sea of Azov, an extension of the Black Sea bordering Russia and Ukraine. There are several other spits in the Sea of Azov, some of which are over 30 km long.

In Virginia, USA, the Willoughby spit in Norfolk is said to have been formed by hurricanes in the 18th and 19th centuries that washed up huge quantities of sand onto the coast.

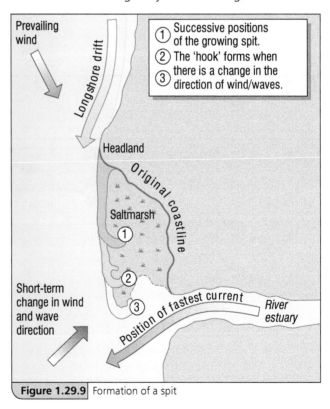

Figure 1.29.9 Formation of a spit

Figure 1.29.10 A tombolo connects an island to the mainland

Tombolos

Occasionally a spit grows away from the shore and becomes attached to an island (see Figure 1.29.10). This is called a **tombolo**. A good example is Scotts Head tombolo in Dominica. The Palisadoes tombolo just south of Kingston, Jamaica, is a highly complex 13 km tombolo that connects several offshore cays. It is the site of Kingston's Norman Manley International Airport.

Bars

A bar is a long narrow deposit of sand or shingle that usually forms parallel to the coast. There are two main types of bar:

1 A **bay bar** is a deposit of sand or shingle that forms across a bay, often trapping a freshwater lake or lagoon behind it (see Figure 1.29.11).

Figure 1.29.11 A bay bar

2 An offshore **barrier bar** is a narrow sand or shingle deposit that runs parallel to the coast just out to sea. It is usually only exposed at low tide. A shallow saltwater lagoon forms behind the bar, topped up at each high tide when water washes over the bar. Over time the offshore bar may form a long narrow island called a barrier beach (see Figure 1.29.12). The Miami suburb of Miami Beach in the USA has been developed on an offshore bar now connected to the mainland by several major bridges. In the Caribbean, two bars along the coast of St Thomas, Jamaica, enclose a lagoon known as the Yallahs Pond.

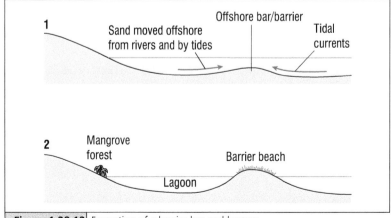

Figure 1.29.12 Formation of a barrier bar and lagoon

Drainage patterns

When viewed on a map or an aerial photo, rivers often form distinctive **drainage patterns**. Look back to Figure 1.25.2, page 67. Notice that the river and its tributaries form a pattern similar to the branches of a tree. This is called a **dendritic** drainage pattern.

There are three common drainage patterns: dendritic, **trellised** and **radial**. They are largely determined by gradient, rock type and geological structure.

Dendritic

This tree-like drainage pattern develops in gently sloping river basins with a uniform rock type (see Figure 1.30.1). Streams flow into each other almost at random. The Caroni River in central Trinidad, which flows over relatively weak sands and clays, is a good example. Dendritic drainage patterns are the most common in the Caribbean.

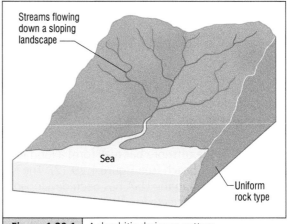

Streams flowing down a sloping landscape

Sea

Uniform rock type

| Figure 1.30.1 | A dendritic drainage pattern |

Trellised

Trellised drainage resembles a rectangular grid, with tributaries joining at right angles. This type of drainage pattern develops in areas with bands of alternating weak and resistant rocks (see Figure 1.30.2). Notice that the bands of rock have been folded and are dipping (plunging) steeply. Tributaries erode the weaker bands of rock and therefore join the main river at right angles. This type of drainage pattern exists in the Northern Range in Trinidad, where folded rocks cause tributaries to join the main rivers at right angles.

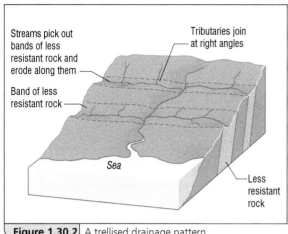

Figure 1.30.2 A trellised drainage pattern

Radial

Radial drainage commonly occurs where rivers flow downhill from a central dome or mountain (see Figure 1.30.3). In the Caribbean, radial drainage is often associated with volcanic islands such as St Lucia, Nevis and Montserrat. Here the rock type is the same (often a lava flow), so it is gradient that determines the pattern of drainage.

Look at the map of Montserrat on Figure 1.30.4. A radial drainage pattern can be seen where rivers flow away from the volcanic centre towards the sea.

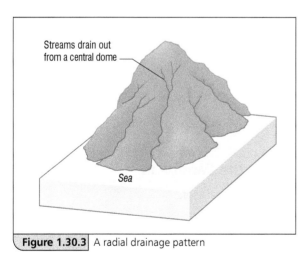

Figure 1.30.3 A radial drainage pattern

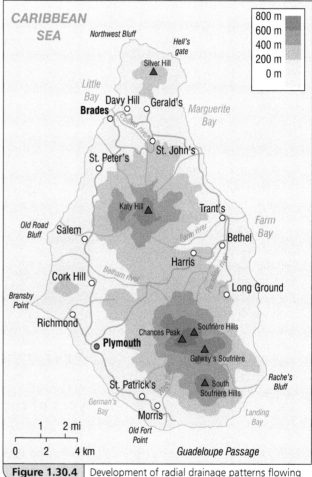

Figure 1.30.4 Development of radial drainage patterns flowing from Montserrat's volcanic centre towards the sea.

DID YOU KNOW?

Coral reefs only account for 0.18 per cent of the marine environment yet they are home to nearly 25 per cent of all known marine species. In the Caribbean, coral reefs support 500–600 species of fish as well as hundreds of other species of plants and animals. One of the most iconic animals associated with the coral reefs in the Caribbean is the endangered sea turtle, which feeds mainly on seagrasses on the sheltered landward side of the reefs.

What is a coral reef?

A coral reef is a hard rocky ridge built up from the seabed by millions of tiny living coral organisms. It is their hard exoskeletons that form the reef itself. Coral reefs are important for several reasons:

- They form one of the richest ecosystems on Earth, supporting many thousands of species of fish, plants and other organisms.
- Millions of people worldwide depend on fish caught from coral reefs, particularly in the developing world. In East Asia, over 1 billion persons are supported by fish caught in neighbouring coral reefs.
- With their stunning beauty coral reefs are popular attractions for tourists in the Caribbean, earning the region an estimated US$10 billion per year (see Figure 1.31.1).
- Coral reefs form a physical barrier to tropical storms and hurricanes, helping to protect the mainland coast from powerful storm surges.
- Algae and sponges on coral reefs have valuable medicinal qualities that scientists believe might be used in the future to treat viruses and some cancers.

Figure 1.31.1 Marine life in a coral reef in the Caribbean Sea

Types of coral reef in the Caribbean

There are three main types of coral reef.

1 Fringing reef

Fringing reefs are shallow-water reefs that run roughly parallel to the coast. They form from the gradual accumulation of coral over a long period of time in ideal environmental conditions (see Figure 1.31.2). A shallow lagoon is often formed between the reef and the shore and this is usually rich in marine life. Storms, such as hurricanes, can occasionally break up fringing reefs to leave behind isolated reefs rather than a single continuous feature.

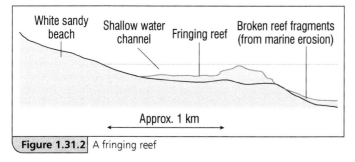

Figure 1.31.2 A fringing reef

2 Barrier reef

Barrier reefs are much more extensive features than fringing reefs and are found further out to sea. The most famous example is Australia's Great Barrier Reef, which runs for some 2,600 km off the east coast of Queensland. The largest barrier reef in the Caribbean (second largest in the world) lies some 25 km off the coast of Belize.

Look at Figure 1.31.3 which shows a barrier reef.

• A barrier reef probably begins life as a normal fringing reef.

• A gradual rise in sea level over a long period of time floods the coastline creating a wide body of water between the shore and the reef.

• While the reef continues to grow it remains some distance away from the coast.

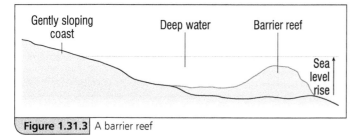

Figure 1.31.3 A barrier reef

3 Atoll reef

A coral atoll is an isolated, almost circular, ring-shaped reef with a deep lagoon in its centre. Coral atolls are largely concentrated in the Pacific and Indian Oceans, for example the Maldives.

Coral atolls often form at submarine seamounts (extinct volcanoes) where the rim of the crater creates the shallow water conditions necessary for coral growth (see Figure 1.31.4). The deep lagoon forms in the extinct volcano's crater, or caldera.

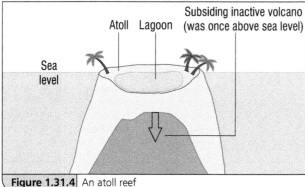

Figure 1.31.4 An atoll reef

Coral formation

Look at Figure 1.31.5. It shows the distribution of coral reefs in the Caribbean. Corals thrive in the Caribbean because conditions are ideal for their growth.

- Temperatures – corals only live in seawater that has an average temperature of 18°C or more. The ideal temperature is 23–5°C
- Salinity – the right amount of salt is needed. Corals thrive best in the open sea away from the freshwater that is found at the mouths of rivers.
- Light – corals thrive in shallow water conditions because the algae on which they feed require light to photosynthesise.
- Clear well-aerated water – polluted water, particularly if it contains lots of sediment, reduces light and can affect the coral's ability to feed. Lack of oxygen can cause the corals to die. They grow fastest where currents bring food.
- Turbidity – some water movement (turbidity) is necessary to provide food and oxygenated water to the coral, but strong currents agitate sediment and this reduces sunlight and smothers coral, preventing feeding and respiration.
- Presence of beneficial algae and fish – coral enjoy a symbiotic (harmless) relationship with algae (zooxanthellae) and fish. Algae live within the coral and provide it with energy (food). Fish shelter in coral reefs and breed there. Corals can consume small fish.

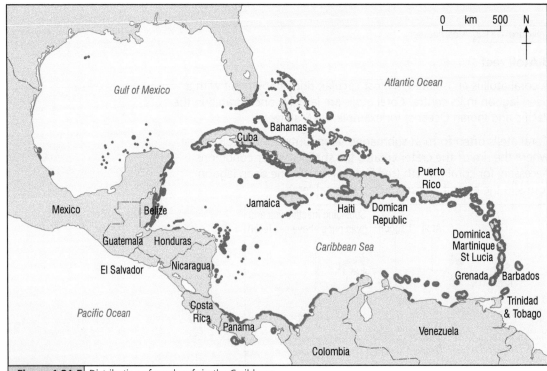

Figure 1.31.5 Distribution of coral reefs in the Caribbean

The importance of coral reefs

Coral reefs are extremely important ecosystems providing a range of benefits. An estimated 500 million people depend on coral reefs for food, coastal protection, building materials and income from tourism. About 30 million people are totally dependent on coral reefs for their livelihoods or because they live on atolls.

The main benefits of corals include the following:

- Coastal protection – coral reefs act as buffer zones, providing vital shoreline protection from storms and tsunami. The shallow water above a reef forces waves to break early before reaching the mainland shore. This reduces coastal erosion and the risk of flooding. Corals also provide sheltered conditions for the growth of mangrove forests, which themselves are important breeding grounds for fish.
- Beach development – the erosion of coral reefs creates the white sand that typically forms the beaches of tropical coastlines. Some of this sand is extracted for the construction industry to make cement.
- Ecological benefits – coral reefs are extremely diverse ecosystems. One hectare of reef off South East Asia was found to support over 2,000 species of fish. Coral reefs are important breeding grounds for fish, offering shelter and food.

Figure 1.31.6 A scuba diver explores a coral reef

- Socio-economic benefits – the global value of the world's coral reefs has been estimated at almost US$30 billion each year. Coral reefs are extremely important commercial fishing grounds, providing some 25 per cent of the Less Economically Developed Countries' (LEDCs) total fish catch. It is estimated that coral reef fisheries in East Asia feed over 1 billion people. Coral reefs are extremely popular tourist destinations, providing a huge source of income and employment for thousands of people. Millions of people visit the Caribbean each year to enjoy its tropical beaches and coral reefs. Coral reefs are also increasingly valued for medicinal purposes. Scientists believe that some coral species could be a fundamental source of life-saving or life-enhacing products.

Mangrove wetlands

What are mangrove wetlands?

Mangrove wetlands or swamps are coastal ecosystems found in tropical and subtropical regions (see Figure 1.32.1). Notice that mangroves are found extensively in the Caribbean as well as in many other regions around the world. One of the largest mangrove swamps in the world is on Florida's south-west coast.

Mangrove swamps are characterised by halophytic (salt loving) trees, shrubs and other plants growing in brackish to saline tidal waters. These wetlands are often found in estuaries, where fresh water meets salt water. They are infamous for their dense maze of woody vegetation.

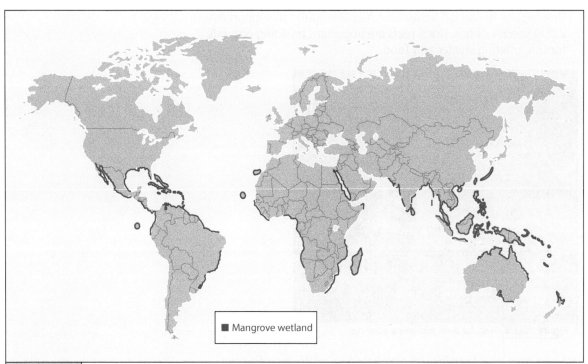

Figure 1.32.1 Global distribution of mangrove swamps

Caribbean mangrove wetland ecosystems

In the Caribbean there are three types of mangrove:

• Red mangroves – these are found closest to the sea and have their roots submerged at high tide. They cope with high levels of salt by obtaining water from the ocean through a process known as 'reverse osmosis'. The long arching aerial woody roots help anchor the plant in the soft muddy sediment. It is through the roots that oxygen is obtained. The roots also trap sediment, helping to stabilise this coastal environment.

- Black mangroves and white mangroves – these are found further inland where conditions are saltier. They do not have the extensive aerial root systems of the red mangroves. They cope by excreting the excess salt onto their leaves. They can transfer oxygen direct to the roots.

Why are mangrove wetlands important?

Mangrove wetlands have several very important functions (see Figure 1.32.2):

- **Coastal protection** – the dense tangle of mangrove roots help to trap sediment. This creates an effective coastal defence to hurricanes, storm surges and tsunami. As sea levels rise due to global warming, mangroves will continue to grow and thrive, providing lasting protection to coastal areas. If the mangroves are removed, the muddy sediment quickly washes away leaving the coastline unprotected.

- **Ecological (biodiversity) importance** – mangrove swamps provide valuable habitats for many species of animal and fish, which benefit from the calm, sheltered waters. These ecosystems sustain billions of worms, protozoa, barnacles and oysters, which in turn feed fish and shrimp. These then support wading birds, pelicans, and the endangered crocodile (see Figure 1.32.3).

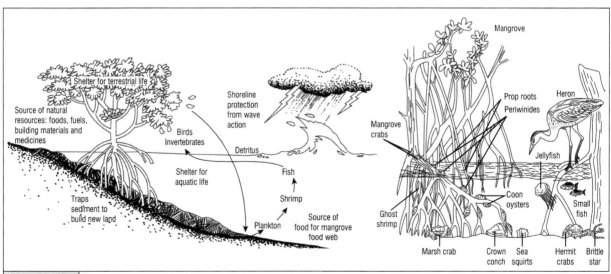

Figure 1.32.2 The importance of mangrove wetlands

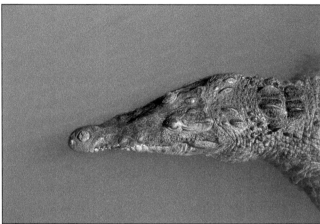

Figure 1.32.3 Crocodile swimming in the Black River, Jamaica

• **Socio-economic benefits** – mangrove swamps are popular tourist attractions despite the biting insects. Visitors can appreciate the wide variety of flora and fauna in their natural habitat. Mangroves provide many products and raw materials and they have significant values for local communities (see Figure 1.32.4).

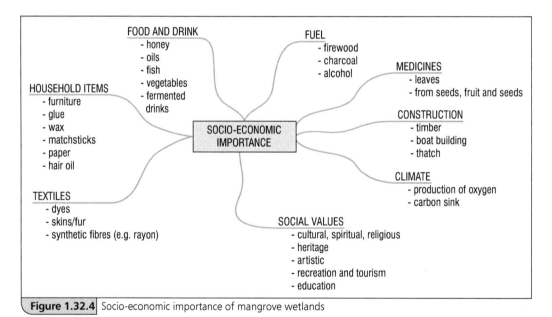

Figure 1.32.4 Socio-economic importance of mangrove wetlands

SUMMARY QUESTION

Construct a summary spider diagram to describe why mangrove wetlands are important natural environments.

CASE STUDY | Black River Lower Morass, Jamaica

The Black River Lower Morass (also known as the Great Morass) is Jamaica's largest wetland (5,700 ha) and is a refuge for two endangered species, the American crocodile (see Figure 1.32.3) and the West Indian manatee. An internationally recognised wetland, it is protected by the Jamaican Wildlife Protection Act.

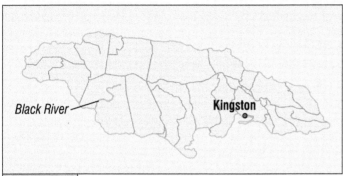

Figure 1.32.5 The Black River, Jamaica

The Black River Lower Morass is an important breeding ground for fish and home to over one hundred species of bird, including ospreys, herons and flamingos. It is a vital economic resource supporting over 20,000 local people by providing opportunities for fishing and tourism. Abundant stands of thatch palm are used by local people for basket making and as a roofing material.

Tourists are attracted to the mangrove wetland, seeing it as wild and mysterious (see Figure 1.32.6). The prospect of viewing crocodiles and birds is a major draw for visitors. Tour operators encourage exploration by kayak, sea bikes and hiking trails. Many local businesses as well as hotels and restaurants have benefited from this example of adventure tourism. With the threat of peat mining (for energy) and agriculture, income generation from tourism has provided an economic benefit that helps to protect and conserve the area from future development and potential damage.

Figure 1.32.6 Tourists visiting the Black River Lower Morass, Jamaica

Natural hazards and natural disasters

What are natural hazards?

A **natural hazard** can be defined as a naturally occurring event, such as an earthquake or a landslide, that poses a threat or risk to people. The catastrophic consequences of such an event, particularly in areas of high population density, are what is called a **natural disaster**.

The term '**risk**' is used to describe the likelihood of a hazard occurring. Those who choose to live close to a volcano are putting themselves at high risk of being affected by a future eruption. Individuals living on the banks of a river are much more at risk from flooding than those who live many miles away.

Vulnerability is a term used to identify those individuals who are likely to be more affected than others by a particular event. For example, the elderly and the very young may be more vulnerable because they cannot move to safety as quickly as others.

Natural hazards in the Caribbean

Look at Figure 1.33.2. It shows some of the main natural hazards that have affected the Caribbean in recent years. Notice that the Caribbean is vulnerable to a range of hazards.

- **Earthquakes and volcanoes**. Several countries lie on or are close to an active tectonic plate margin and are at risk from earthquakes and volcanoes. Some recent eruptions and earthquakes are shown on Figure 1.33.2, including the devastating Haiti earthquake of 2010, which killed some 230,000 persons.
- **Hurricanes**. The Caribbean is often struck by tropical storms and hurricanes that have been formed in the North Atlantic and drift westwards with the trade winds. In 2011, Hurricane Irene caused flooding and damage in the Bahamas.
- **Landslides**. Landslides are common in mountainous regions of the Caribbean. Triggered by heavy rainfall or earthquakes, they can bury villages, block roads and destroy crops. (See 'Mass movement' on pages 22–3.)
- **Floods and storm surges**. Tropical storms and hurricanes can dump huge quantities of rainfall during the summer months, often leading to flash floods. Flat coastal zones are at risk from rapid rises in sea level called storm surges which are associated with passing hurricanes. (See 'Hurricanes' on pages 42–5.)

Figure 1.33.1 Haitians negotiate a flooded street in Haiti after Hurricane Tomas battered the country with heavy rains

Trends in natural hazards

In recent decades there has been an increase in the number of individuals affected by hazards. There are several reasons for this trend:

- An increase in population resulting in individuals living in more hazardous locations, such as close to the sea or on steep slopes.

- Deforestation has increased the likelihood of landslides and flash floods.
- More families living in poverty lack the resources to respond effectively to the threat of an event such as an earthquake. They may, for example, live in poorly constructed houses that are vulnerable to collapse during an earthquake or a hurricane.
- Changes to the natural environment, such as climatic cycles (e.g. El Niño) and global warming that might be increasing the magnitude and frequency of storms.

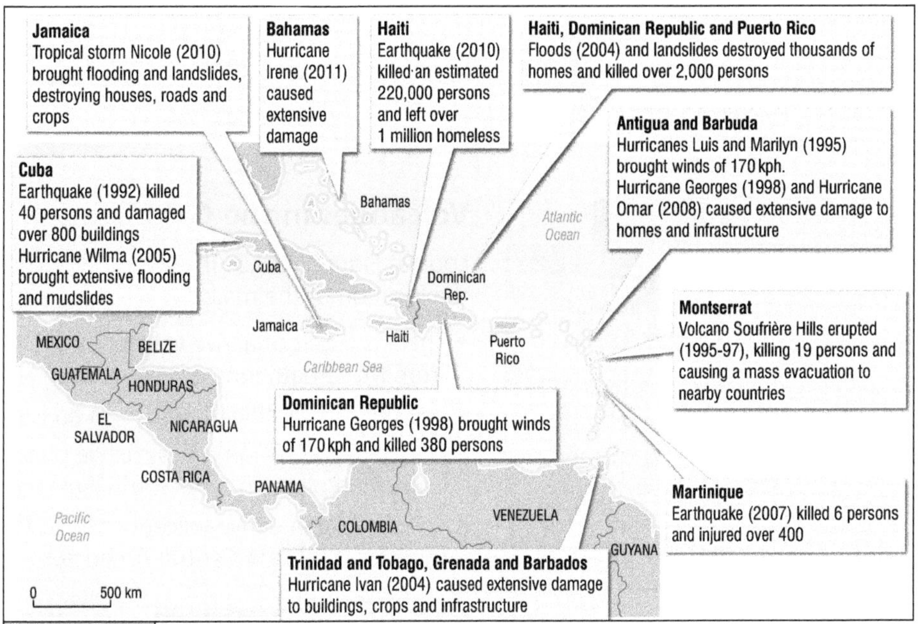

Figure 1.33.2 Natural hazards in the Caribbean

Responses to natural hazards

Short-term responses

Immediately after an event has occurred everyone is concerned with providing emergency help to those who have been affected. Search and rescue is the immediate response. Locals will often dig with their bare hands to search for those trapped or buried. Shortly afterwards the main focus is on providing medical care, food, water and emergency shelter. These responses, that take place in the first few hours, are short-term responses.

Long-term responses

In the days and weeks after an event such as an earthquake or a flood, attention shifts to consider rebuilding houses, shops and offices. Communication systems such as roads may need rebuilding and services damaged by the event (e.g. water, sanitation and electricity) will need to be reconnected.

Government agencies may improve information for preparedness and guidelines may be developed to improve the design of buildings, which leads to improved building codes. Areas that are most vulnerable to natural events may be mapped and actions taken to restrict these areas for uses such as agriculture, savannas and reserves.

Aid

Responding to a disaster requires a huge amount of money and considerable expertise. Often foreign countries, trading blocs (such as the European Union) and charities offer financial support or expertise such as specialist search and rescue teams or helicopters. This support is called **aid** and countries affected by natural disasters usually welcome it.

DID YOU KNOW?

The Haiti earthquake in 2010 killed more than 200,000 persons, making it one of the 'top 40' natural disasters ever recorded. In the Caribbean, Jamaica has recorded the greatest number of hazard events, including earthquakes, hurricanes, floods and landslides.

- Describe the pattern of volcanoes in the Caribbean.
- Understand the hazards associated with Caribbean volcanoes.
- Understand the impacts and responses associated with the eruption of Soufrière Hills volcano on Montserrat.

DID YOU KNOW?

Known as the 'Emerald Isle', Montserrat is a British protectorate whose primary income came from tourism. With the opening of a new airport in 2005, tourism is starting to recover, particularly volcano tourism!

Volcanoes in the Caribbean

Look at Figure 1.33.3. It shows the plate margins in the Caribbean and the location of the major active volcanoes. Notice the following patterns:

- There is a belt of active volcanoes in the eastern Caribbean, stretching from Mt St Catherine on Grenada to Soufrière Hills on Montserrat.
- The belt of volcanic islands form an island arc.
- The volcanoes lie on a destructive plate margin at the boundary of the Caribbean plate and the South American plate.
- The only other active volcanoes lie at the western edge of the Caribbean plate in Central America.

Volcanic hazards in the Caribbean

The volcanoes in the Caribbean are typical of volcanoes found at destructive plate margins. They are explosive and potentially extremely destructive. In the past they have caused considerable devastation and loss of life.

The following are the main hazards associated with volcanic eruptions in the Caribbean:

- **Pyroclastic flows**: probably the most deadly hazard. They are superheated clouds of ash and rocks that move at tremendous speeds (up to 200 m/s) down the sides of a volcano. Nothing can survive the destructive force of a pyroclastic flow.

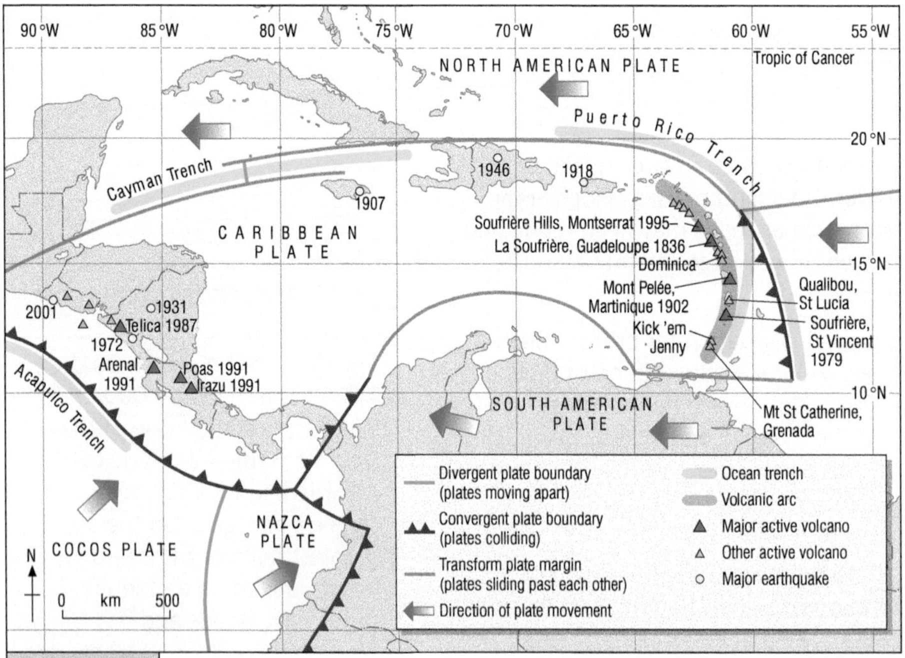

- **Ashfalls** can be very extensive and can bury settlements, roads and agricultural land. House roofs collapse under the weight of deposited ash.

- **Lahars** are mudflows, often resulting from snowmelt or heavy rainfall washing ash down the volcano's sides. Like pyroclastic flows, lahars can move at tremendous speeds and can be extremely destructive.

- **Landslides** can be triggered by volcanic eruptions, especially on the steep sides of a volcano when loose rocks (tephra) have been deposited.

Figure 1.33.3 Tectonic hazards in the Caribbean

Event

- In July 1995, after a dormant period of some 350 years, Soufrière Hills volcano burst into life.
- There were several small eruptions throughout 1995–96 leading to a major eruption in June 1997.
- The volcano has continued to show signs of activity to the present day. It last erupted in 2010.
- Eruptions have involved pyroclastic flows, ashfalls and lahars.

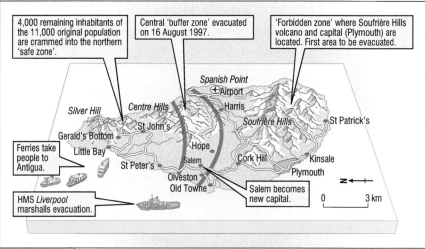

4,000 remaining inhabitants of the 11,000 original population are crammed into the northern 'safe zone'.

Central 'buffer zone' evacuated on 16 August 1997.

'Forbidden zone' where Soufrière Hills volcano and capital (Plymouth) are located. First area to be evacuated.

Ferries take people to Antigua.

HMS *Liverpool* marshalls evacuation.

Salem becomes new capital.

Spanish Point
Airport
Centre Hills
Silver Hill
Harris
St John's
Souffrière Hills
St Patrick's
Gerald's Bottom
Little Bay
Hope
St Peter's
Salem
Cork Hill
Kinsale
Olveston
Old Towne
Plymouth

0   3 km

Figure 1.33.4 | Impact of the eruption of Soufrière Hills volcano, Montserrat

Impacts

- Ash and lahars buried much of the capital, Plymouth, and destroyed St Patrick's village.
- Vast areas of productive farmland were covered by ash and crops were destroyed.
- 19 people were killed in the 1997 eruption.
- Montserrat's thriving tourist industry was destroyed.

Responses

- After the first eruptions in 1995, people were evacuated from settlements in southern Montserrat, including the capital Plymouth. Some people moved to safety in the north of the island. Others were transported by ferry to Antigua. About two-thirds of the population was evacuated.

- The UK government provided £41 million in aid to support the local people who had been evacuated.

- While much of southern Montserrat remains a 'forbidden zone' some foreigners have continued to visit their holiday homes in the area, putting themselves at risk from future eruptions.

- The volcano is monitored for further activity. Scientists study patterns of earthquakes, composition of gases and changes in the physical shape of the volcano.

Figure 1.33.5 | Lava flowing down the Soufrière Hills volcano

LEARNING OUTCOMES

- Describe the patterns of earthquakes in the Caribbean.
- Understand the hazards associated with earthquakes.
- Understand the impacts and responses to the Haiti earthquake in 2010.

DID YOU KNOW?

Scientists have recently published a warning of a possible tsunami risk in the Caribbean. A 1 million tonne block of rock on the northern flank of Morne aux Diables volcano on Dominica is being undercut by coastal erosion. If it collapses into the sea, it could trigger a 3 m tsunami that could devastate the coast of Guadeloupe and threaten the lives of 30,000 persons.

Earthquakes in the Caribbean

Look back to Figure 1.33.3 on page 98. Notice that earthquakes occur in a zone running roughly parallel to the tectonic plate margins. They are a common occurrence in the Caribbean and represent a significant threat to individuals and property.

Look at Figure 1.33.6. It shows the location of large earthquakes from 1610 to 2004. Notice the following patterns:

- Earthquakes occur in a narrow band through the islands of the Lesser Antilles and the Greater Antilles.
- Another narrow band of earthquakes stretches along the west coast of Central America.
- Most of the earthquakes have a shallow focus, particularly along the transform plate margin between the Caribbean plate and the North American plate. These are particularly destructive earthquakes.
- Some deep-focus earthquakes occur at the destructive plate margin to the east.
- Some earthquakes trigger tsunami.

The earthquake hazard

Earthquakes are a serious threat to many people living in the Caribbean. As recently as 2010 some 230,000 persons lost their lives after a powerful earthquake struck Port-au-Prince on Haiti.

The Richter scale measures the magnitude of an earthquake. This is a logarithmic scale that does not have an absolute upper limit. Most destructive earthquakes have a Richter scale value over 5.5. The Haiti earthquake in 2010 measured 7.0.

The *effects* of an earthquake are measured by the Modified Mercalli scale.

The following are the main earthquake hazards:

- **Ground shaking** – over 95 per cent of deaths from earthquakes occur when buildings collapse following ground shaking.
- **Liquefaction** – when silt sediments are shaken they become jelly-like, often causing buildings to lean or collapse.
- **Landslides** – these are often triggered by earthquakes and can destroy buildings and cause loss of life. They can hamper rescue efforts by blocking roads.

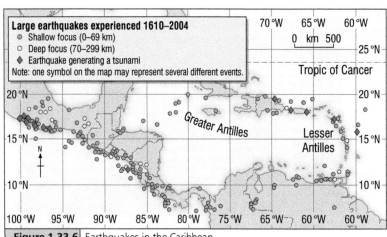

Figure 1.33.6 Earthquakes in the Caribbean

- **Tsunami** – when earthquakes occur in the ocean, displacement of the seabed can trigger waves which, as they approach the shore, rise to heights of 10 m or more and flood the land.

| CASE STUDY | Haiti earthquake (2010) |

Event

- Shortly before 5 p.m. on 12 January 2010, a powerful 7.0 magnitude earthquake struck Haiti, with its epicentre just 25 km west of the capital Port-au-Prince.

- The earthquake resulted from a sudden shift along a fault line running parallel to the transform plate margin separating the Caribbean plate and the North American plate.

- Violent ground shaking caused tremendous destruction throughout Haiti.

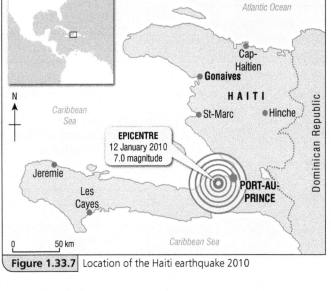

Figure 1.33.7 Location of the Haiti earthquake 2010

Impacts

- An estimated 230,000 persons were killed and over a million made homeless; many thousand were still living in appalling conditions in camps over a year after the event.

- Approximately 250,000 homes were destroyed.

- Public buildings such as hospitals and schools were destroyed, and services such as water and electricity were cut off. The airport and sea port were badly damaged, preventing emergency supplies from entering the country.

- Ninety per cent of Port-au-Prince was damaged by the earthquake.

- Diseases such as cholera became widespread in the temporary camps – over 4,000 died from cholera.

Responses

- Immediate responses focused on search and rescue and the provision of water, food and shelter.

- Makeshift hospitals were set up and medics operated on people in the open air, often without anaesthetic.

- The US military, United Nations, other Caribbean countries and aid agencies provided emergency supplies and assisted in maintaining law and order.

- In the months that followed, a massive rebuilding programme began.

Figure 1.33.8 Haiti after the earthquake

- Describe the patterns of hurricanes in the Caribbean.
- Understand the hazards associated with hurricanes.
- Understand the impacts and responses to Hurricane Ivan (2004).

The deadliest Atlantic hurricane occurred in 1780. Well over 25,000 persons were killed as the hurricane tore into the Lesser Antilles. Winds of over 300 kph devastated Barbados and caused widespread damage in Martinique and St Lucia.

Hurricanes in the Caribbean

Hurricanes are the most violent and frequent hazards to strike the Caribbean. During the hurricane season, which runs from June to November, powerful tropical storms track westwards from the warm Atlantic Ocean towards the Caribbean. Some of these storms develop into hurricanes, which have the potential to cause widespread destruction and loss of life.

Look at Figure 1.33.9. It shows the tracks of North Atlantic hurricanes in 2004, a year when several powerful storms lashed the Caribbean. Notice the following patterns:

- Most hurricanes are formed in the Atlantic Ocean, west of Africa. However, some hurricanes form closer to the Caribbean and may even form in the Caribbean Sea towards the end of the season.
- Hurricanes track from east to west across the Caribbean driven by the trade winds.
- They tend to curve northwards in the direction of the USA and across the north Atlantic Ocean towards Europe. This is because of the effect of the Earth's rotation.
- Hurricanes tend to intensify as they move westwards over the warm sea. When they hit land, they begin to lose their intensity as they are cut off from their energy source (evaporated water).

Hurricane hazards

Hurricanes are huge storms up to 800 km across. They can achieve wind speeds in excess of 250 kph and dump huge quantities of rainfall, which can cause extensive flooding.

The strength of a hurricane is measured by the Saffir–Simpson scale. The most powerful hurricane is a category 5 storm, which has the potential to cause extensive damage and loss of life. The following are the main hazards associated with hurricanes:

- Very strong winds with sustained speeds in excess of 125 kph (hurricane force) and gusts of over 200 kph. These winds will strip roofs, upturn mobile homes and flatten trees and crops.
- Heavy rainfall, with the potential to cause flooding and trigger landslides.

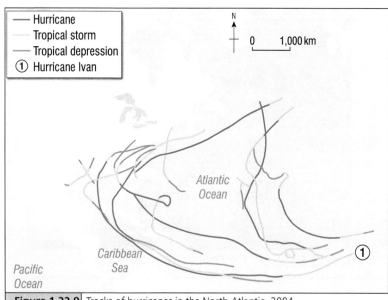

| Hurricane |
| Tropical storm |
| Tropical depression |
| ① Hurricane Ivan |

Atlantic Ocean

Pacific Ocean

Caribbean Sea

Figure 1.33.9 Tracks of hurricanes in the North Atlantic, 2004

- Storm surges are often the greatest killers. A storm surge is a temporary rise in sea level, often by several metres, causing seawater to surge inland. It results from the intense low pressure associated with the hurricane (low pressure enables the water to expand upwards) combining with the extremely strong winds driving the hurricane onshore. Figure 1.33.10 describes the impacts of a storm surge.

Figure 1.33.10 A storm surge caused by a hurricane

| CASE STUDY | Hurricane Ivan (2004) |

Hurricane Ivan was one of a number of powerful hurricanes to pass through the Caribbean during 2004. Its path (track) is shown in Figure 1.33.9.

Event

- Hurricane Ivan was the fourth major hurricane of the active 2004 season, reaching category 5 on the Saffir–Simpson scale.
- It first struck Grenada on 7 September before passing over Jamaica and Grand Cayman, and clipping Cuba. It made landfall in Alabama, USA on 16 September.
- Winds reached speeds of 270 kph at the height of the storm as it passed close to Grand Cayman on 11 September.
- The hurricane spawned several devastating tornadoes.

Impacts

- Many people were evacuated from coastal regions as Hurricane Ivan approached, including 500,000 persons in Jamaica.
- A total of 212 persons were killed by the hurricane, 64 of whom were in the Caribbean (mainly Grenada and Jamaica).
- In Grenada, 85 per cent of the island was totally devastated, with property damaged, services cut off and crops destroyed. 39 people were killed. Damage was estimated at over US$800 million.
- In Jamaica, floods and storm surges killed 17 people and left 18,000 homeless.

- Grand Cayman also suffered considerable damage to property.

Responses

- Thousands were evacuated as the hurricane approached.
- Emergency support (food, water, medical aid and shelter) was provided to the many thousands who were affected by the hurricane.
- Rebuilding homes and the infrastructure took many months.
- Economic growth slowed dramatically due to damage to industry, farming and tourism.

Figure 1.33.11 Devastation in Grenada's capital, St George's, after Hurricane Ivan

Figure 1.33.12 | Immediate responses following the 2010 earthquake in Haiti

Short-term and long-term responses

When an event such as an earthquake or a hurricane strikes a community, the community responds. Short-term responses occur in the first few hours and days after an event. They usually involve **local communities** helping themselves and each other. Longer-term responses take place in the following weeks and months.

Short-term

- In the first few hours, those who have survived will concentrate on search and rescue. They will try to find other people who are alive but who may be buried or trapped.
- Medical attention and the supply of water, food and shelter are all short-term considerations.
- Emergency help will probably arrive from both national and international sources.

Long-term

- Long-term response involves reconstruction, such as repairing houses or building new ones. In most cases they will be built using strict building codes to enable them to better withstand a similar event in the future.
- Infrastructure, such as roads and railways, may need repairing.
- Services, such as water, electricity and sanitation, may need to be restored.
- Businesses that have been destroyed may need financial help to enable them to start up again. This is important to provide employment for people.

CASE STUDY | Jamaica's Office of Disaster Preparedness and Emergency Management

Jamaica has been severely affected by natural hazards, particularly flooding associated with hurricanes. Established in 1973, this permanent disaster management organisation is committed to preventing or reducing the impacts of natural hazards in Jamaica.

Its professionally trained staff work with local communities and other national and international organisations to reduce people's vulnerability to natural hazards. Achievements so far include:

- Establishment of a National Emergency Operations Centre to take control when the country is affected by an event.

- Development of disaster management plans and establishment of parish disaster committees to coordinate activities at the local level.
- Relocation of persons at high risk from natural hazards to disaster shelters in each community.
- Coordination of post-disaster assessment and clean-up activities.
- Establishment of community flood-warning systems.
- Development of websites and printed material to provide information to people so that they can be better prepared.

- Plans to reduce the impact of future events will be made. This may include improving building standards or increasing people's awareness through education.

National responses

Natural hazards are common in the Caribbean, and all countries are aware of the need to make preparations to minimise the impacts. An **Office of Disaster Preparedness and Emergency Management** has been established in Jamaica, Antigua and Barbuda, Barbados, and Trinidad and Tobago to oversee disaster management.

Figure 1.33.13 A van is trapped by a bridge after floods swept it off a road in Grenada

Regional responses

In 1981, following severe floods and hurricane damage, the Pan Caribbean Disaster Prevention and Preparation Project was established. In 1991, this became the **Caribbean Disaster Emergency Response Agency (CDERA)**. There are currently 16 participating states within the Caribbean. CDERA's motto is 'Managing Disasters with Preparedness'. The institution was reorganised in 2009 and was given a new name. It is now called CDEMA, the **Caribbean Disaster Emergency Management Agency.**

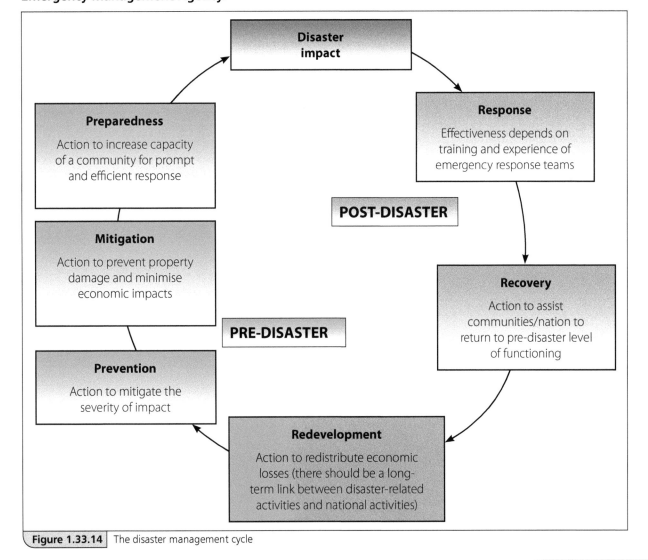

Figure 1.33.14 The disaster management cycle

The following are CDEMA's main functions:

• Make an immediate and coordinated response to any disastrous event in the participating states. This includes man-made disasters such as oil spills and aircraft accidents as well as natural hazards.

• Reduce vulnerability of individuals to natural disasters by providing information and guidance.

• Collate accurate information about disasters in the region.

• Provide training for disaster management personnel.

• Maintain a dynamic website to provide up-to-date information, for example weather forecasts.

CDEMA responds to events that are beyond the capacity of the affected country or countries. Hurricane Ivan (see the case study, page 103) in 2004 is an example of an event which caused such widespread devastation that those individual countries (particularly Grenada) simply could not cope.

Managing natural hazards: floods, landslides, volcanoes and earthquakes

It is possible to identify two distinct approaches to managing natural hazards:

1 **Physical approaches** – these involve attempts to prevent hazards occurring or building structures to prevent or reduce their impacts.

2 **Behavioural approaches** – these involve adapting people's behaviour so that they become less vulnerable. Examples include warnings and forecasts, evacuation, education and awareness, land-use zoning, hazard mapping and insurance.

Physical approaches in reducing the flood hazard

Flooding, a common hazard in the Caribbean, is usually caused by torrential rainfall associated with tropical storms or hurricanes. A number of physical techniques have been used to contain floodwaters and reduce their impacts on people and property.

• **Check dams** – these are small dams, usually formed of rock or timber, that are built across small channels and gullies to slow down the flow of water.

• **Gabions** – wire cages filled with rocks can help to support and strengthen river banks (see Figure 1.33.15).

• **Levees** – raised river embankments that can increase the capacity of a river channel, making flooding of adjacent land less likely.

Figure 1.33.15 Gabions in Barbados

- **Paved drains** – wide and deep paved drains are common sights alongside roads in towns (see Figure 1.33.16). While these may be dry for most of the year, they are capable of containing large volumes of water during heavy rainstorms.

Managing landscapes to prevent landslides

Most landslides are triggered by seismic activity or heavy rainfall. However, human activities such as deforestation and construction often make slopes more vulnerable to collapse. Landscapes can be managed to reduce the risk of landslides by:

- planting trees
- stabilising slopes using pins or steel bolts
- improving drainage
- re-profiling a slope to reduce its angle.

Figure 1.33.16 Paved drain in St Johns, Antigua

'Build back better': earthquake-proof buildings in Haiti

Much of the loss of life caused by the Haiti earthquake of 2010 resulted from the collapse of poorly built houses. Many of the schools and homes had brittle walls and unreinforced masonry that simply fell apart when ground shaking occurred.

As the Haitian capital Port-au-Prince is rebuilt, there is a desire to 'build back better'. This means constructing new buildings that are built to withstand ground shaking. While no building can be 100 per cent earthquake proof, it is possible to build more rigid constructions that are less likely to collapse.

DID YOU KNOW?

At 1,156 m high, the volcano Mount Liamuiga on St Kitts is one of the highest peaks in the Caribbean. It is clothed with rainforest and has a 1 km crater, which contains a crater lake.

CASE STUDY | Volcano hazard risk mapping: St Kitts

In 2001, scientists from the University of the West Indies published a volcanic hazard assessment map for St Kitts to identify those areas most at risk from future eruptions of Mt Liamuiga. While the volcano has not erupted since 1843, there have been periods of earthquake swarms in 1974, 1988 and 2000, indicating that the volcano is still active and likely to erupt at some point in the future.

Figure 1.33.17 shows the different hazard zones on St Kitts. Notice that the highest hazard zone is in the north of the island. Even the yellow zone to the south is at risk from ash falls.

Mt Liamuiga, in common with other active volcanoes in the Caribbean, is constantly monitored for signs of activity.

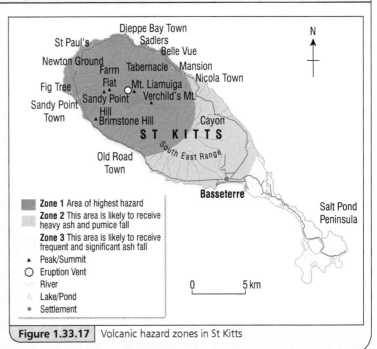

Figure 1.33.17 | Volcanic hazard zones in St Kitts

Earthquake-resistant features include using reinforced concrete (concrete with steel rods to give added support), supporting walls and roofs with diagonal cross beams, and bolting buildings to their foundations.

Hazard mapping

Hazard maps can be used to provide information that can influence people's behaviour and reduce their vulnerability to natural hazards such as flooding, landslides and volcanic eruptions.

Based on historic events and scientific surveys, zones of different levels of risk can be identified. Governments may decide to restrict developments in high-risk zones or devise detailed evacuation plans. By identifying the areas at greatest risk, actions can be taken to reduce the likely impacts of an event.

For example, on Montserrat, the southern half of the island is an exclusion zone, where no admittance is permitted apart from for scientific monitoring.

How can the hurricane hazard be reduced?

Tropical storms and hurricanes are common in the Caribbean and are capable of causing considerable devastation. Look back to page 103 to see how Hurricane Ivan caused extensive damage to Grenada in 2004.

Hurricanes are enormously powerful storms that cannot be controlled or prevented. This means that people have to find ways of reducing the impact of the strong winds, heavy rainfall and storm surges. These are some examples:

- Land-use zoning – hurricane damage tends to be focused on low-lying coastal areas and alongside rivers where flooding is a major hazard. National governments can devise land-use plans to keep vulnerable groups and expensive land uses away from these areas.
- Building regulations – new buildings can be constructed with strong walls, doors, windows and roofs to withstand strong winds.
- Communications – telephone and electricity lines can be kept well away from coastal areas or installed underground.

Figure 1.33.18 The Malecón sea wall in Havana, Cuba

- Levees and embankments – these can be constructed to reduce the flood risk and sea walls can be built to protect against storm surges (see Figure 1.33.18).
- Trees – planted along coastal areas, trees (e.g. mangroves) help to break up the power of waves and reduce the impact of a storm surge.
- Hurricane tracking, prediction and evacuation – this is often the most effective approach.

Tracking hurricanes

Hurricanes are very distinctive features and they can easily be tracked by satellites as they move across the ocean towards land. Computer models based on past hurricane tracks help scientists to predict the likely course of a hurricane. This enables warnings to be issued, giving people time to respond before the hurricane arrives. Most hurricanes affecting the Caribbean are tracked by the National Hurricane Center in Miami, USA.

Issuing warnings

When a hurricane seems likely to strike a country two levels of warning are issued:

1 **Hurricane watch** – this is issued when there is a threat of a hurricane within 24–36 hours.

2 **Hurricane warning** – this is a higher level of warning and is more of a probability than a possibility. It is issued when hurricane conditions are expected in 24 hours or less.

Once a warning has been issued, everyone starts to take precautions by boarding up windows, turning off gas, water and electricity supplies and seeking shelter, possibly in a designated hurricane shelter. Advice is available in printed booklets, posters, on the radio and television, and on the internet.

CASE STUDY | Tracking Hurricane Ivan (2004)

Look at Figure 1.33.19. It shows the predicted track of Hurricane Ivan at 11 a.m. on Thursday, 9 September 2004. It has just passed over Grenada, causing widespread devastation and killing 39 persons. Notice the following:

- A predicted track for the centre of the hurricane has been drawn through to 8 a.m. on Sunday, 12 September.
- The predicted track takes the form of a cone, allowing for an increasingly wide margin of error further into the forecast period.
- Based on the predicted track, warnings have been issued, for example Jamaica has a 'Hurricane Warning'.

The predicted track will be constantly updated and refined, allowing for greater precision in the issuing of warnings. According to Figure 1.33.19, Jamaica is directly in the firing line, to be followed by Cuba. Look back to Figure 1.33.9, page 102, to see whether these countries were hit by Hurricane Ivan.

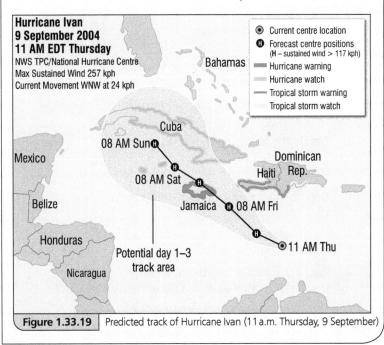

Figure 1.33.19 | Predicted track of Hurricane Ivan (11 a.m. Thursday, 9 September)

SECTION 1: Practice exam questions

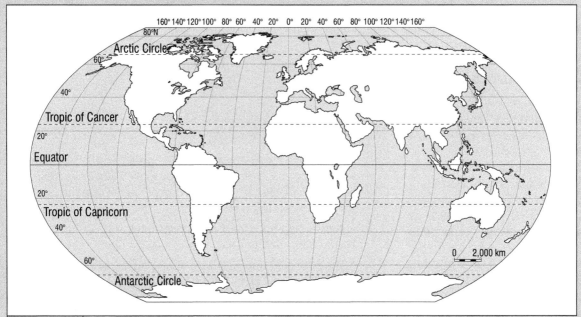

Figure 1 | World outline map

1 a On the map provided (Figure 1), insert and name two ranges of fold mountains, and give the map an appropriate title. (5)

b Describe, in one or two sentences, each of the following:

   i a dyke (4)
   ii a sill. (4)

c Account for the formation of volcanoes near subduction zones. (12)

2 a Draw a diagram to show two effects of soil creep. (5)

b Define the following processes:

   i weathering (4)
   ii erosion. (4)

c Describe and account for the occurrence of:

   i landslides (6)
   ii soil creep. (6)

3 a Figure 2 shows a river basin. Identify the features labelled A, B, C, D and E. (5)

b Describe the four processes of erosion by a river. (8)

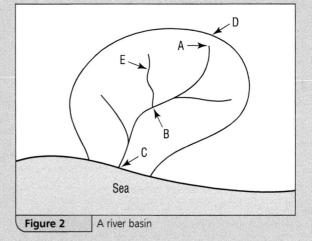

Figure 2 | A river basin

c Account for the formation of waterfalls and the gorge downstream of a waterfall. (12)

4 a Figure 3 is a diagram of the water cycle. Identify the five processes labelled A, B, C, D and E. (5)

b Describe, in about four sentences, how oxbow lakes are formed. (8)

c Account for, and compare, trellis and radial drainage patterns. *(6)*

d Account for the development of deltas. *(6)*

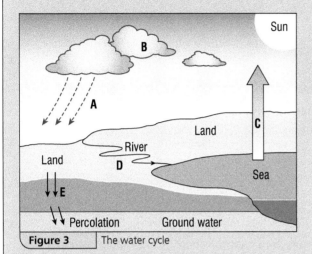

Figure 3 | The water cycle

5 a Draw a diagram of a limestone area to show four features (two on the surface and two underground). *(4)*

b Define the terms 'carbonation' and 'mass wasting'. *(4)*

c Describe two processes of physical weathering. *(4)*

d Account for the development of four (surface and/or underground) landforms in limestone areas in the Caribbean, other than those you named in **a**. *(12)*

6 a Draw and label two diagrams to show the difference between a barrier reef and a fringing reef. *(5)*

b State four conditions needed for coral reef formation. *(8)*

c Account for the formation of caves in limestone areas. *(6)*

d Account for the formation of spits. *(6)*

7 a Draw four isobars to show the centre of a hurricane. Indicate the pressure and wind direction. *(4)*

b Define the following terms:

i weather *(2)*
ii cold front *(2)*
iii tropical wave *(2)*
iv ITCZ. *(2)*

c Explain fully how relief influences the weather and climate in the Caribbean. *(12)*

8 a On the world map provided (Figure 4), insert and name two areas of tropical rainforests. *(5)*

b Describe the characteristics of the vegetation of a tropical rainforest. *(8)*

c How are the soils of the tropical rainforest biome affected by the climate and the vegetation? *(12)*

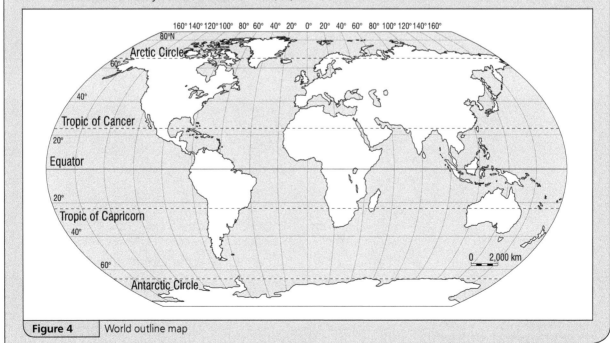

Figure 4 | World outline map

2 Human systems

2.1 Global population distribution and density

LEARNING OUTCOMES

- Understand the global patterns of population distribution and density.
- Understand the factors affecting population distribution and density.

Global population distribution

Population distribution describes the location of individuals in an area. Look at Figure 2.1.1. It is a **dot map** showing population distribution in the world. Notice that each dot represents 100,000 persons. Imagine how the map would look if every person in the world was shown by a single dot.

Notice the following patterns:

- Population is not distributed evenly across the world.
- Some areas have high concentrations of population, such as western Europe, India, eastern China, south-east Africa and southern Japan.
- Some regions have few people, such as central, eastern and northern Russia; much of Canada and Australia; northern Africa (away from the coast).
- Many coastal regions have high population concentrations.

Advantages and problems of using dot maps

Dot maps show densely and sparsely populated areas clearly, both between countries and within a country. In China the great majority

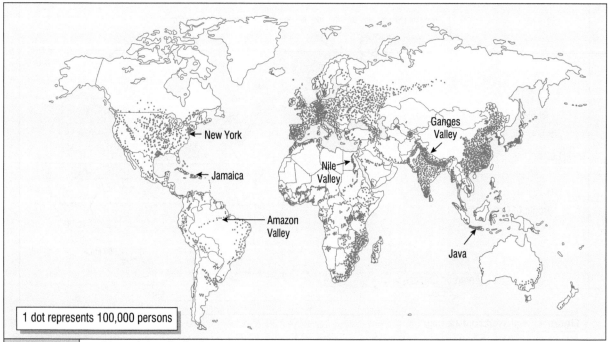

1 dot represents 100,000 persons

Figure 2.1.1 World population distribution

of people live in the eastern half of the country, avoiding the difficult desert and mountainous regions in the west. Choosing the ideal value for dots is difficult. If a dot represents fewer people there are too many dots and they merge, which can confuse the person using the map. However, if a dot represents a high number of people it becomes impossible to show how people are spread across a sparsely populated area such as western China.

Global population density

Population density is defined as the number of people per km^2, the relationship between people and the space they occupy. Cities have higher population densities than rural areas because people are concentrated into a smaller area. Here are some examples to illustrate this:

- Manila (Philippines) has 46,000 people/km^2 (see Figure 2.1.3).
- Kibera (a slum district of Nairobi, Kenya) is thought to have 90,000 people/km^2.
- Kingston (Jamaica) has 1,358 people/km^2 – rather lower population density.

Compare this data with rural St Andrew Parish (Barbados), which has <300 people/km^2.

Figure 2.1.2 is a choropleth map showing global population density. This is how a choropleth map works:

- A colour scale is devised to represent the range of population density data.
- The colours are related to each other in the colour wheel – yellow/orange/red/brown is usually used for population density.
- The darker the colour, the higher the value it represents.

EXAM TIP

Look for these features on Figure 2.1.1: the labels on the map will give you clues.

- Rivers attract people – the Ganges, Nile and Amazon valleys stand out as lines of red dots.
- Islands concentrate populations – as shown, for example, in Java and Jamaica.
- Global cities stand out as concentrations of dots, for example New York.

Identify other densely and sparsely populated areas across the world.

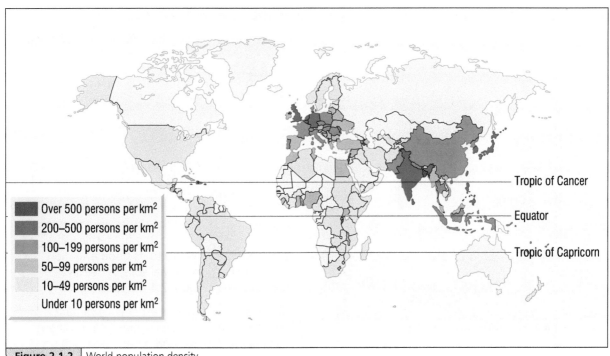

■	Over 500 persons per km^2
■	200–500 persons per km^2
■	100–199 persons per km^2
■	50–99 persons per km^2
■	10–49 persons per km^2
■	Under 10 persons per km^2

Tropic of Cancer
Equator
Tropic of Capricorn

Figure 2.1.2 World population density

Figure 2.1.3 | Densely populated housing in Manila, Philippines

Notice the following patterns on Figure 2.1.2:

- the areas of very high population density are north-west Europe (especially the UK and Germany); southern Asia (India, Pakistan and Bangladesh); China and Japan; Indonesia
- the areas of lowest population density include large parts of the southern hemisphere (South America, southern Africa and Australia) as well as sections of northern Africa and the Middle East. Canada and Russia stand out in the northern hemisphere.

Advantages and problems of using choropleth maps

Choropleth maps are relatively easy to draw and are better for making comparisons between countries than dot maps. However, the single shading in choropleths suggests population is evenly spread across the country, which we have already seen is not true in China. The USA and Australia also have low overall densities, but their people are spread very unevenly. Figure 2.1.1 indicates a high concentration of people along the eastern seaboard of Australia and large almost empty areas elsewhere.

Factors affecting population distribution and density

There are several factors that affect where individuals live and therefore influence patterns of population distribution and density.

1 **Physical geography** – Some environments experience hostile living conditions, such as deserts, high mountains and dense forests. These areas tend to have fewer people than areas with natural advantages such as fertile flat land and well-watered river valleys. In China, for example, few people live in the Himalayan mountains where the climate is extremely cold, the soils are thin and infertile and the slopes are too steep for farming. In contrast, the flat fertile valley of the Yangtze River, with its good irrigation opportunities and alluvial soils, is heavily populated (see Figure 2.1.4 opposite).

2 **Climate** – Some places experience climatic extremes, such as polar regions (e.g. northern Canada and Siberia) and deserts (e.g. Sahara Desert in Africa). Few individuals choose to live

Figure 2.1.4 | The Yangtze River in Shanghai

in these areas where it is hard to make a living (see Figure 2.1.5). Elsewhere, climatic conditions in temperate and tropical regions are less hostile to human settlement and these regions tend to have higher population concentrations.

3 **Proximity to the coast** – An estimated two-thirds of the world's population live within 500 km of the coast and many live on the coast itself. The main reasons for this are trade with other countries, the development of fishing and, more recently, the development of tourism.

4 **Resources** – The presence of resources, particularly energy resources such as coal, has had an important influence, particularly in Europe and in parts of the USA. In Europe, the Industrial Revolution was based on the extensive coal resources in the UK, France and Germany. This explains the high concentration of persons in this region.

5 **Rivers** – Some major rivers are responsible for high concentrations of persons. The River Nile in Egypt acts as an important transport route and provides much-needed water for irrigation in an otherwise extremely arid country (see Figures 2.1.6 and 2.1.7).

Figure 2.1.5 | A Bedouin camp in the Sahara Desert

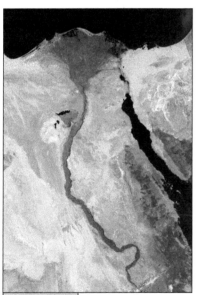

Figure 2.1.6 | The River Nile

Figure 2.1.7 | Irrigation using River Nile water

EXAM TIP

Make links between resources given to you in an examination. For example, Figure 2.1.1, the population distribution dot map (page 112), shows a line of dots along the River Nile. Figure 2.1.6 shows vegetation and/or agriculture along the River Nile. If you were given these two figures in an examination, you should identify and explain the links between them.

Population distribution and density in the Caribbean

- Describe population patterns in the Caribbean.
- Explain variations in population distribution and density in the Caribbean.
- Understand population density in Jamaica.

DID YOU KNOW?

Guyana has the lowest population density in the Caribbean, with just 3.5 persons per square kilometre. This compares to the population density of Jamaica which is 249 persons per square kilometre.

Population patterns in the Caribbean – reasons for high and low population densities

Look at Figure 2.2.1, which shows population density in the region. Caribbean islands have higher densities than countries on the surrounding mainland of North and South America. Globally, islands attract people. In the Caribbean this is true of several islands, but particularly true of Haiti and Martinique.

Haiti and Barbados, for example, have the highest population densities, with >1,000 people/km². Caribbean islands favour settlement because the climate encourages agriculture and tourism. Ports such as Bridgetown and Port-au-Prince are important trade hubs for the export of produce, including sugar.

The Dominican Republic has relatively low population density: mountainous relief discourages settlement and most settlements have coastal locations.

Key factors in population distribution and density in Jamaica

- Relief and height of the land, rock type and drainage are key factors:
  - The steeper the slope, the more difficult it is to build on – the Blue Mountains in Jamaica repel larger settlements.
  - Steep slopes also lead to thin soils, too poor to farm effectively.

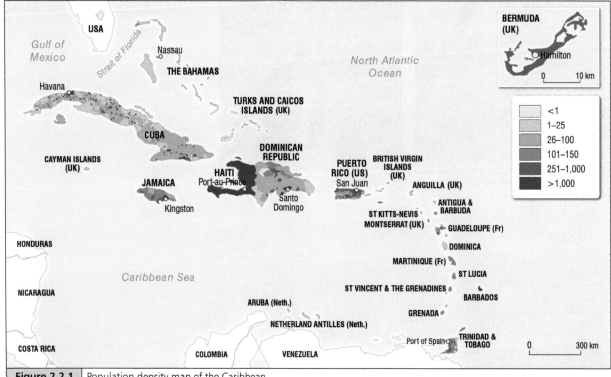

| **Figure 2.2.1** | Population density map of the Caribbean |

- Rock types such as limestone create entirely unique landscapes, generally of little value for agriculture due to lack of surface water, while attracting limited numbers of tourists to see the unique landscape, for example Cockpit Country, Jamaica.
- Coastal plains provide flat land for building homes and businesses, as well as for constructing transport routes. Of the global population, 56 per cent of people live less than 200 m above sea level.

- Rivers flowing towards the sea cross coastal plains, providing water-supply and other port opportunities such as fishing and trade. These two factors, plus the development of tourism, explain the original location and recent expansion of Kingston in Jamaica.

- Socio-economic factors are important – economic factors are to do with money and jobs; social factors involve health, education and other public services. For example, many Caribbean settlements have grown recently because of the pull factors of available jobs, especially in tourism. Jobs may be seasonal (which is a disadvantage), but people take what is on offer. The larger the settlement the more services, for example retailing and banking, are required for the population.

Opportunities in rural areas remain limited, leading to continuing rural to urban migration in the Caribbean.

CASE STUDY | Population density in Jamaica

Look at Figure 2.2.2. It shows population density in Jamaica. Notice that the population density for most of the country is greater than 100 persons per square kilometre. While much of the country has a similar population density, there are some notable variations, which are largely the result of physical factors.

- **Kingston** – The population density here is over 1,000 persons per square kilometre. Kingston is the capital of Jamaica and, with its thriving port, shops and industries, it attracts a lot of people to live in the area.

- **Blue Mountains** – Here the population density is less than 100 persons per square kilometre. High altitudes (Blue Mountain Peak rises to 2,256 m) and steep slopes create problems for farming and communications. Few people choose to live here.

- **Cockpit Country** – This is an extensive area of limestone. It also has a very low population density (less than 100 persons per square kilometre). The landscape is rocky, very undulating and severely weathered. There are few resources and limited opportunities for farming.

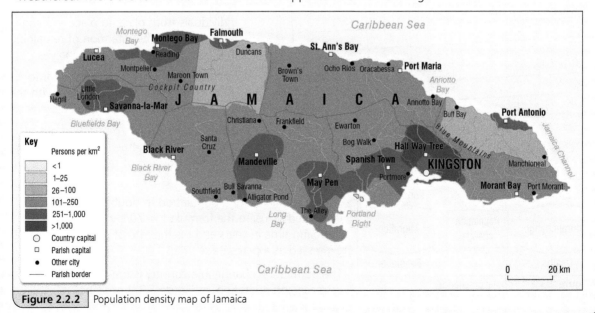

Figure 2.2.2 | Population density map of Jamaica

2.3 — Population change

LEARNING OUTCOMES

- Understand key population change terms.
- Understand the demographic transition model as a background to understanding population change in the Caribbean.

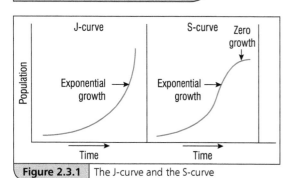

Figure 2.3.1 The J-curve and the S-curve

EXAM TIP

Know your Caribbean data

Caribbean country	Total population (million)	BR/ 1,000/ year	DR/ 1,000/ year	Net migration/ 1,000 people
Haiti	9.996	22.8	7.9	−4.12
Jamaica	2.930	18.4	6.7	−4.83
Trinidad and Tobago	1.223	13.8	8.5	−6.42
Barbados	0.289	12.0	8.4	−0.30
St Lucia	0.163	13.9	7.3	−3.13

Data source: *The CIA World Factbook 2015*

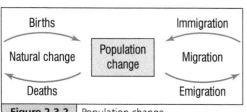

Figure 2.3.2 Population change

Population change key terms

There are a few important geographical terms that you need to know when studying population growth:

- **Birth rate** (BR) – number of babies born alive per 1,000 persons per year.
- **Death rate** (DR) – number of individuals dying per 1,000 persons per year.
- **Natural change** (NC) – the difference between the birth rate and the death rate, but expressed as a percentage (per 100 persons) rather than per 1,000 persons.
- **Natural increase** (NI) – this is where there is a positive natural change, that is, the birth rate is higher than the death rate.
- **Natural decrease** (ND) – this is where there is a negative change, that is, the birth rate is lower than the death rate.
- **Infant mortality** – this is the number of deaths in the age group 1–12 months per 1,000 live births per year.
- **Child mortality** – this takes account of all deaths of children up to the age of 5, per 1,000 children in that age group.
- **Life expectancy** – this is the number of years that individuals are expected to live from birth in a particular country.
- **Migration** – this is the movement of individuals from place to place – changing residence with the intention of remaining in the new place for at least one year.
- **Immigration** – this is movement into another country to settle there – with the intention of remaining for at least one year.
- **Emigration** – this is movement out of one's country to settle in another country – with the intention of remaining there for at least one year.

The time it takes for a population to double in size can be estimated by using the formula $t = 70/r$, where t is the doubling time in years and r is the rate of population growth expressed as a percentage.

The population change in a country is the result of natural increase and migration, as Figure 2.3.2 explains.

Calculating natural change

Barbados

BR	= 12.0 per 1,000
DR	= 8.4 per 1,000
Migration	= −0.3 per 1,000
Natural change	= 12.0 − 8.4 = 3.6 per 1,000
	= +0.36 % (natural increase)
Population change	= natural change (+3.6 per 1,000)
	+/− migration (−0.3 per 1,000)
	= 3.3 per 1,000

Carry out your own calculations for Trinidad and Tobago to find natural change and population change.

BR	= 13.8 per 1,000
DR	= 8.5 per 1,000
Migration	= −6.42 per 1,000

Population change – the demographic transition model

Look at Figure 2.3.3. It is a graph that shows population change over time. It is called the **demographic transition model** (*demography* is the study of population). The demographic transition model (DTM) shows the changes in birth rate (red line), death rate (blue line) and total population (green line). It does not, however, take account of migration.

Notice that on the graph it is possible to identify natural change between the birth rate line and the death rate line.

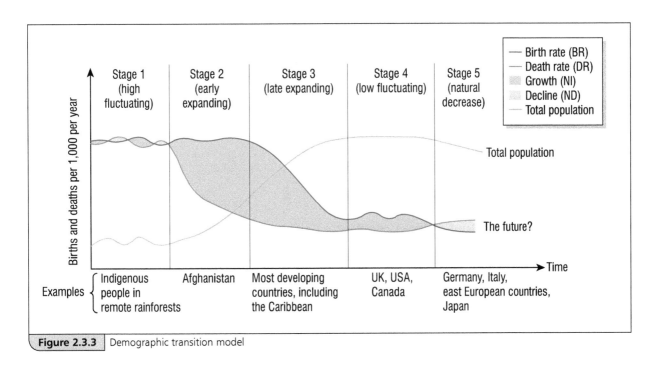

Figure 2.3.3 Demographic transition model

119

- Natural increase (shaded pink) occurs where the birth rate is higher than the death rate.
- Natural decrease (shaded blue) occurs where the death rate is higher than the birth rate.

The demographic transition model shows the theoretical changes that take place in a country's population over several hundred years as it becomes developed. It is possible to place a country into one of five stages according to its population characteristics.

Note that the demographic transition does not follow a smooth movement along the various stages.

Demographic transition model stages

Stage 1

- Birth rate and death rate are both high and fluctuating.
- Birth rates are high owing to high infant mortality, lack of birth control and need for children to work on the land.
- Death rates are high owing to famines, wars and disease.

Figure 2.3.4 | Stage 1 – Shuar family of the Ecuadorian rainforest

Stage 2

- Death rate starts to fall. Natural increase rises as does the total population.
- Death rates fall as medicines are introduced, health care improves, and there are better diets and improved living conditions (safe water and sanitation). Children are still needed for labour.

Figure 2.3.5 | Stage 2 – extended family of farmers in At-Bashi, Kyrgyzstan

Stage 3

- Birth rate starts to fall rapidly, natural increase declines as does the rate of total population growth. An increased standard of living means that children go to school rather than work.
- Birth rate falls owing to reductions in infant mortality (better medicines, vaccinations), decisions to reduce family size, women entering careers and family planning.

Figure 2.3.6 | Stage 3 – Caribbean brothers and sisters waiting for the bus to school

Stage 4

- Birth rate and death rate now low and fluctuating. Total population levels off.
- Slight variations reflect short-term changes, such as 'baby booms' or economic growth/decline.

Figure 2.3.7 | Stage 4 – couple and their two daughters playing on the beach

Stage 5

- Birth rate falls below death rate and total population declines.
- Very low birth rates result from women's choice to follow careers, leading to them having children later, or not at all. Remember that women's fertility reduces with age.

Most Caribbean countries can be placed towards the end of stage 3 or the start of stage 4. Notice that some countries, such as Japan in stage 5, are likely to experience a decline in their future populations.

Figure 2.3.8 | Stage 5 – One-child European family

Population structure

Population pyramids

The total population of an area, such as a country, a region or a city can be subdivided into different age groups. It can also be divided into male and female. This information can be plotted as a series of horizontal bars to create a diagram called a **population pyramid**.

Population pyramids can be used to identify trends in birth rates, death rates and life expectancy. They are extremely useful to governments for planning purposes, for example, in providing enough school places for a growing population or health care and support services for an ageing population.

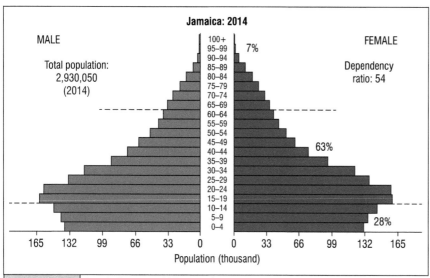

Figure 2.4.1 | Population pyramid for Jamaica

Source: Indexmundi and *The CIA World Factbook 2015* (Total population and Dependency ratio data)

Jamaica's population pyramid

Look at Figure 2.4.1. It shows Jamaica's population pyramid. Notice that Jamaica has youthful and young adult populations with a high proportion of individuals aged 0–30 years. While there has been a recent decline in the birth rate, Jamaica's population does have a broad lower half and narrow top, which is typical of developing countries. In the future, the 0–30 'bulge' of the pyramid will work its way up, resulting in a larger number of middle-aged and elderly people.

Comparing population pyramids

Now look at Figure 2.4.2 and compare the population pyramids for Nigeria (a developing country) and Australia (a developed country).

- In Nigeria, the very broad base indicates a high birth rate and suggests that the population is likely to rise in the future.
- In Australia, the narrow base indicates a low and stable birth rate.
- The roughly parallel sides of Australia's population pyramid suggest that life expectancy is high and the population is fairly stable.
- Nigeria faces challenges associated with a high birth rate and rapidly growing population whereas Australia faces challenges associated with an ageing population.

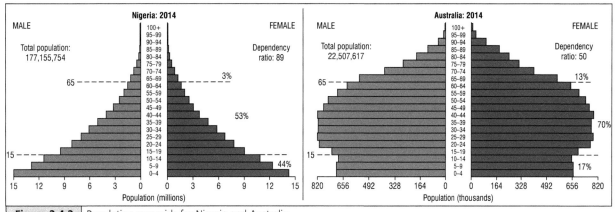

Figure 2.4.2 | Population pyramids for Nigeria and Australia

Source: Indexmundi and *The CIA World Factbook 2015* (Total population and Dependency ratio data)

Population pyramids and the demographic transition model

Look at Figure 2.4.3 to see how the different stages of the demographic transition model can be represented by population pyramids. Notice that in stage 1 the population pyramid has a very broad base and narrow top. By stage 5 it has been transformed to have a narrow base with roughly parallel sides and a high broad top.

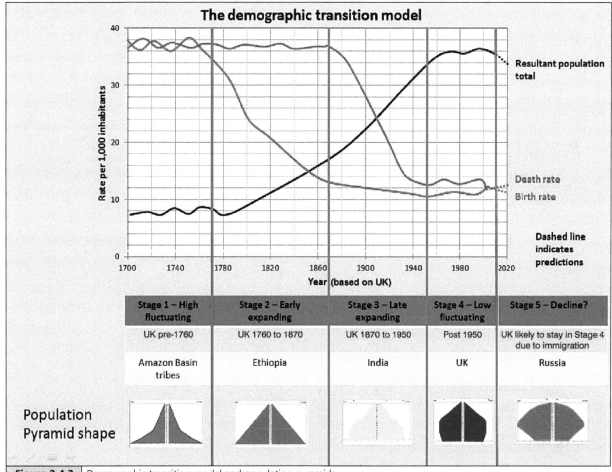

Figure 2.4.3 | Demographic transition model and population pyramids

Population growth case studies

- Compare the demographic transition models for Jamaica and China.

Jamaica: a developing country

In 2014 Jamaica had a total population of 2,930,050. Having grown rapidly between 1950 and 2000, it is now growing much more slowly, at a rate of just 0.7 per cent per year. The reduction in population growth since about 1998 is the result of reduced natural increase and the emigration of young adults and young families.

Look at Figure 2.5.1. It shows Jamaica's demographic transition model. Notice that Jamaica is currently towards the end of stage 3 in the model. The death rate has fallen and is now low and the birth rate is falling too. When the birth rate starts to level off Jamaica will enter stage 4. Here is some more information about stages 1–3:

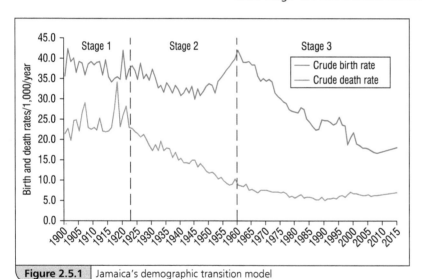

Figure 2.5.1 Jamaica's demographic transition model

- Stage 1 (1900–23). The birth rate and death rate were both high during this period. Poor living conditions and outbreaks of disease resulted in high and fluctuating death rates. High infant mortality and a need to have children to support families and work on the land accounted for the high birth rates.

- Stage 2 (1923–60). Improvements in medicine and better living conditions resulted in a steady drop in the death rate. The birth rate remained high and, for a short time, even increased between 1952 and 1965.

- Stage 3 (1960–2015, then beyond). Birth rates started to fall during this period. Infant and child mortality rates fell due to improvements in health care. Full-time education resulted in women choosing to follow careers rather than starting a family at an early age. Contraception became more widely available and more acceptable.

Look at Figure 2.5.2. It shows the expected changes in Jamaica's population structure from 2000 to 2050.

- 2000–25. The narrowing bars at the base of the pyramid suggest that the birth rate will fall. The bars towards the middle and top of the diagram are becoming wider suggesting a low death rate and increasing life expectancy.

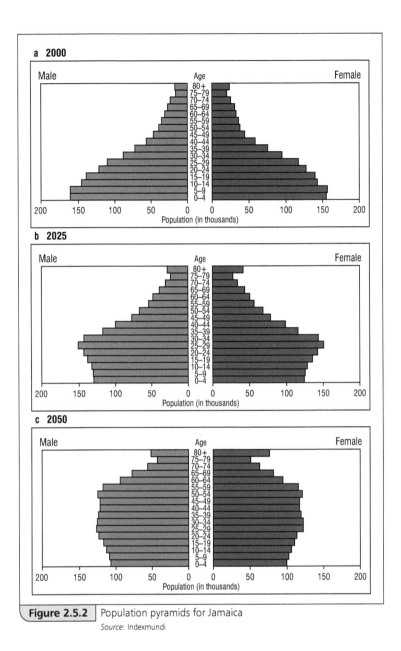

a 2000

Male / Age / Female
Population (in thousands)

b 2025

Male / Age / Female
Population (in thousands)

c 2050

Male / Age / Female
Population (in thousands)

| Figure 2.5.2 | Population pyramids for Jamaica |

Source: Indexmundi

- 2025–50. The birth rate becomes low and stable by 2050. The population becomes older, with more individuals living to middle and old age. This is now a typical developed world population pyramid. In the future, Jamaica will have to cope with issues associated with an ageing population.

China: a rapidly growing economy

China is an increasingly wealthy country in eastern Asia. As the largest population in the world, it had 1.35 billion people in 2014. Its pattern of growth has not followed the demographic transition model very closely.

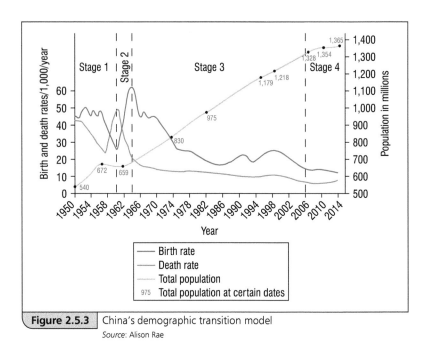

Figure 2.5.3 China's demographic transition model
Source: Alison Rae

Figure 2.5.3 shows China's progress through its demographic transition, which is rather different from Jamaica's experience on page 124.

- China was in Stage 1 until around 1960. Children were important as they were needed to work the land. The Communist government provided reasonable health care. The birth rate was high and the natural increase rapid. Rapid industrialisation took people off the land and the food supply reduced. In the resulting devastating famine almost 30 million people died of starvation. The death rate rose and the birth rate fell, giving a period of dramatic natural decrease.

- After the famine China moved into stage 2 with a baby boom and rapid natural increase. The government was concerned that the population would again outgrow resources, so in 1979 the one-child policy was designed to reduce family size (see Figure 2.5.4). The policy included these measures:

  - Later marriage was encouraged, leaving little time to have children.

  - Only one successful pregnancy was allowed.

  - Sterilisation after the first child was often forced.

  - Very late abortions were performed.

  - Couples who obeyed the rules were given benefits; those who did not were financially penalised.

Figure 2.5.4 One-child policy billboard in China

- China's birth and death rates are now low and stable and it can be classified as a stage 4 country. Soon it will be overtaken in population size by India.

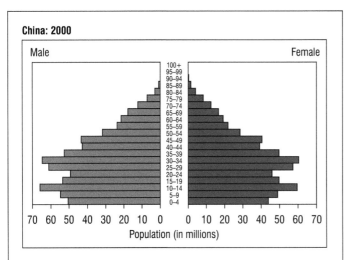

China: 2000

China: 2007

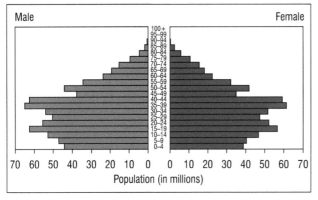

China: 2025

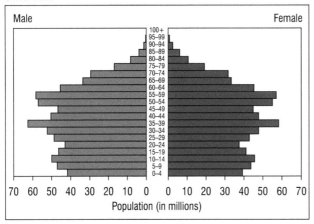

Here are some of the results of China's one-child policy:

- Sons were preferred and some girls were abandoned or placed in orphanages. Some were adopted by British and American couples.

- Chinese children are sometimes called 'Little Emperors' because many are over-indulged as only children.

- Today a gender imbalance exists – young men have trouble finding a wife.

- Girls are now valued as much as boys and urban women especially are very career-focused.

- China will soon become an ageing population and more young people are needed to look after the elderly. Since China overturned its one-child policy in late 2015, the number of couples having two children has progressively increased.

Urbanisation in the Caribbean

What is urbanisation?

Urbanisation is the growth in the proportion of individuals living in towns and cities. **Urban growth** is the increase in the number of urban dwellers.

In 2011, 56 per cent of people lived in towns and cities; in 1960 the figure was 34 per cent. By 2030, an estimated 60 per cent of the world's 8.1 billion inhabitants are expected to be urban dwellers. However, this figure varies enormously from country to country.

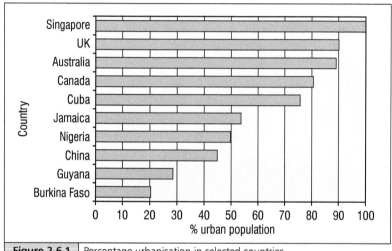

Figure 2.6.1 | Percentage urbanisation in selected countries

The steady increase in urban population arises from two factors:

1 **Rural–urban migration**, as individuals seek to improve their lives by moving from the countryside to towns and cities.

2 **Rapid natural increase** in urban areas, usually owing to the influx of young couples from rural areas. These are people in their child-bearing years. Towns and cities usually have a younger population than rural areas.

Figure 2.6.2 | A young family in a squatter town in Cambodia

Rural–urban migration

Most individuals who move from rural to urban areas choose to do so. They weigh up the advantages and disadvantages of such a move. It is possible to identify **push factors** and **pull factors** (see Figure 2.6.3):

• **Push factors** – these are negative aspects of rural areas that encourage individuals to move away, for example crop failure, poor standards of living, poor services and infrastructure, lack of educational and employment opportunities, and limited entertainment.

- **Pull factors** – these factors draw individuals towards a town or city, rather like a magnetic force. They are positive factors and include better opportunities for education and health care, better-paid jobs and wider choices of entertainment. Often these advantages are what individuals *think* will be available – they may well be disappointed when the reality turns out not to be quite so good!

Urbanisation in the Caribbean

Look at Figure 2.6.4. It uses pie charts to show the levels of urbanisation in the Caribbean. Notice that some countries are more urbanised than others:

- In Cuba, Martinique, Puerto Rico and Trinidad and Tobago, over three-quarters of the population live in urban areas, mostly in the capital cities.
- In contrast, less than half the populations of Haiti, St Vincent, Guyana, Montserrat and Antigua and Barbuda live in urban areas.

Compared to the rest of the world, the Caribbean region has high levels of urbanisation. In 2000, just under 50 per cent of the world's population lived in towns and cities whereas in the Caribbean the figure was nearly 65 per cent. By 2025, the urban population in the Caribbean is expected to rise to 76 per cent.

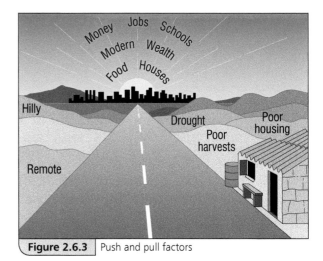

Figure 2.6.3 | Push and pull factors

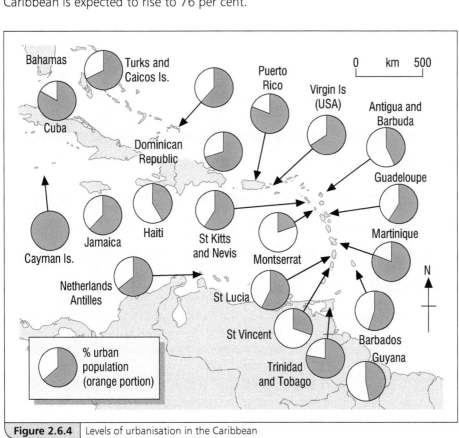

Figure 2.6.4 | Levels of urbanisation in the Caribbean

Impacts of urbanisation

Urbanisation has impacts on both rural areas and towns and cities.

Impacts on rural areas

The high rate of rural–urban migration has led to a fall in the population in many rural areas in both the Caribbean and in other parts of the world. This is called **rural depopulation**.

Rural depopulation can bring advantages – with fewer persons there is less pressure on limited resources, such as food, water, employment and shelter. However, it often creates problems, for example:

- **An ageing population** – mostly it is young men or couples who move to urban areas in search of better opportunities, leaving the older individuals behind.
- **Decreasing food production** – older individuals are less able to cope with the physical demands of farming so production may decrease.
- **Loss of services** – as the population reduces, some public services, such as schools and transport, may be affected. Shops may close with fewer customers living in the area. As services decline, more individuals will be tempted to move away and so the cycle continues.

Impacts on urban areas

The rapid influx of newcomers to towns and cities has provided much-needed labour and created a thriving market for goods and services. However, it has also brought with it these problems:

- **Urban sprawl** – this is the physical growth of the city at the edges, mostly caused by more and more people needing housing. Urban sprawl can destroy valuable farmland and natural vegetation close to the city.
- **Lack of appropriate housing** – housing shortages have led to the development of poor-quality housing areas, sometimes called squatter settlements. Here the houses are poor quality and residents often have inadequate services, such as education and health services, access to water, waste disposal and sanitation.
- **Urban poverty** – the reality of city life may not live up to expectations and some individuals are unable to get a job. The level of poverty in urban areas is high.
- **Transport and congestion** – transport systems may fail to cope with the sheer number of persons so 'all-day rush hours' may result as vehicles clog the narrow streets.
- **Crime** – levels of crime can be high in some cities, particularly where there are high levels of poverty, alcoholism and drug abuse.

DID YOU KNOW?

Around 8 per cent of the world's population live in massive cities called 'megacities'. A megacity is defined as a city with a population of over 10 million. According to the United Nations, the world's largest megacity is Tokyo in Japan, with a population of 38 million in 2016.

Primate cities

One characteristic of urbanisation in the Caribbean has been the concentration of persons into a single urban area. This is sometimes called a **primate city**.

A primate city has a population of at least twice that of the next largest city. In most Caribbean countries, over 30 per cent of the population live in a single primate city, which is usually the capital. Figure 2.6.5 lists the primate cities in Jamaica, Barbados and Antigua. Notice how much larger they are than the second cities.

Primate cities can cause an imbalance of investment, resulting in the formation of a thriving economic **core** area based on the primate city and a relatively poor, more rural, **periphery**. In an ideal world, it is good to balance out development over the whole of a country.

Country	Largest city		Second city	
	Name	**Population**	**Name**	**Population**
Jamaica	Kingston	584,627	Portmore	182,153
Barbados	Bridgetown	99,100	Speightstown	3,600
Antigua	St John's	24,451	All Saints	3,900

Figure 2.6.5 Selected primate cities in the Caribbean

Figure 2.6.6 Bridgetown, the capital of Barbados

Urban agglomeration	Country	Population 2014 (000s)	Rank 2014	Population 2030 (000s)	Rank 2030
Tokyo	Japan	37,833	1	37,190	1
Delhi	India	24,953	2	36,000	2
Shanghai	China	22,991	3	30,751	3
Mexico City	Mexico	20,843	4	23,865	10
São Paulo	Brazil	20,831	5	23,444	11
Mumbai	India	20,741	6	27,797	4
Osaka	Japan	20,123	7	19,976	13
Beijing	China	19,520	8	27,706	5
New York/Newark	USA	18,591	9	19,885	14
Cairo	Egypt	18,419	10	24,502	8

Figure 2.6.7 Top 10 megacity populations and rankings (2014) with predictions to 2030

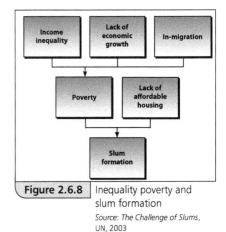

Figure 2.6.8 Inequality poverty and slum formation

Source: The Challenge of Slums, UN, 2003

Problems of urbanisation in the Caribbean: Kingston, Jamaica

- Understand the causes and impacts of urbanisation in Kingston, Jamaica.

Problems caused by urban growth

The problems of urban growth in the Kingston built-up area include:

- development of squatter settlements – the Global Housing Policy Indicators report of 2011 showed that 20 per cent of households in the Greater Kingston area lived in informal squatter settlements
- substandard housing
- high rents for the quality of housing available
- overcrowding
- inadequate transport networks
- environmental degradation
- high crime rates.

Kingston: a primate city

Jamaica's capital city, Kingston, is the largest city in the English-speaking Caribbean with a population of 584,627 (2011 census). Over 30 per cent of the population of Jamaica live in Kingston. It is a classic example of a primate city, being more than three times larger than the second city, Portmore.

The location of Kingston

The city of Kingston lies on the coast of the bay of Kingston in the south-east of Jamaica. Look at Figure 2.7.1. Notice that the city is sited on relatively flat land bounded by mountains to the north and east, and the sea to the south. Much of the land to the west is heavily wooded and swampy. The Palisadoes spit has created an excellent natural harbour, which is one of the main reasons for the growth of the city.

Population growth in Kingston

The population of Kingston has grown rapidly from 379,980 in 1960 to its current level approaching a million. This is mainly the result of:

- high rates of natural increase (birth rate of 22 per 1,000 and death rate of 6 per 1,000)
- rural–urban migration.

In recent years, migration from the countryside has decreased, with natural increase being the main cause of Kingston's growth. Emigration rates, particularly to the USA, are quite high. Without this, the rate of Kingston's growth would be even higher.

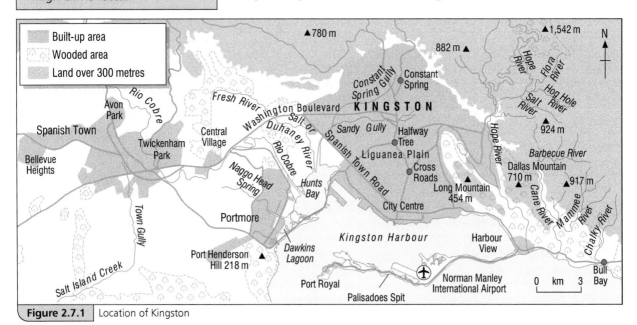

Figure 2.7.1 Location of Kingston

Kingston's urban landscape

As the population has increased, Kingston has expanded physically to cover much of the Liguanea Plain (see Figure 2.7.2) and is expanding into the foothills of the Blue Mountain range.

Kingston is divided into several different districts. To identify these, locate Cross Roads on the map shown in Figure 2.7.1.

* To the south is **Downtown**, mostly comprising the harbour, industrial areas and low-income housing. This is the busiest part of the city, with many retail and commercial enterprises, and many government offices. Some of the housing in districts such as Trench Town is low quality, being poorly maintained and often subdivided. This is where a building that was originally occupied by a single family has been converted into flats or apartments to house several families, each with only a small amount of living space.

* To the north is **Uptown**, which is mostly made up of modern offices, entertainment, restaurants and higher-income housing. The area known as New Kingston is popular with tourists.

Downtown Kingston is characterised by a **grid-square** road layout. However, as the city has expanded outwards (urban sprawl) to engulf smaller villages, this regular street pattern cannot be found on the outskirts of the city.

The city of Kingston can be called a **conurbation** since its growth has engulfed former free-standing towns and villages.

Problems of urban growth in Kingston

While the growth of Kingston's population has provided much-needed labour for industrial development and a huge market for goods and services, it has led to a number of social and environmental problems:

* **Housing poverty** – many individuals live in cramped and poorly maintained houses in the Downtown district of the city (see Figure 2.7.3). Up to a quarter of Kingston's population is unemployed, which means that they have very little money to spend on home improvements. Crime is widespread, often related to drug abuse. Despite some attempts to improve housing, such as loans from the National Housing Corporation, many individuals still live in poverty.

* **Urban decay** – a number of buildings in the Downtown district have been poorly maintained and have deteriorated. The government has responded to the issue by redeveloping the waterfront, which was completed in 1975. In the 1980s, the Urban Development Corporation upgraded Parade Square and since 1995 the Urban Renewal Tax has funded additional improvements in the area.

* **Transport** – congestion and pollution have been a problem for many years. Older cars are often poorly maintained, adding to the problems of air pollution. New roads constructed for commuters have increased the number of cars funnelled into Kingston's dense city-centre road network. Despite investment in public transport, transport remains a major issue in Kingston.

Figure 2.7.2 Liguanea Plain, Kingston

DID YOU KNOW?

Kingston is home to three of Jamaica's largest newspaper companies, several television and radio stations and sports stadiums, including the famous Sabina Park cricket ground. Indeed, Jamaica is referred to as the 'Holiday Home of Cricket'! The great Sir Garfield Sobers scored 365 not out at Sabina Park against Pakistan in 1958. Jamaica is also referred to as the 'Track capital of the world' as it is the training ground for three of the fastest men in the world.

Figure 2.7.3 Low-income housing in Trench Town, Jamaica

What are the problems of urbanisation?

Urbanisation can cause a number of problems:

- As city populations increase there is pressure on jobs, housing and services.
- Cities face increasing problems of unemployment, crime, building decay, congestion and pollution.
- The growth of a single primate city often leads to inequalities within a country.
- Rural areas suffer from problems of rural depopulation such as lack of investment and an ageing population.

How can these problems be solved?

Countries in the Caribbean have tried to address these problems by:

- **Decentralisation** – encouraging new developments to take place away from capital cities, thus reducing primacy.
- **Green belts** – the use of planning measures to create a 'green belt' around cities where development is restricted. Not only does this prevent urban sprawl but it helps to protect farmland and conserve wildlife.
- **Investing money in rural areas** – improving services, transport and living conditions so that people will choose to stay and work in the countryside rather than moving to towns and cities.

CASE STUDY | Barbados and Cuba

Barbados

In Barbados, a series of Physical Development Plans (1970, 1986, 1998 and most recently 2003) have attempted to reduce the inland physical growth of the capital Bridgetown and encourage investment in the countryside.

The main features of the 2003 Development Plan are as follows:

- The designation of an **urban corridor** along the south and west coast of Barbados that includes Bridgetown and other major settlements. It is within this zone that most new developments will be concentrated. Notice on Figure 2.8.1 that the urban corridor will prevent the inland expansion of Bridgetown.

- The designation of the existing communities of Speightstown, Holetown, Oistins and Six Cross Roads as Regional Centres. They will be developed as mixed-use centres, with housing and commercial developments being permitted.
- Investment in other smaller settlements outside the urban corridor (rural settlements with growth potential), such as Ellerton, in an attempt to reduce rural depopulation.
- Some housing and commercial developments will be permitted in villages within the National Park, such as Bathsheba.
- In an attempt to boost farming and reduce rural depopulation there will be opportunities for people to buy land to establish small farms.

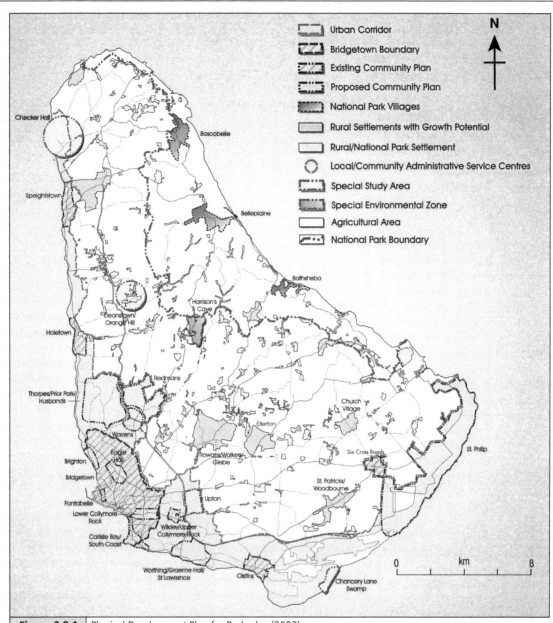

Figure 2.8.1 | Physical Development Plan for Barbados (2003)

Legend:
- Urban Corridor
- Bridgetown Boundary
- Existing Community Plan
- Proposed Community Plan
- National Park Villages
- Rural Settlements with Growth Potential
- Rural/National Park Settlement
- Local/Community Administrative Service Centres
- Special Study Area
- Special Environmental Zone
- Agricultural Area
- National Park Boundary

Cuba

The Cuban government exerts much greater control over the lives of its people than happens elsewhere in the Caribbean, and policies here have tended to be more successful. Since the 1960s the government has invested heavily in educational and welfare programmes in the countryside to reduce the flow of individuals to the capital city, Havana. The focus on improving schools, health clinics and agriculture in rural areas has been very successful in reducing rural depopulation (see Figure 2.8.2).

Figure 2.8.2 | Rural developments in Cuba

International migration in the Caribbean

- Understand the types and causes of migration.
- Understand the trends in migration in the Caribbean.
- Understand trends of immigration and emigration in the Cayman Islands and Jamaica.

EXAM TIP

Make sure you know the difference between emigration and immigration – also be careful with spelling.

DID YOU KNOW?

Caribbean immigrants to the UK, USA and Canada have introduced a rich cultural heritage, including reggae music, fashion and cooking, such as Cajun and Jerk dishes. In the UK, the annual Notting Hill Carnival is a celebration of West Indian culture and heritage centred in the Notting Hill district of London. Traditional steel bands and colourful floats create a vibrant Caribbean atmosphere in the centre of London, and hundreds of food stalls line the streets. Millions of people from around the world are attracted to the carnival each year.

What is migration?

Migration is the movement of individuals from place to place. While some forms of migration are short term, such as commuting to work or going on holiday (which is called **circulation**), the term is usually applied to those who move to a new place, often in a new country, with the intention of remaining there permanently or for at least a year.

Most migration is **voluntary**. Individuals weigh up the advantages and disadvantages before deciding to leave one place and move to another. Often this is to do with employment or the desire to live closer to relatives. However, some migrations are **forced**. These may result from a natural disaster, such as an earthquake or volcanic eruption, or they may be the result of political persecution and 'ethnic cleansing'.

Individuals who move out of a country are called **emigrants**. Individuals who move into a country are called **immigrants**.

International migration in the Caribbean

The Caribbean has been greatly affected by international migration for hundreds of years.

- During the colonial era from about 1500, many individuals from Spain settled in the Caribbean. They brought with them African slaves to work on plantations.
- The Spanish were followed by the British, French and Dutch who later colonised the islands in the Caribbean.
- Following the abolition of slavery in 1834, there were large-scale movements of people within the Caribbean from Barbados and Jamaica to less populated countries such as Guyana and Trinidad. In recent decades individuals have moved from Haiti, the western hemisphere's poorest country (which also suffers from earthquakes and hurricanes) into the neighbouring Dominican Republic to work on the sugar cane plantations.
- During the 1950s, many West Indians decided to move to the UK and other European countries in search of work. In the 1961 UK census, over 170,000 Caribbean-born people were found to be living in the UK compared with just 15,000 in 1951.
- In the 1960s, changes to the immigration laws in the USA and Canada made migration from the Caribbean easier. In 2000, there were nearly 3 million Caribbean-born persons living in the USA, mostly in the states of New York and Florida. Most had travelled to the USA in search of work or education, or to buy land.
- More recently, there have been several major development projects in the Caribbean funded by China and other Asian countries, such as improvements to Kingston's harbour and the construction of a cricket ground on Dominica. During construction, Chinese workers were brought to the Caribbean, and they then returned home when the contract was complete.

Cayman Islands: high immigration

The Cayman Islands has the highest rate of immigration in the Caribbean. Recent economic growth, particularly in tourism, construction and financial services, has resulted in a rapid expansion of employment opportunities. Between 1970 and 2014, the population grew from 10,068 to almost 55,000.

Most of the immigrants to the Cayman Islands have come from nearby Jamaica where there are fewer opportunities for employment. Increasingly, the Cayman Islands is a 'halfway house' for Cubans wishing to migrate to the USA.

Immigration has brought wealth and development to the Cayman Islands. However, there has been a negative impact on the environment, particularly widespread deforestation.

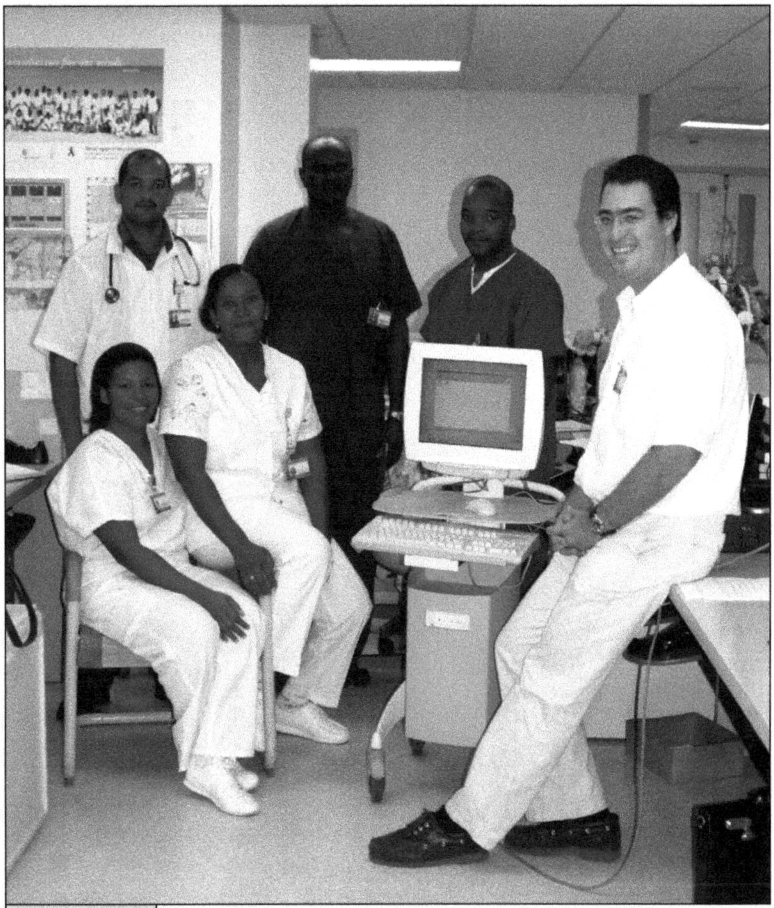

Jamaica: high emigration

In contrast to the Cayman Islands, Jamaica has experienced one of the most rapid rates of emigration in the Caribbean. An estimated 2.6 million Jamaicans live abroad – a similar number to those currently living in Jamaica. The greatest concentrations are in the USA, Canada and the UK. The main reason for emigration has been to seek better opportunities for employment.

Figure 2.9.1 Workers from foreign countries in the Cayman Islands

- UK – most emigration took place in the late 1950s before the 1962 Immigration Act in the UK restricted immigration. From the late 1960s some of the immigrants moved back to Jamaica, although a large number still live in the UK.

- USA – over 173,000 Jamaicans were admitted into the USA between 1991 and 2000. Most live in the urban centres, such as New York and Miami.

- Canada – most Jamaicans are concentrated in Toronto.

The emigrants have brought benefits to Jamaica. Many send or remit money home to their families. This money is added to the economy and can be used by family members to start up businesses. Indirectly, emigration has reduced pressure on jobs and social services in Jamaica.

Economic sectors in the Caribbean

- Understand the four sectors of economic activity.
- Understand economic sectors in the Caribbean.

What is economic activity?

Economic activity is the way that individuals and countries produce, distribute or consume products or services. Economic activity provides the money needed for governments to spend on services such as health and education, water and electricity as well as for building roads, hospitals and schools (infrastructure).

It is possible to identify four main types or **sectors** of economic activity:

1 **Primary sector** – this involves the extraction of raw materials from the earth, for example farming, quarrying and fishing.
2 **Secondary sector** – this involves making (manufacturing) products using the raw materials from the primary sector. Examples of secondary industries include food processing, e.g. taking sugar cane and processing it to make sugar. Clothes made from cotton and cars made from steel and other raw materials are also examples of secondary sector industries.
3 **Tertiary sector** – these are economic activities that provide a service to people. Examples of workers in the service sector include teachers, shop workers, hotel staff, health care providers and the police.
4 **Quaternary sector** (finance, trade, research and development, advertising, consultancy) – this sector involves individuals who provide information and expertise for others to use. This may involve training, consultancy and research and development. A lot of individuals working with information technology are included in this sector. This is a relatively recent sector and is really just a branch of the service (tertiary) sector.

Importance of economic sectors in selected countries

Look at Figure 2.10.1. It shows the importance of the economic sectors in some selected countries according to their contribution to the wealth of the country (gross domestic product – GDP). Notice that the information is arranged in a slightly different way, using agriculture, industry and services as the main types of economic sector. Figure 2.10.2 shows the employment in each sector.

Composition of GDP (%)			
Country	Agriculture	Industry*	Services
Jamaica	7	29	64
Barbados	3	14	83
Trinidad and Tobago	1	57	42
Guyana	21	38	41
Canada	2	28	70
China	10	45	45
UK	1	20	79
India	17	17	66
Nigeria	31	43	26

Figure 2.10.1 Economic sectors by contribution to GDP
  * Includes mining/fishing

- For most countries, the service sector is the most important. In the Caribbean, many individuals are involved in tourism. In countries such as the UK, large numbers of individuals work in retailing and in the financial sector.
- Industry is the dominant sector in China, where many people are involved in the manufacturing of clothing and electronics. In Trinidad and Tobago, a lot of wealth is generated by the oil and gas industry, food processing and in manufacturing cement.

- In the Caribbean, agriculture is an important sector in Guyana. It is less important in Jamaica, Barbados and Trinidad and Tobago.
- Figure 2.10.2 shows that developed countries, such as Canada and the UK, have few people working in the agricultural sector. They also have large service sectors. Poorer countries, such as Bangladesh and Ethiopia, are very dependent on agriculture and have much smaller service sectors.

Economic sectors by employment (%)			
Country	Agriculture	Industry*	Services
Jamaica	17	19	64
Barbados	10	15	75
Trinidad and Tobago	4	33	63
Guyana	30	27	43
Canada	2	19	79
China	40	27	33
UK	1	25	74
Bangladesh	45	30	25
Ethiopia	80	8	12

Figure 2.10.2 Economic sectors by employment
* Includes mining/fishing

Economic sectors in the Caribbean

Primary sector (raw materials)

The primary sector has traditionally been very important in the Caribbean:

- In farming, production of traditional crops, such as sugar cane, has been widespread and still employs many workers in countries such as Jamaica and Guyana.
- Fishing employs many people throughout the Caribbean.
- In Trinidad and Tobago, oil and gas is an extremely important source of income and employs about 20,000 people (see Figure 2.10.3).

Figure 2.10.3 Extraction of oil in Trinidad and Tobago

Guyana is one of the poorest countries in the Caribbean. It still has a large number of low-income individuals working on the land owing to the lack of modern machinery.

Secondary sector (manufacturing)

By adding value to raw materials (by processing them), such as food products and fish, the secondary sector provides important export revenues for countries in the Caribbean. Trinidad and Tobago has one of the largest secondary sectors in the Caribbean. This is the result of the processing of foods, oil and gas, and the manufacture of cement. Elsewhere, food processing (see Figure 2.10.4) and the manufacturing of clothes are important industries in the Caribbean.

Tertiary sector (services)

Tourism is a rapidly growing industry throughout the Caribbean. It provides an important source of income and generates a large number of jobs. Retailing also employs a lot of individuals and increasing numbers are working in public services, such as education and health care.

Quaternary sector (information and expertise)

The provision of information, together with activities such as research and training, is increasing in the Caribbean. One recent development has been the creation of **call centres**, where individuals ring for advice about banking, travel, insurance or cellphone services. Modern technology means that call centres can be located almost anywhere in the world. One reason for the growth of call centres in the Caribbean is because wages are lower than in countries such as the USA or the UK.

Figure 2.10.4 A citrus processing factory in Belize

Resources and their locations

- Understand the locations of resources in the Caribbean.
- Understand the factors affecting industrial location.

Renewable and non-renewable resources – what are the differences?

Renewable resources are those which can be used repeatedly – they are **infinite** and therefore do not run out. There are two types:

- A flow of nature – wind, tides, waves and the sun provide renewable energy.
- Living things – trees, ecosystems and soil are renewable as long as people do not use them faster than they can be replaced.

Non-renewable resources, on the other hand, are **finite** – they will run out. Examples include coal, oil and natural gas, and minerals such as gold and bauxite.

Technology and simple common sense can help people extend the use of both types of resource. Here are some examples:

- If fish stocks are over-used, fishermen can be excluded from certain areas to allow regeneration. In the European Union there are rules on the size of fish that can be caught – small ones must be thrown back to mature.
- Selective cutting in rainforests allows the whole ecosystem to remain while exploitation takes place.
- Soil needs to be looked after to prevent erosion.
- High-tech mining equipment allows previously inaccessible coal in the UK to be mined. Improved oil exploration has revealed new, previously unknown supplies globally.

Figure 2.11.1 Surviving Caribbean forests

Examples of resources in the Caribbean

In the Caribbean, agriculture and natural resource extraction are the basis of many islands' economies.

Forests

Figures 2.11.2 and 2.11.3 show forest and farmland resources in Guyana and Jamaica. Forest is scattered in Jamaica but is found in sufficient areas to be sustainably exploited.

Guyana has large areas of forest, much of which is tropical rainforest.

Fishing

Fishing is carried out across the Caribbean region, using trawling, lines, seining (boats dragging huge nets behind them) and pots for shellfish, largely for the home market. Care needs to be taken to conserve resources.

Oil and natural gas

Oil and natural gas exploitation is particularly important to Trinidad and Tobago as well as in Cuba and to a lesser extent to Barbados (see Figure 2.11.4).

Trinidad is the Caribbean's largest producer of oil and gas. BP (British Petroleum) is the main company involved. In terms of gas, Trinidad and Tobago is becoming a major global gas centre. In addition to the three countries shown in Figure 2.11.4, the Bahamas may have 4.3 million barrels of oil (according to the US Geological Survey 2012). There may be gas resources off Aruba and Costa Rica, though exploitation in Costa Rica is unlikely due to environmental risks.

Figure 2.11.2 Tropical rainforest in Ocho Rios, Jamaica

Figure 2.11.3 Coffee plantation in the Blue mountains, Jamaica

	Proven resources Crude oil (million barrels)	Proven resources Natural gas (billion cubic feet)
Trinidad and Tobago	716.0	23,450
Cuba	750.0	2,500
Barbados	2.5	5
Total Caribbean	1468.5	25,955

Figure 2.11.4 Caribbean oil and natural gas reserves

Source: Caribbean Fact Sheet
http://www.geni.org/global energy/library/national_energy_grid/cuba/carib.shtml

Bauxite

Bauxite (or alumina – aluminium oxide, Al_2O_3) is the ore of the metal, aluminium. It is an important global resource and the Caribbean is a key location. Bauxite needs to be heated to 600°C to extract the metal and this takes a huge amount of energy. Bauxite is processed to a limited extent in the Caribbean but much is exported to cheap energy locations such as Iceland with its geothermal and hydroelectric power. For Jamaica, this is the second most important foreign exchange earner. Jamalco and Alcoa are key companies.

Figure 2.11.5 Limestone in a quarry in Port-au-Prince, Haiti

Limestone

Limestone is quarried primarily for making cement for the construction industry (see Figure 2.11.4). There is considerable demand for this as tertiary and quaternary businesses need new buildings. Jamaica, Barbados, the Dominican Republic, and Trinidad and Tobago all have such businesses.

Rock being blasted out of the landscape causes considerable scarring. It is essential to have contracts that include a commitment to regenerate the landscape to its previous appearance.

Gold

Jamaica worked gold deposits until 2005. More recently Hispaniola (Haiti and the Dominican Republic) has been the important location for gold exploitation. Hispaniola is bisected by a central ridge of high land containing precious metal deposits in both countries. The two key mines are:

• Mont Organisé in Haiti
• Pueblo Viejo in the Dominican Republic (see Figure 2.11.6).

Other, smaller companies continue to search for viable mines. Canadian companies are interested in mining in the Dominican Republic, but the mining process threatens the very environment

DID YOU KNOW?

Industry aims to cut costs by being as close to its resources and raw materials, labour and market as possible. The heavier and bulkier the inputs and/or outputs, the closer they need to be to the other hubs of the industry. Here are some examples:

• Limestone and bauxite are heavy and it is cheaper to carry them by sea.
• Vegetables such as yams need to be close to market as they are heavy compared to most other vegetables and are therefore more expensive to transport.
• Crops that deteriorate quickly also need to be near the market.
• Oil and gas are transported via pipelines, which are expensive to construct but efficient to run.

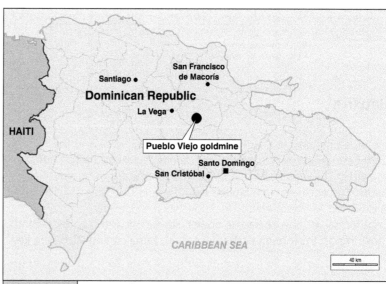

Figure 2.11.6 Location of Pueblo Viejo goldmine in the Dominican Republic

that supports tourism. Cyanide, a highly toxic chemical, is used to extract the gold. The daily requirement of cyanide is 24 tonnes just at the Pueblo Viejo site. Cyanide gets into the hydrological cycle and poisons aquatic ecosystems and perhaps even human water supplies.

Factors affecting the location of industry

Human/Economic

- **Labour** – factories often need to employ large numbers of workers and for this reason it is an advantage to be located in a town or city. Some industries require highly skilled university-educated workers. In the UK, several industries of this type are found in the university cities of Oxford and Cambridge.
- **Markets** – industries need markets for their products. Sometimes a market can be another industry (e.g. components for the car industry) or just the general public (e.g. clothes and processed food).
- **Transport** – good transport links are essential for many industries to bring in raw materials and take away finished products. For this reason many industries are close to main roads, railway terminals or ports.
- **Capital** – industries rely upon investment in buildings, equipment and training. This may come from governments or wealthy individuals and can affect location.

Political

Government policies – governments often encourage industrial location in certain areas by providing grants or tax-free incentives. In the UK, this has happened in older industrial areas such as South Wales where heavy industries have closed down causing widespread unemployment. The government of the Dominican Republic has established free-trade zones to encourage new industries to locate there.

Physical

- **Raw materials** – heavy and bulky raw materials, such as sugar, coal and bauxite, are expensive to transport.
- **Energy** – in the past, industries were very tied to power sources, such as coal and water. Today, most industries use electricity, which is available almost anywhere at the flick of a switch, so this factor is less important than it used to be.
- **Relief** – industries often need extensive areas of flat land for building and storage (see Figure 2.11.7).
- **Environmental quality** – increasingly, industries are choosing sites that are attractive and provide pleasant working conditions for their employees.

Figure 2.11.7 Sugar mill in La Romana, Dominican Republic

Primary sector case study: fishing

Figure 2.12.1 Cuban stamp illustrating the fishing industry – a bonito is a small tuna, rather like a mackerel

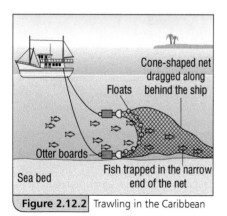

Figure 2.12.2 Trawling in the Caribbean

Fishing in the Caribbean

Fish are abundant in the warm waters of the Caribbean and have always been an important source of food (see Figure 2.12.1). All countries in the Caribbean have developed small-scale fishing industries and freshly caught fish, such as flying fish and mahi-mahi, are popular in restaurants.

Fishing occurs throughout the year in the Caribbean. Over 10,000 workers are employed in Guyana and several thousand are employed in Barbados and Trinidad and Tobago.

Fishing methods in the Caribbean

Fishing in the Caribbean mostly involves the use of small boats and nets to catch fish close to the shore.

Seining

Seining involves a net that is kept vertical in the water by corks floating on the surface. Two boats draw the net together encircling a school of fish. The net is then dragged onto the boats or to the shore and the trapped fish are removed. Seining is used to catch king fish, shark and carite.

Trawling

In some countries, such as Trinidad and Tobago and Barbados, fishing has become more commercialised with the introduction of fleets of trawlers. Guyana now has over 250 shrimp trawlers. **Trawling** involves a cone-shaped net being dragged through the water by a large boat (trawler). Fish become trapped in the narrow end as the net is drawn up to the boat (see Figure 2.12.2). Trawling is often used to catch fish that live near to the sea floor. The main fish caught by trawling are shrimp, carite, snapper and cavali.

Other methods of fishing involve the use of **fish pots**, to catch red snappers and jacks, and **long lines** with up to 1,000 hooks that are towed behind boats to catch tuna, swordfish, grouper and shark.

Why is fishing important in the Caribbean?

There are several reasons why the Caribbean has developed a fishing industry:

- The shallow coastal waters around Trinidad and Tobago and Guyana are rich in nutrients washed into the sea by rivers such as the Orinoco in Venezuela and Essequibo in Guyana.
- Abundant marine life provide food for fish in the coral reefs.

- Mangrove swamps provide important habitats and breeding grounds for fish and shrimps.
- Many islands have good natural harbours for fishing boats and ports for export.
- There is a long tradition of fishing for food and trade.
- Tourism provides an important market for fresh fish in restaurants and hotels, as well as sports fishing.

How are fish marketed?

A lot of fish are sold locally from the harbourside to 'middlemen', who then sell the fish on to retailers or restaurant owners. This small-scale marketing is common in villages in Jamaica, St Vincent, Dominica and St Lucia and in major tourist areas.

Wholesale markets have developed in Guyana, where companies such as the Guyana Food Processors and Georgetown Seafoods and Trading Company buy from the fishermen.

Once caught, fish are processed to preserve them. This can involve salting, common in Barbados and Tobago, smoking and filleting, or quick freezing. In the 1990s and early 2000s, the Tobago Sea Products Fish Processing plant in Shaw Park, Tobago processed about 200,000 kg of flying fish, snapper, grouper, wahoo and king fish annually.

Future challenges for the fishing industry.

A number of challenges face the Caribbean fishing industry:

- **Over-fishing**, often involving catching and killing young fish which cannot then mature and breed. This reduces fish stocks and is unsustainable. Some widely available species are under-used at present.
- **Pollution** in both rivers and the sea from oil, sewage and waste can contaminate fish and kill off fish stocks.
- **Destruction of mangrove swamps** for building and tourist developments removes important fish breeding grounds and habitats.
- **Lack of investment** in refrigeration and marketing restricts the quantity of fish that can be sold.

CASE STUDY	Belize

With an extensive 457 km length of coastline rich in mangrove swamps and coral reefs, Belize has one of the best fishing grounds in the Caribbean. Over 1,670 people are employed in fishing, most belonging to a small number of cooperatives that own the modern fish-processing plants.

The most important fish products are lobsters, caught in wooden traps or by divers in the shallow waters along the coral reefs. They account for over 50 per cent of the export earnings. Conch, found on beds of sea grass, is exported to the Far East and shrimp (caught by Honduran trawlers) are processed and exported to the USA.

Fish stocks have declined in recent years as a result of over-fishing and damage done to coral reefs by hurricanes, such as Hurricane Keith in 2000. Some fishermen have moved into the tourist industry, taking charter boats out to sea in search of deep-sea fish. Despite these issues, fishing continues to be an important industry contributing some 5 per cent to Belize's gross domestic product (GDP).

Stricter regulations have recently been introduced to enable fishing to be more sustainable in the future. These include limiting the number of shrimp trawlers to a maximum of eight in any one year, the introduction of closed seasons and enforcement of minimum sizes/weights for fish (e.g. conch shell length must exceed 18 cm). The government is also trying to encourage individuals to make greater use of the less popular under-used species.

Look at the following website for more information: ftp://ftp.fao.org/FI/DOCUMENT/fcp/en/FI_CP_BZ.pdf

2.13 Primary sector case study: crude oil and natural gas in Trinidad and Tobago

LEARNING OUTCOMES

- Understand the formation, discovery and exploitation of oil and gas.
- Understand the importance of oil and gas to Trinidad and Tobago.

Millions of years ago, plants and animals living in the sea (mostly plankton) died and collected on the seabed.

↓

Buried and compressed by overlying sediments, these organic deposits became heated and slowly transformed into crude oil and natural gas.

↓

Trapped by overlying impermeable rocks, the oil and gas remained deep underground without migrating and being lost to the surface.

↓

The result was the creation of huge **reservoirs** of oil and gas trapped underground and available to be tapped and exploited.

Figure 2.13.1 Formation of oil and gas

'Black gold' in the Caribbean

Crude oil is one of the world's most valuable natural resources. For this reason it is sometimes known as 'black gold'. Trinidad and Tobago is fortunate in having large reserves of both crude oil and natural gas, which explains why it is one of the wealthiest countries in the Caribbean.

The extraction of crude oil and natural gas is a good example of a primary industry. Once extracted, the oil is used to make gasoline, diesel and kerosene. The gas is used both as a fuel to generate electricity and as a raw material in the manufacture of plastics and fertilisers, which are secondary industries.

The extraction and refining of crude oil and natural gas provides cheap energy supplies in Trinidad and Tobago and supports many secondary industries. This explains the high percentage of workers employed in this sector compared with other Caribbean countries (see Figure 2.10.2, page 139).

Formation and discovery of crude oil and natural gas

The formation of oil and gas occurred many millions of years ago and involved the stages shown in Figure 2.13.1.

The first oil well was drilled in the south of Trinidad in 1857. For 100 years oil exploitation was restricted to the land as it was much easier to extract oil on land than at sea. Offshore drilling began in the 1950s as technology improved. Today, the largest operations are offshore, particularly off the east and west coasts of Trinidad. Many of the onshore oilfields are becoming depleted, with oil being expensive to extract.

Extraction of crude oil and natural gas

Look at Figure 2.13.2. It shows the location of the oil and gas fields in Trinidad and Tobago. Notice the following features:

- The oilfields occur in a discontinuous band roughly east–west through southern Trinidad. Some of the oilfields are offshore in the Gulf of Paria and the Atlantic Ocean.
- All the gasfields are offshore with the greatest concentration being in the Atlantic Ocean to the east of Trinidad.
- Some gasfields are found to the north of Trinidad and to the west of Tobago.
- Pipelines are used extensively to transport oil and gas to terminals on Trinidad.

- Oil tankers operate out of Galeota Point, Point Fortin and Pointe-à-Pierre, transporting oil to markets such as the USA.
- There is a major oil refinery at Pointe-à-Pierre where the oil can be processed.

Importance of crude oil and natural gas

The oil and gas industry is extremely important to the economy of Trinidad and Tobago. It brings in over 70 per cent of foreign exchange and accounts for 23 per cent of gross domestic product (GDP) there. It has fuelled massive growth in the country's economy and has given many a good standard of living.

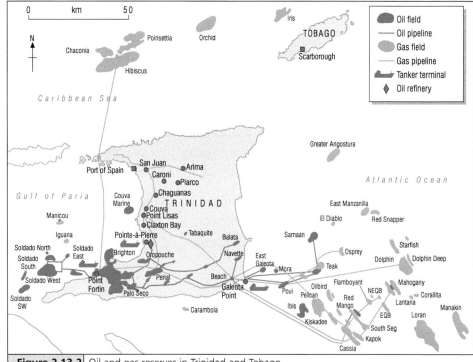

Figure 2.13.2 Oil and gas reserves in Trinidad and Tobago

Source: *Philip's Certificate Atlas for the Caribbean* (6th edition), 2011

There are several other benefits:

- Over 20,000 persons are directly employed by the oil and gas industry and many thousands are employed in related industries.
- Using oil and gas profits, Trinidad and Tobago has invested money in other industries, such as a large steelworks.
- There is an extensive network of gas pipelines providing a reliable supply of energy throughout the country.
- Money has been invested in services (e.g. education, health) and infrastructure.
- The service sector has grown (e.g. retailing) and this provides yet more jobs.

Where does Trinidad and Tobago sell its oil?

Most Caribbean oil is transported the short distance to North America. Transport costs are therefore relatively low. Americans prefer to trade with stable governments in the Caribbean rather than with those with political problems in the Middle East.

Challenges for the future

Oil and gas are examples of **non-renewable** resources. They are not being formed today and, therefore, they are finite. While Trinidad and Tobago has reserves to last until at least 2050, eventually exploitation will be too expensive. Alternative activities will need to be developed to maintain economic growth.

DID YOU KNOW?

Several international **trans-national companies** (TNCs) are involved in the extraction of oil and gas in Trinidad and Tobago, including BP (British Petroleum) and BG (British Gas). The state-owned Petroleum Company of Trinidad and Tobago (Petrotrin) is involved in both extraction and the operation of the oil refinery at Pointe-à-Pierre.

Secondary sector case study: food processing in the Caribbean (CARICOM)

DID YOU KNOW?

Grenada has an international reputation for manufacturing a liqueur made from nutmeg. De la Grenade Industries started producing the liqueur as a small cottage industry in 1996. Following the success of the product it has recently constructed a modern factory to mass produce the popular drink.

CARICOM, the Caribbean Community Market, is an organisation of 15 nations established in 1973. Its main aim is economic cooperation. These are the members:

- Antigua and Barbuda
- Bahamas
- Barbados
- Belize
- Dominica
- Grenada
- Guyana
- Haiti
- Jamaica
- Montserrat
- St Kitts and Nevis
- St Lucia
- St Vincent and the Grenadines
- Suriname
- Trinidad and Tobago

Types of food processing

Food processing is an important manufacturing industry in the Caribbean. Food is processed to preserve it and to add value before it is sold. A huge range of agricultural products is processed in the Caribbean, including sugar cane, cocoa, citrus fruit, fish, meat, nuts (such as cashews and peanuts), milk, coffee, vegetables and preserves of local fruits. Processing involves canning, drying and smoking. The industry employs several thousand workers across the region and contributes significantly to exports. Some large multinational companies such as Nestlé are involved, but 80 per cent of the companies are cottage industries or family businesses. Many are owned and run by women. These businesses are generally growing.

Location of food-processing factories

There are two main types of location:

1 In food-producing areas, such as where sugar cane, cocoa and cattle are farmed. This is because the raw materials are bulky and expensive to transport. They may also be perishable and need rapid processing once harvested.

2 In coastal sea ports/towns where there is a nearby workforce, a large local market and opportunities for exporting the finished products. Most food-processing plants in the Caribbean import the ingredients in bulk, and package and process them near the port.

Examples of food-processing locations in the Caribbean

Jamaica

Look at Figure 2.14.1. Notice that the sugar-cane processing factories are located in the main sugar-producing areas and that the rum factories, which use processed molasses, are located nearby. They are usually extensions of the sugar mills and are owned and operated as an end stage in the process. Other food-processing factories, including a flour mill, are concentrated in the Kingston area benefiting from the urban workforce, a large local market and export opportunities. The flour mill processes imported flour, which explains its port location.

Guyana

In Guyana, food processing is concentrated at the coast (see Figure 2.14.2) for the following reasons:

- Nearby food-producing areas (sugar cane, cattle, vegetables).
- Close to fishing grounds that provide fish for processing.
- The capital Georgetown and other coastal towns provide a workforce and a large domestic market.
- Ports enable processed products to be exported.

In the south of Guyana there is a large modern meat-processing factory at Lethem, located within a major ranching region. Here, beef is processed for sale in Guyana and nearby Brazil. There are plans to develop an organic beef industry in the area. In addition to beef, there is a cashew nut processing factory.

Guyana can already feed itself and has a seven-year plan to increase production to process and export.

Advantages of the Caribbean for food processing

These industries continue to be important and growing. Below are some of the reasons why:

- Raw materials are mostly from local farming and fishing, so they do not have to travel far from source to processing site and then to market. This cuts production costs.
- Efficient transport networks (road and port) already exist.
- There is a readily available supply of experienced workers.
- New technologies for storing food products are used whenever possible.
- Some Caribbean countries place high import taxes on imported food products to make home-produced goods more competitive.

Challenges for food processing in the Caribbean

While food processing remains a growth industry in many CARICOM countries, there are potential problems. Many raw materials come

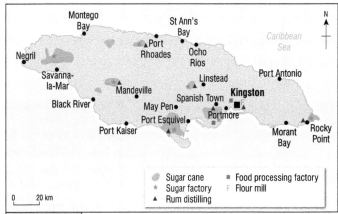

Figure 2.14.1 Location of food processing in Jamaica

Figure 2.14.2 Location of food processing in Guyana

from small-scale producers with gardens, orchards or fishing boats. These suppliers are not always consistent in their production, limiting the capacity of the food-processing factories. Pressure to build houses in Belize has reduced the area of orange orchards, reducing juice manufacturing capacity in Trinidad and Tobago. Hurricanes may also reduce agricultural production.

Some fruit crops have suffered as a consequence of disease, for instance:

• the citrus tristeza virus reduces citrus harvests in Trinidad and Tobago
• the pink hibiscus mealybug has attacked pineapples in Dominica and Guyana.

Since the majority of companies involved are very small, staff training and research and development are not prioritised. Competition from larger companies, such as those in the USA, threatens future Caribbean success.

The future of food processing in CARICOM countries

Despite difficulties discussed above, many CARICOM countries are planning to develop their food processing industries further.

Expanding populations, within some Caribbean countries and in those to whom the food products are sold, mean more food is needed. Using as much as possible of what the Caribbean produces itself cuts import costs. For example, food processing can utilise fruit not quite good enough for exporting, and that is consumed within the Caribbean. Some food-processing businesses are based on imported foodstuffs, such as New Zealand dried milk which is converted in the Caribbean into condensed milk for typical local recipes.

With governments backing food processing there is the potential to grow further; food processing is likely to remain an important part of the secondary economy of the CARICOM countries.

Figure 2.14.3 Processed sauces produced in the Caribbean

A secondary sector comparison: food processing in Singapore

Development of large-scale food-processing industries in Singapore

Over 42 million people live in the Caribbean, and 5.3 million live in Singapore, only slightly more than in St Lucia. The food-processing industry in Singapore, with over 800 factories earning over US$4 billion in 2011, is much larger than that in the CARICOM countries.

As one of the earliest manufacturing industries in Singapore, food processing is today one of its largest. It began as small-scale businesses, based on local culture and traditions, and there are still such businesses thriving. Overall, therefore, there are clear similarities and differences with the Caribbean pattern.

Singaporean food manufacturing industries went through periods of severe difficulty caused by regional and global political and economic issues, including:

• the economic recessions of 1986 and 2008
• the Asian financial crisis (1997)
• the bird flu epidemic (2003).

Nevertheless, food processing remains the seventh largest manufacturing industry in terms of income generated.

Below are the similarities and differences between the Singaporean and CARICOM food-processing industries.

How are Singapore and CARICOM countries similar?

• The majority of businesses (95 per cent in Singapore) are classed as small and medium-sized enterprises (SMEs) with up to 200 employees; the remaining very large ones tend to be multinationals.
• Export markets are important as a source of GNP (see 'Did you know?').
• Efficient road and port networks operate to make distribution and export effective.

How is Singapore different from CARICOM countries?

• Businesses are most commonly located on industrial estates.
• Most raw materials are imported as Singapore has limited amounts of agricultural land.
• Labour supplies in Singapore include migrant workers as well as local people; a total of 19,000 people are involved compared with 13,000 in CARICOM countries.
• High-tech equipment dominates, and research and development is very important.
• Government involvement in Singapore is greater – suitable buildings are provided; products are duty free; taxes are kept low.

Challenges for the future

Salaries in Singapore are relatively high compared with the rest of Asia, meaning foreign competition can sell at lower prices, and, since Singapore's population is only 5.3 million people, that limits the local market. Global prices for raw materials tend to rise. In order to be more in control of their costs, some Singaporean companies are buying land in China to grow their own raw materials on huge farms.

Consumers are increasingly aware of what they are eating from the health and nutrition point of view. Eating too much processed food does not form a well-balanced diet. Positive images and good advertising are important.

Singapore is a global centre of finance and investment and therefore has the financial backing and flexibility to meet future challenges.

Figure 2.14.4 Food-processing factory in Singapore

Tertiary sector case study: tourism in the Caribbean

Tourism is travel for pleasure. More than 100 years ago, only the very wealthy could afford it, but it has now become increasingly common for people to have holidays. During the 20th century Europeans and Americans began to visit the Caribbean islands, mainly choosing their previous colonies:

- The British visited Jamaica and Barbados.
- The French liked Martinique.
- The Dutch preferred Curaçao.
- The Americans often chose Cuba and the Bahamas.

The importance of tourism

Tourism is an example of a tertiary industry because it provides services for tourists in resorts, hotels and restaurants. Tourism also supports secondary industries, particularly those involved in the production of crafts, furnishings and processed foods. It also supports primary industries such as farming and fishing.

In the Caribbean, it is for most countries the fastest-growing and most important industry, providing much-needed foreign income and supporting thousands of jobs (see Figure 2.15.1).

- In 2014, almost 26.3 million tourists visited the Caribbean, up from 18.5 million in 2005. This could rise to 28 million by 2021.

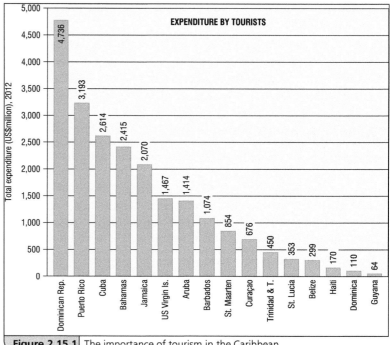

Figure 2.15.1 The importance of tourism in the Caribbean

- In 2014, 14.6 per cent of the Caribbean's gross domestic product (GDP) came directly or indirectly from tourism. This is the highest contribution of any region in the world and shows how dependent the Caribbean is on tourism.
- In 2014 some 2,231,500 jobs were directly or indirectly supported by tourism in the Caribbean, equivalent to 13 per cent of the workforce. By 2025 this is expected to rise to 2,788,000 (14.4 per cent of the workforce).

Figure 2.15.2 Tourist attractions in the Caribbean

What are the attractions of the Caribbean?

The Caribbean has much to offer tourists as Figure 2.15.2 illustrates. Attractions include the following:

- The area has a warm year-round climate, particularly popular during the winter (December–March) when conditions are cold and dark in the USA and much of Europe.
- There are spectacular landscapes, with beautiful beaches, warm seas, forested mountains and volcanoes.
- The Caribbean has a rich cultural heritage and direct connections with many European (former colonial) countries.
- The area is mostly free from the insect-borne diseases associated with exotic locations elsewhere in the world.
- English is widely spoken and locals are friendly, relaxed and welcoming.
- 'The paradise' image is portrayed by books and films, such as *Pirates of the Caribbean*.

Why has tourism grown rapidly in recent years?

Tourists first started to arrive in the Caribbean during the 18th century. They were mostly wealthy Europeans taking part in what became known as the 'Grand Tour'.

Mass tourism, involving thousands of ordinary individuals, took off from the 1960s and has increased rapidly since the 1990s. There are several reasons for this rapid growth in tourism:

- Greater availability of relatively cheap flights and cruises from Europe and the USA.
- Increased incomes with more money available for travel and holidays.
- Increased available leisure time, with paid holidays now commonplace.
- People living longer, healthier lives and often wishing to travel the world after retirement.
- Increased awareness of opportunities for tourism in far-off places through advertising, television and, most recently, the internet.

As more and more tourists have flocked to the Caribbean, there has been a massive increase in the provision of resorts, hotels, bars and cafes. Sites for tourism, such as plantation houses, natural wonders such as Harrison's Cave in Barbados, and beach resorts have all been developed in recent years.

2.15 (continued)

Trends in tourism

Look at Figure 2.15.3. It describes some trends in tourism in the Caribbean. Notice the following important points:

- The vast majority of tourists (nearly 50 per cent) come from the USA. This is because the islands are relatively close and many tourists choose to take their holiday during the winter when the weather in the USA is often cold and gloomy.

- There are large variations in the number of tourists visiting different countries. Huge numbers (mostly Americans) visit Puerto Rico, the Dominican Republic, Cuba and the Bahamas.

- European tourists often visit ex-colonial countries where there is a common language. So, for example, many British tourists visit

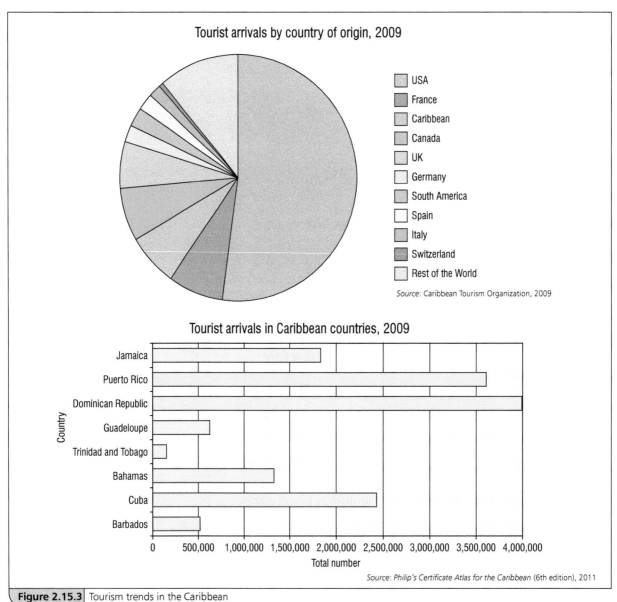

Figure 2.15.3 Tourism trends in the Caribbean

154

Jamaica and Barbados whereas the French are more likely to visit countries such as Martinique.

• While mass tourism is popular in countries such as Puerto Rico, expenditure per tourist is highest in the smaller, more exclusive islands such as the US Virgin Islands and the Cayman Islands that appeal to very wealthy businessmen and celebrities.

The advantages and disadvantages of tourism

Tourism brings many obvious advantages, such as foreign income and employment opportunities. There are, however, a number of disadvantages too. Figure 2.15.4 lists the main advantages and disadvantages. Try to relate these general points to your home territory.

Advantages of tourism	Disadvantages of tourism
Employment – many persons are directly employed to serve tourists as guides, waiters, cleaners, cooks, etc. Indirectly, many persons gain employment too, for example, in construction, food supply, electrical and plumbing businesses, and in making crafts and souvenirs.	*Environmental damage* – tourist developments, particularly at the coast, can damage or destroy natural ecosystems, such as mangrove swamps and coral reefs. Naturally attractive landscapes can become scarred by poorly designed developments.
Foreign income – tourists spend their money in US dollars, euros and British pounds, which provides an important source of foreign income. Spending on goods and services in the Caribbean also helps to boost the economy by providing tax income.	*Pollution* – waste management can be a problem if tourism develops rapidly, leading to contamination by sewage and untreated waste.
Agriculture and fisheries – tourists provide a huge market for food crops, such as fruit, salads and vegetables, as well as demand for fresh fish.	*Economic dependency* – some countries can become over-dependent on tourism, so that any reduction in numbers (e.g. owing to global economic recession or terrorism) can have catastrophic effects.
Multiplier effect – tourism has many useful knock-on effects on the economy such as improvements in infrastructure (roads, airports, electricity and water), construction, retailing and other industries.	*Social issues* – occasionally tourism can lead to problems of drugs, crime and prostitution. This can cause social conflicts between tourists and locals.

Figure 2.15.4 The advantages and disadvantages of tourism in the Caribbean

> **DID YOU KNOW?**
>
> According to Orbitz, an online travel company, the 'best scuba island' in the Caribbean is Turks and Caicos, the 'best natural wonders' are on Dominica, the 'best beaches' are on Barbados and the 'best adventure island' is Jamaica. Do you agree?

Tourism case studies: Jamaica and Belize

- Understand the characteristics of tourism in Jamaica and Belize.
- Understand the principles of ecotourism.

Jamaica

- Jamaica is the Caribbean's fifth most visited country after Puerto Rico, the Dominican Republic, Cuba and the Bahamas. Almost 2 million tourists visit the island each year.
- 80 per cent of tourists come from the USA and about 10 per cent from the UK, many arriving on cruise ships.
- Tourism is an important source of foreign income and accounts for about 20 per cent of GDP.
- Tourist attractions include the extensive sandy beaches with warm tropical seas, water sports, fishing and golf, wildlife, and historical and cultural sites, such as plantation houses, and Jamaica's music.
- Tourism directly supports some 220,000 jobs in shops, hotels and restaurants, and many thousands in, for example, construction, food production, transportation and crafts.
- Jamaica faces competition from other Caribbean islands. This explains the development of specialist types of tourism such as adventure tourism, ecotourism and community tourism.

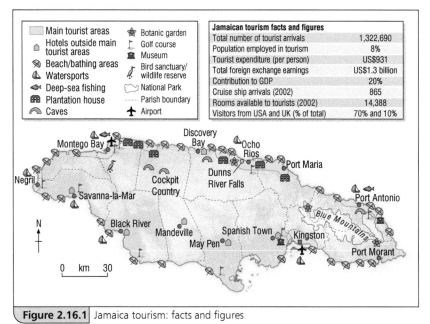

Jamaican tourism facts and figures	
Total number of tourist arrivals	1,322,690
Population employed in tourism	8%
Tourist expenditure (per person)	US$931
Total foreign exchange earnings	US$1.3 billion
Contribution to GDP	20%
Cruise ship arrivals (2002)	865
Rooms available to tourists (2002)	14,388
Visitors from USA and UK (% of total)	70% and 10%

Figure 2.16.1 Jamaica tourism: facts and figures

Adventure tourism includes activities such as cliff diving at Negril, bouldering at Dunn's River Falls and ziplining in Montego Bay. A number of companies offer holidays involving these activities.

Ecotourism involves small specialist trips focusing on nature. Jamaica has abundant birdlife and natural wonders. Tours include wildlife watching in the Blue Mountains and bamboo raft trips to explore the rainforest along the Rio Grande.

Community tourism consists of tourists being provided with overnight accommodation in local people's homes. This enables them to get to know local communities and experience the Jamaican way of life.

Figure 2.16.2 Jamaica: trends in visitors

Belize

What is ecotourism?

- **Ecotourism** involves small special groups experiencing and learning about the natural world.
- Ecotourism conserves the environment, making use of local building materials and avoiding environmental damage and pollution.
- Local people are employed as guides, resources such as water and energy are conserved, waste is recycled and tours usually involve walking or rafting.
- Ecotourism is an example of **sustainable development** in that communities benefit without suffering environmental damage. It is a long-lasting form of tourism.

Ecotourism in Belize

- Belize boasts a large number of national parks and natural reserves which, together with its extensive coral reefs, wild stretches of coastline and tropical rainforest, make it an ideal location for ecotourism.
- Many hotels and lodges make use of rainwater for washing and showers, use renewable supplies of energy to generate electricity and make use of local building materials in construction.
- Tour guides and adventure providers are well trained to pass on information to tourists about environmental conservation, for example ways of protecting rather than damaging coral reefs.
- People are encouraged to be sensitive to local traditions, not to purchase artefacts or natural souvenirs such as shells, not to approach wildlife, and to dispose of waste in designated containers.
- Among the most popular attractions for ecotourists are the Maya temples and ruins, coral reefs and beaches, hiking or biking the many jungle trails, visiting the Belize Jaguar Preserve, kayaking on the rivers and streams and visiting the many underground caves and caverns.

Figure 2.16.3 Male loggerhead turtle off Turneffe Atoll, Belize

Figure 2.16.4 A Belize stamp showing the importance of wildlife

---

CASE STUDY | Black Rock Lodge, Belize

Black Rock Lodge is nestled in dense rainforest overlooking the Macal River in the foothills of the Maya Mountains just two-and-a-half hours west of Belize City. There are opportunities for canoeing down the Macal River, horseback riding to the Flour Camp Caves or hiking up the various canyon trails to spot the wild birds and animals.

Electricity is supplied by a customised hybrid system involving a micro-hydro scheme and solar power. All water is supplied from a local spring and is conserved and reused where possible. Locals act as guides and work at the lodge, and much of the food is produced locally and is organic. Waste is recycled or composted and waste water passes through a wetland system where it is filtered and cleaned.

Figure 2.16.5 Bird watching at Black Rock Lodge, Belize

Quaternary sector case study: ICT industries and call centres

The quaternary sector is the part of the economy which deals with providing information and expertise. A quaternary business serves other businesses. Examples include customer relations, call centres, training, research and development. Known as **footloose industries**, they do not rely on the locations of raw materials or markets. Communication is primarily by phone, the internet and satellite, which are available almost everywhere. The key location factor is a suitable workforce.

ICT industries in the Caribbean

ICT industries are an important route to economic development in any country in the world. Most Caribbean countries are now well-provided for in terms of telecommunications, especially landline and mobile phone systems. Nevertheless, infrastructure distribution is uneven and expensive to construct.

Jamaica

Jamaica now has 15 cable TV channels and there has been considerable growth in 'new media'. Traditional radio and TV channels are now supplemented by niche and community-based radio stations as well as independent television providers. However, the change from traditional to new media systems that is happening globally remains slower than average in the Caribbean because of low levels of growth in internet and fast broadband services.

Nevertheless, the Jamaican government recognizes ICT as a tool for economic growth. A commitment to ICT education in schools ensures skills for the next generation. At the same time, local businesses can be slow to adopt new technologies due to current lack of skills or finance, which does limit growth.

Haiti – a special case

Even Haiti with its history of regular hurricane and earthquake events likely to disrupt such communications, has reasonable landline, mobile and internet services in urban areas. In contrast, rural areas often lack phone lines, internet and even simple electricity lines. There is potential for improvement in these systems, but one can understand that major companies are unwilling to invest in high-risk areas, limiting regeneration.

Telecommunications in the Caribbean

The ICT industry of Costa Rica

Costa Rica was previously dependant on agriculture and then on eco-tourism, but has recently developed a modern ICT industry, ahead of other Caribbean countries. Intel, the giant microchip processor company, located a base there in 1998. Other related industries were therefore attracted to Costa Rica and adjacent Caribbean countries. Costa Rica is involved in the manufacturing of both integrated circuits and related electronics, which is essentially secondary industry. The quaternary aspect here is research and development into new systems for manufacturing and export, boosting the Costa Rican economy. The share of ICT businesses in Costa Rican exports grew from $1,100 million in 2008 to 2,100 million in 2012, from 11 per cent to 22 per cent of GDP (Source PROSIC 2013).

Figure 2.17.1 ICT education in a school

Costa Rica's government has a policy of supporting ICT companies and of using these skills to provide ICT equipment (computer labs) and skills education in schools (see Figure 2.17.1). ICT companies pay taxes to the Costa Rican government, which funds educational development, as well as being an investment in computer systems supporting secondary and tertiary industries, plus operating government systems. Overall, ICT industries, including quaternary research and development, have a positive impact on the country's economy.

Call centres in the Caribbean

The Caribbean is increasingly attractive to quaternary sector businesses and to call centres in particular. The region can provide plenty of well-educated workers at relatively low pay levels. Call centres in the UK and USA have often closed down due to competition from countries such as India and Indonesia where the organisations were more cost effective due to lower wages. Caribbean and Indian hourly wages are around US$16.50, compared with US$29 in the USA. British and American companies therefore moved their call centres to Asia.

Figure 2.17.2 A Caribbean call centre worker

However, some users of Asian centres found difficulty understanding the spoken English of the call handlers. English is the first language in many Caribbean countries, giving them a clear advantage in this market. Some Caribbean governments are offering tax and other incentives to attract new, long-term contract clients.

Main call centre countries in the Caribbean include Jamaica, Barbados, Trinidad, the Dominican Republic and Puerto Rico (see Figure 2.17.2). These last two can offer services in Spanish as well as in English. In 2015, 41 million Americans (13 per cent of the population) used Spanish as their first or only language.

This all sounds very positive but there are inevitably some drawbacks. Set-up costs are high due to the expense of bringing in high-tech equipment. From time to time cultural differences have led to some difficulties. Nevertheless, growth in Caribbean call centres has been rapid. The number grew from 44 call centres across the whole Caribbean in 2001, with 11,000 workers, to over 55,000 by 2008.

Agriculture in the Caribbean

- Understand the characteristics of small-scale farming and commercial plantations.
- Understand the importance of agriculture.
- Understand the patterns and trends in agriculture.

DID YOU KNOW?

Historically, the colonial plantation system dominated agriculture, and indeed the whole economy of the Caribbean. Originally, the labour force consisted of slaves. The system existed to export raw materials to Europe. Today's sugar plantations are large-scale, modern operations (see the case study, page 173). Smaller-scale farms also produce sugar cane.

History and development of agriculture in the Caribbean

Agriculture involves growing crops and raising livestock on the land. It is an example of a primary industry.

In the Caribbean a dual agriculture economy has developed.

1 **Small-scale family-owned farms**, where a variety of crops are grown and livestock is reared (see Figure 2.18.1). The produce is used by the household as well as being sold locally at markets and to supermarkets. This is a traditional type of agriculture.

2 **Commercial plantations** were developed during the colonial era alongside the smaller traditional farms. These plantations concentrated on growing a single crop such as sugar cane, making use of large numbers of workers to maximise production and profit. Many plantations still exist today, concentrating on producing food products for export (see Figure 2.18.2).

The importance of agriculture in the Caribbean

- Agriculture contributes to gross domestic product (GDP) and to export earnings. Several countries' economies are very reliant on agriculture, for example Haiti (24 per cent of GDP), Guyana (21 per cent) and Dominica (16 per cent). Generally, the trend in the Caribbean is for this to fall as the service sector grows.
- Thousands of individuals are employed in agriculture. In Haiti 38 per cent of the workforce is employed in agriculture.

Figure 2.18.1 Small-scale traditional farm in the Caribbean

Figure 2.18.2 Caribbean banana plantation

Elsewhere, Dominica (40 per cent), Guyana (30 per cent) and St Lucia (22 per cent) are also heavily dependent on agriculture for providing jobs. The widespread increase in the use of machines and chemicals means that the number of individuals employed is declining.

- Farming provides a great deal of food for locals, reducing the need to rely upon expensive food imports.
- Agriculture provides raw materials for secondary industries such as food processing and the manufacture of rum.
- Incomes generated by farming supports local services such as shops and cafes.

Figure 2.18.3 Caribbean market

2.18 (continued)

Agricultural land use in the Caribbean

Look at Figure 2.18.4 which shows land use in the Caribbean.

Notice that the pie charts have been drawn in proportion to the total land area of each country. Cuba has the largest land area and the biggest pie chart, followed by the Dominican Republic and Haiti. Each pie chart has been split into the relative land uses.

- Cuba has the largest land area in the Caribbean and over 50 per cent of all the Caribbean's farmland. This helps to explain the high rate of agricultural employment in Cuba. More land has been brought into production in Cuba (50 per cent in 1975, increasing to over 61 per cent by 2011).

DID YOU KNOW?

Despite falls in production, both commercial and subsistence systems of agriculture remain important in the Caribbean as sources of:

- local foodstuffs
- family income
- foreign exchange.

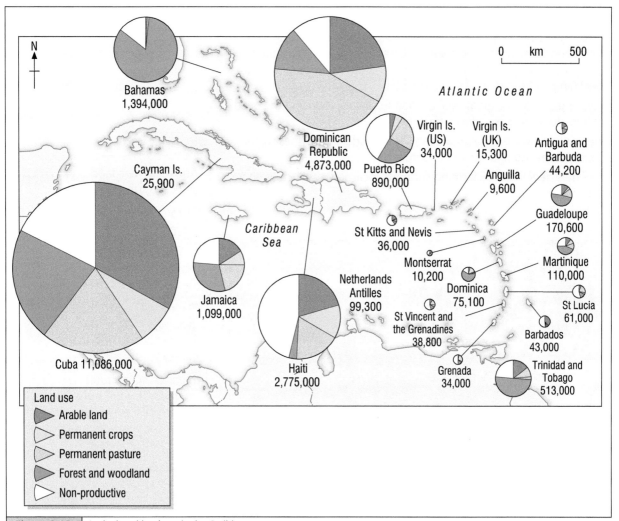

Figure 2.18.4 Agricultural land use in the Caribbean

Land use: Arable land, Permanent crops, Permanent pasture, Forest and woodland, Non-productive

- Cuba, the Dominican Republic and Haiti account for 90 per cent of the region's farming area.

- Agricultural land occupies 44 per cent of Barbados and Jamaica. This is declining owing to urban and tourist-related developments.

- There is great contrast across the region. For example, the Bahamas has a high proportion of forest and woodland as does Dominica, Trinidad and Tobago and Guadeloupe. Barbados has a high proportion of arable land whereas the Dominican Republic has a high proportion of permanent pasture. This variety is largely the result of physical geography (relief, rock type) and historical factors.

Recent trends in Caribbean agriculture

- The agriculture workforce declined from 50 per cent in 1960 to 20 per cent in 2010. This is largely the result of increased use of machines, together with the growth of employment opportunities in the service sector.

- Increased productivity led to an increase in exports in the 1970s and 1980s (more than 6 million tonnes in 1986). However, since the 1990s, exports have fallen, reducing to as low as 2 million tonnes in 2001. This can be linked to an increase in service industries and a wider range of jobs available. Reasons for the decline were, among other things, a ruling of the World Trade Organization that removed the protected market arrangements for former colonies, as well as hurricane damage.

- Fertiliser use increased between the 1960s and 1980s but later reduced when it was proved that its over-use can be a problem.

- There has been a gradual loss of protected markets for sugar, bananas and other crops because of competition from low-cost producers in South and Central America.

- The development of organic farming and Fair Trade bananas has helped the Caribbean to provide for a high-priced niche market in Europe, and some farms have remained in business. The major Caribbean Fair Trade banana producers are Dominica, the Dominican Republic and Grenada.

- Other plantations have diversified their production, including growing flowers and providing vegetables for the local markets.

- In Guyana, the rice farmers have developed specialised rice varieties to improve yields. They have also targeted their sales by developing parboiled rice products to sell this higher-priced commodity to more Caribbean countries.

DID YOU KNOW?

In Barbados, the amount of productive farmland has decreased in recent years, especially along the west coast. This is because farmers have sold land for housing and tourist developments, especially all-inclusive resorts. Some farmland is left unused while waiting for developers to make a sufficiently high bid to purchase the land.

LEARNING OUTCOME

• Understand the characteristics of commercial farming in Jamaica.

Patterns of land use in Jamaica

Less than a third of Jamaica is suitable for farming. There are several reasons for this:

• About 50 per cent of the country is over 300 m high and much of this land is made of steep slopes (1:5 or 20 per cent or more). Access is often difficult and machines cannot be used on steep slopes.

• Limestone areas develop thin soils and have little surface water (limestone is a permeable rock that allows water to pass through it).

• Some of the slopes have become vulnerable to soil erosion following widespread deforestation for timber and charcoal production.

DID YOU KNOW?

In 2005, Jamaica suffered from a serious drought between January and April. Later in the year it was struck by two powerful hurricanes, Dennis and Emily. These climatic events caused considerable damage to Jamaica's agricultural sector. Some 40 per cent of the coffee harvest was lost and the banana industry was almost totally destroyed.

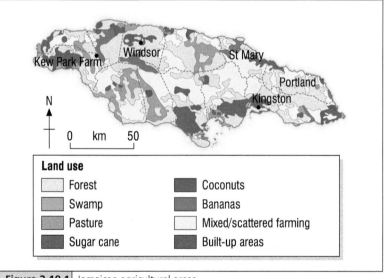

Figure 2.19.1 Jamaican agricultural areas

Look at Figure 2.19.1. It contains information about farming in Jamaica. Notice the following:

• The main land use in Jamaica is forest (24 per cent of the total land area).

• While a variety of commercial crops are grown, sugar cane is by far the most important in terms of land use and production.

• Large concentrations of sugar cane are found close to the coast, particularly in the south and the west.

• Banana production is extensive in the rainier north-east, such as Portland and St Mary.

- Small concentrations of coconut plantations are found on the east and north coasts.
- Traditional small-scale farming is scattered across Jamaica, particularly within areas of scrub and woodland.

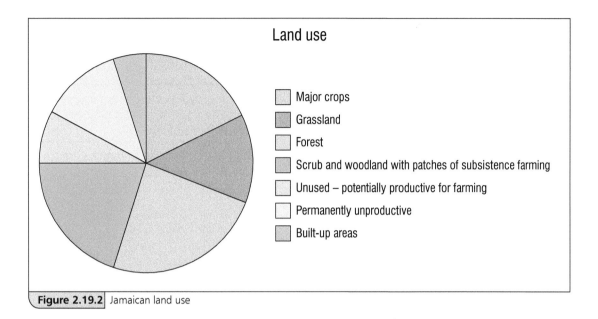

Figure 2.19.2 Jamaican land use

Land ownership and size of farm

Jamaica functions as a dual agricultural economy. Average farm size has increased, but inequalities in land ownership created in colonial times remain. Plantations were owned by wealthy people for commercial export. This situation continues, except that large-scale family businesses have often been replaced by big companies, some multinational.

This inequality is illustrated by these facts:

- The largest 1,400 holdings – at least 20 hectares (ha) each – make up 54 per cent of Jamaica's farmland.
- 60 per cent of farms are less than 1 ha.
- Another 17 per cent are between 1 ha and 2 ha.

Family farms have become less common and corporate business now has an increasing role in Jamaica's agricultural economy. Large-scale holdings often have the best land, while small farmers remain on the poorer land. Security of tenancy is also an issue for poorer farmers – some pay rent, although there is always the risk that their landlord will decide to sell the land.

	Commercial arable	Small-scale farming
Location	Kew Park Farm, about 10 km south of Montpelier	Farms close to Windsor in Cockpit Country
Farm size	385 hectares (ha)	Small, mostly less than 1 ha. Land is very fragmented. Farmers often have to cycle between plots of land.
Labour	40 full-time workers and up to 100 part-timers during coffee harvesting. Some live on site, others travel from nearby villages. Wages are low.	Family labour only. Most farmers are older (60 per cent over 50).
Crops/livestock	Mostly commercial beef cattle ranching (700 animals). Also 16 ha coffee, 2 ha citrus fruit, 2 ha lychees, over 2,500 pigs and 2,000 free-range chickens.	Some sugar cane is produced as a cash crop, otherwise a variety of arable food crops (e.g. yams, maize, sweet potatoes and cabbage), tree crops (breadfruit, avocado and coconuts) and livestock (goats and cattle) are produced.
Markets	All produce is sold. Coffee is partly processed on site then sent to Kingston to be graded, roasted and packed. Fruit and eggs are sold locally. Pigs are sold to local processor, Grace Food Processors.	Sugar cane is processed at the Long Pond factory. Excess food is sold at local markets.

Figure 2.19.3 A comparison of farming in Jamaica

Labour, capital and technology

Capital inputs into commercial holdings reduce the demand for labour. Figure 2.19.3 illustrates a large commercial farm with only 40 full-time workers. This surprisingly low number is the result of dependency on mechanised farm equipment. This means high energy use from unsustainable fossil fuel sources, which is expensive and polluting.

Administration and communication with customers is largely done via the internet. Large-scale commercial agriculture is capital intensive and technology dependent.

Jamaica's farming practices and products

Monoculture dominates large-scale holdings in Jamaica – this is what makes them efficient. Inputs, processes and outputs are consistent, reducing costs and improving profits. Production is purely for profit and the result is increased food output. Machinery becomes almost more important than employees.

KEY TERMS

Monoculture: the production of a single crop, usually with high inputs of capital, machinery, technology, quality seed and fertilisers. A single crop will take the same nutrients out of the soil every year, reducing the fertility of the soil and sometimes damaging its structure. Chemical fertilizers are used to feed the crops, but in large quantities they can still damage the soil.

The main commercial Caribbean products are sugar, bananas, tobacco, rice, cotton, cocoa and coffee. Jamaica prioritises sugar cane, bananas and coffee.

Markets

The UK and mainland Europe are the main markets for Jamaica's (and the Caribbean's) food exports. The British market used to be protected for Caribbean bananas, but the World Trade Organization (WTO) insisted Latin American producers be treated equally after 2006. Sugar prices were fixed at a much higher level than average global prices, but again the WTO has intervened to the detriment of Caribbean producers. Caribbean rum was imported into Europe duty free and still benefits from low duty. Montserrat and Curaçao, as French and Dutch overseas territories, have duty-free privileges on crops such as rice.

The future

Natural disasters have affected Jamaican farming during the 2000s, reducing yields, and this may continue. Changes in European Union (EU) policies remain a problem, although the UK leaving the EU may be beneficial for Caribbean producers since Britain will no longer be controlled by EU rules.

In the future, sugar will become the key crop – 200,000 tonnes of raw sugar per year – with three products in different markets:

• Raw sugar is mainly exported.

• Molasses is used in rum manufacture.

• Ethanol is produced for fuel – this is the likely growth area. Brazil currently produces most ethanol for biofuel, but there is plenty of future capacity.

Figure 2.19.4 Interior view of a rum plant in Marie Galante

Recent changes in Caribbean commercial agriculture

Employment

In recent years there has been a decline in the number of individuals employed in agriculture (see Figure 2.20.1). The largest declines have occurred in the Dominican Republic, Guadeloupe and Martinique. Significant declines have also occurred in Barbados and Puerto Rico.

There are several factors responsible for the decline in agricultural employment:

- Decreased agricultural production, for example sugar cane, reducing job opportunities.
- Increased mechanisation replacing manual labour.
- Alternative better-paid employment in urban factories and in tourism.

Agricultural employment in Haiti declined from 85 per cent in 1950 to 62 per cent in 2000. Haiti is a poor country that still relies heavily on agriculture and has few machines or alternative jobs in industry. However, natural disasters are a serious limitation. In 2010 there were two earthquakes in January, followed by Hurricane Tomas in November. Hurricane Matthew also hit Haiti in October 2016.

In Trinidad and Tobago relatively few individuals are employed in agriculture owing to the large industrial sector based on the oil and gas industry.

Contribution to GDP

Agriculture contributes about 25 per cent of gross domestic product (GDP) in the Caribbean, mostly from the export of major commercial crops such as sugar cane and bananas. The contribution to GDP is highest in Haiti (28 per cent), Guyana (25 per cent), Dominica (20 per cent) and the Dominican Republic (11.5 per cent).

The trend in most countries is a fall in contribution to GDP owing to the expansion of the service sector, particularly based on retailing and tourism, and the growth of light manufacturing. For example, in Barbados, the contribution has fallen from 38 per cent in 1958 to 6 per cent today. In St Kitts and Nevis, it has fallen from 40 per cent in 1964 to less than 3 per cent today. The rapid growth in tourism is largely responsible for these changes. Tourism offers more attractive and less physically demanding employment.

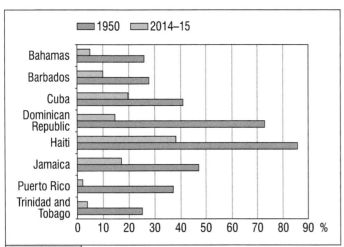

Figure 2.20.1 Changes in agricultural employment

Changes in agricultural land area

The Caribbean accounts for just 0.25 per cent of the world's agricultural land. Over 90 per cent of the region's agricultural land is in Cuba, Haiti and the Dominican Republic.

Look at Figure 2.20.2. Notice that since 1981 there have been some changes in agricultural land areas.

- Some countries, such as Cuba, Dominica and Haiti, have shown an increase in agricultural land. This may be because of the clearance of forests or improving land (by drainage or irrigation) that was previously unsuitable for farming.
- Some countries have shown a significant decline in agricultural land, such as Grenada, Puerto Rico, St Kitts and Nevis and the Virgin Islands (US). This may be because of the development of tourism and the growth of built-up areas.

Country	Area (thousand km²)	Percentage of agricultural land	
		1981	2008
Antigua and Barbuda	0.4	27.3	29.5
Aruba	0.2	11.1	11.1
Bahamas	14	1.1	1.3
Barbados	0.4	44.2	44.2
Belize	23	4.3	6.7
Cayman Islands	0.3	11.3	11.3
Cuba	111	55.3	62
Dominica	0.8	25.3	30.7
Dominican Republic	49	54.3	51.7
Grenada	0.3	47.1	35.3
Guyana	215	8.7	8.5
Haiti	28	58.1	64.9
Jamaica	11	45.9	42.8
Puerto Rico	8.9	52.6	21.1
St Kitts and Nevis	0.4	57.7	19.6
St Lucia	0.6	32.8	18.0
St Vincent and the Grenadines	0.4	30.8	25.6
Trinidad and Tobago	5	18.5	10.5
Turks and Caicos	0.9	1.1	1.1
Virgin Islands (US)	0.3	45.7	11.4

Figure 2.20.2 Changes in agricultural land areas in selected countries
Source: World Bank http://data.worldbank.org/indicator/AG.LND.AGRI.ZS

Food security

Women have a very important role in local food production. They grow food for themselves and to sell to their neighbours. This increases their incomes while also allowing their neighbours to have food security. While some women have taken the opportunity to commit their working hours to food production as a source of income, it is also possible for any woman to produce on a small scale alongside her normal job and/or domestic responsibilities. The Kitchen Garden and Backyard Garden Projects allow women to receive training in growing organic fruits and vegetables not only for home consumption but also for sale locally.

Diversification

Diversification involves developing alternative sources of income. This might involve developing new markets for existing agricultural products, for example using sugar cane as a source of fuel. It can also involve growing different crops, such as introducing mixed farming on sugar plantations.

2.20 (continued)

Other forms of diversification include the development of farm shops or providing bed and breakfast accommodation for tourists.

Changes in marketing

Marketing agricultural produce usually involves one of two options:

1 Direct selling to the public at local markets, and to hotels, restaurants and supermarkets. This has changed little over the years.
2 Selling to companies and organisations, often for processing in factories at home and abroad. This is the most common option with commercial crops such as sugar cane, bananas, coffee and cocoa.

In the past, most of the companies involved with agricultural processing and export were foreign. This is because they had the expertise and money to invest in the Caribbean.

In recent years, some Caribbean countries have reduced the influence of foreign companies through nationalisation and sales to local entrepreneurs. Now it is small farmers who dominate exports in crops such as bananas in the Windward Islands and yams in Jamaica.

Charities such as Fair Trade have had an increasingly important influence in the Caribbean to ensure that farmers receive a fair return for their crops.

Biofuels

Biofuels are in increasing demand globally as a means to reduce dependence on fossil fuels. This also encourages agricultural production in locations such as the Caribbean and Brazil. Sugar cane is an ideal crop to produce biofuels.

Brazil's economy now relies heavily on sugar-based biofuels for its energy needs. Ethanol increasingly fuels vehicles. Not only does the home economy gain from cheap, clean fuel, ethanol is increasingly exported. In the future the Caribbean could benefit in a similar way.

Value-added

An increase in small-scale local production could lead to food processing at cottage industry level. Both local and tourist markets could be served. Cooperatives of local growers should receive government support. Cooperatives reduce costs by members purchasing and selling as a group. They can buy at lower prices and sell at higher ones.

DID YOU KNOW?

Food security means that everyone has access to enough nutritious food at an affordable price. During the 2000s CARICOM countries have reduced production levels and earnings from traditional crops, increasing dependence on imported food. As a result, some people have become poorer and have a poor diet, which can lead to diet-related diseases. To correct this there needs to be increased support for small-scale farmers producing local food.

DID YOU KNOW?

Yam was never produced on foreign-owned estates. It was always a small farmers' crop, but as a result of diversification it has become one of the non-traditional exports, especially to countries such as the USA, Canada and the UK, which have many Jamaican immigrants.

Technology and shade houses

Flat and undulating land is limited in the Caribbean, so people are forced to utilise steeper slopes. This limits the use of machinery that might improve yields. Nevertheless, technology can offer help in other ways – shade houses have great potential. These are simple constructions that protect plants from the direct glare of the sun, reducing water consumption yet increasing production and income. Relatively cheap darkened plastic materials are used to minimise glare.

New markets

Changes in European Union (EU) policies have limited the potential of the Caribbean exporting to Europe. Brexit (the process of the UK leaving the EU) may limit EU purchases, but the UK may well independently make new and beneficial agreements with CARICOM.

Overall, Caribbean producers need to search for new markets within the region and in North America. Costs of transport are minimal within a limited area, plus the large-scale size of the market may bring increased security.

Impact of agriculture on economic development in the Caribbean

Farming remains a major land use in the Caribbean, taking up more land than any other economic activity. It produces, on average, 24 per cent of the region's GDP. In general, the poorer the country, the greater is the proportion of income from agriculture. As jobs decrease in this sector, they tend to increase in the tertiary sector, in particular tourism. Figure 2.20.3 shows employment across the economic sectors in selected Caribbean countries.

Country (in order of agriculture as a percentage of the workforce)	Agriculture (%)	Industry (%)	Services, including tourism (%)
Dominica	40.0	32.0	28.0
Cuba	18.0	10.0	72.0
Jamaica	17.0	19.0	64.0
Barbados	10.0	15.0	75.0
Trinidad and Tobago	3.8	33.2	63.0
Virgin Islands	1.0	19.0	80.0

Figure 2.20.3 Employment across the economic sectors in selected Caribbean countries

As exports such as sugar and bananas decline, light manufacturing, tourism, offshore financial and IT sectors increase. Where agriculture has limitations, as in the drier Leeward Islands, this process is faster than in more favoured agricultural regions (e.g. the Windward Islands). Nevertheless, in nine of the 15 CARICOM countries food products account for 20 per cent or more of their exports. In Dominica this represents 60 per cent of export earnings. Bananas are the dominant crop.

Since 1970 farmland area has expanded in some Caribbean countries and reduced in others. In Cuba, with the greatest percentage and area increase, three million hectares of new land have been brought into production, bucking the general trend of reduction of arable land.

Sugar cane in the Caribbean

In 1961, sugar cane from the Caribbean accounted for 20 per cent of world production. In recent decades this has fallen dramatically and it is now less than 4 per cent.

One of the main reasons for this decline is the high cost of production and the fact that it can be produced elsewhere in the world (from sugar beet) more cheaply. In addition, some plantation land is being sold for tourist developments.

Cuba is the region's largest producer, accounting for 75 per cent of total harvest. Jamaica and Guyana are the other two major producers in the Caribbean.

Across the Caribbean, the sugar industry is still an important source of foreign income and it supports 150,000 unskilled and semi-skilled workers. In Barbados, sugar cane accounts for a third of all agricultural production by value.

Sugar cane production

Sugar cane is a tall grass growing to a height of 2.5–4.5 m. It can be grown on flat or hilly land; if machinery is used, it is usually grown on flat land.

Sugar cane is harvested by hand or by harvester machines (see Figure 2.21.1). The stumps are left in the ground for up to five years (new canes, called ratoons, shoot from these stumps) before they are dug

Figure 2.21.1 Mechanised harvesting of sugar cane

up and replaced with new plants. Harvesting takes place during the drier months after a growth period of between 8 months (for a ratoon cane) and 18 months (for new cane).

When cane is harvested by hand, the fields are often burned before harvesting to destroy old leaves, get rid of pests and diseases and to make it easier to harvest. Occasionally these fires burn out of control and they can destroy cane that has yet to be harvested.

CASE STUDY | Sugar cane production in Guyana

Location

Guyana is one of the largest sugar cane producers in the Caribbean region. The ideal location is along the eastern coastal strip, for these reasons:

- The area has deep alluvial soil, with high nutrient content and a light texture for easy cultivation.
- There is high rainfall – around 2,000 mm/ year – and sugar cane is a 'thirsty' crop. Two wet seasons per year mean two crops can be harvested annually.
- The coastal plain is densely populated, providing plenty of labour.
- The coast road provides a key transport link to the three ports of Georgetown, Skeldon and Blairmont.

Sugar factories are located within the sugar plantations, so the distance from harvest to processing is minimal. As in Jamaica, both large companies and medium-sized farms produce sugar cane. They, too, are located close to processing centres to minimise transport costs.

In Guyana, sugar creates:

- 7 per cent of jobs
- 13 per cent of GDP
- 24 per cent of foreign exchange.

Farming methods

A network of canals within the plantations allows easy, cheap transport. These also act as a drainage system. However, some flooding is beneficial as the water washes unwanted salts from the soil and adds new nutrients, reducing the need for expensive artificial fertilisers. Pest control has been improved by using biological methods (introducing predators), replacing high

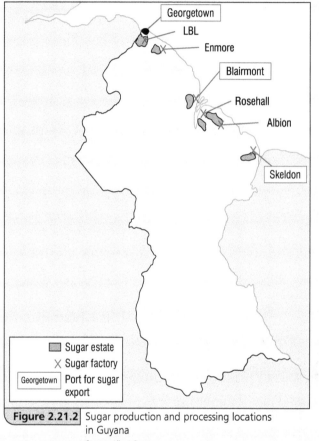

Figure 2.21.2 Sugar production and processing locations in Guyana
Source: Alison Rae

usage of chemicals. This has an environmental benefit.

Guyana employs less mechanisation in sugar production than many other parts of the Caribbean. This is a result of its sugar often being produced on gentle slopes. These help good drainage but make use of machinery more difficult. Some soils are too soft to support the weight of heavy machinery. One set of plants can produce up to five crops within a short time, then ploughing and replanting are needed.

The cane may be cut up into short lengths on site (see Figure 2.21.3) before being transported (usually by road) to a processing factory.

Figure 2.21.3 Farm worker cutting sugar cane in Barbados

Here, the cane is crushed and the juice is extracted. It is then purified and heated to produce sugar crystals. The sugar crystals are treated to form brown sugar, which can then be packaged and exported. It is further refined in the receiving country to produce white sugar.

Recent trends in sugar cane production

Recent trends in Caribbean sugar cane production include the following:

- Increased use of machinery for planting, spraying and harvesting.
- Reduction in the production, workforce and land area planted with sugar cane.
- Reduced involvement of foreign companies.
- Loss of preferential trade arrangements and protected markets.
- Increasing expense with maintaining or replacing old sugar-cane refining infrastructure.
- Reduction in available cane cutters as individuals move to work in towns and cities (rural depopulation).
- Sugar cane is also grown on thousands of small farms, yet most of these are unproductive, as they are too small to benefit from the use of machinery.

Is diversification the way forward?

In the face of increasing competition and falling demand for sugar, a recent trend in the Caribbean has been **diversification**. This involves finding alternative products and markets for sugar cane.

- A large number of products can be made from sugar cane, including antibiotics, alcohol, vinegar and animal foods. In Barbados, the authorities are considering the use of sugar cane bagasse to generate electricity. In Brazil, sugar cane is used to produce fuel for cars.
- In Trinidad and Tobago, Caroni (1975) Limited was the largest company involved in sugar cane production. It was responsible for producing over 90 per cent of Trinidad's sugar. In the 1980s and 1990s it converted some of its sugar cane fields to growing alternative commercial crops such as rice, mangos, pineapples and nuts. Livestock was reared using animal food made from sugar cane and, in 1992, ponds were created to farm Malaysian prawns. In 2003, the Trinidad and Tobago government closed down the company owing to mounting debts. Some Caroni land has been leased to 8,400 former Caroni workers to grow crops for local consumption and niche crops for export, such as hot peppers (Trinidad Daily Express).

DID YOU KNOW?

In 1992, Caroni (1975) Limited decided to diversify into aquaculture. Freshwater ponds were constructed to produce Malaysian prawns and cascadura for export to Toronto, London and New York. Cascadura are highly valued fish in Trinidad and Tobago. They live in murky water, grow to a length of about 15 cm and have bony plate-like scales to provide protective body armour.

Challenges facing the Caribbean economies

Globalisation

A current process that no country's economy can avoid is globalisation, which increases competition and makes markets more difficult to find, affecting profits. For example, Europe was the key market for Caribbean bananas and sugar, but today other countries such as Colombia, Peru, Ecuador, Panama, Brazil, Côte d'Ivoire, Cameroon and Ghana compete for the UK market, lowering prices and therefore profits. Wages for Caribbean workers fall as a result. Trading together in groups helps Caribbean countries maintain markets.

Some nations remain dependant on particular crops. For example:

* sugar – Cuba, Guyana
* bauxite – Jamaica; bauxite earns more than 50 per cent of the export income (see Figure 2.22.2)
* bananas – the Windward Islands.

Relying on a single product or two leaves a country's economy more vulnerable.

Chinese investment in the Caribbean

China has invested billions of dollars in the Caribbean by supporting the development of tourist projects, financing roads and port developments and buying companies. This investment has provided employment for construction workers brought in from China and has enabled the Caribbean economy to develop (see Figure 2.22.1). Little local labour was used.

* In 2005, the Chinese government spent US$55 million constructing a brand new cricket stadium on the island of Grenada in preparation for the 2007 World Cup.
* In 2011, the Chinese government announced an investment of US$2.4 billion in a new 3,800-room resort in the Bahamas that would include the largest casino in the region. Some 5,000 Chinese workers were involved in construction.
* Other investments announced in 2011 include port and harbour improvements in Suriname, resort development at Punta Perla in the Dominican Republic and a US$17 million cricket stadium in Dominica.

Many residents welcome the increased investment and economic ties with China. However, some are concerned that the massive investment will lead to an influx of Chinese goods into the Caribbean and an increased influence on the region's economy.

While globalisation has brought many advantages to the Caribbean, such as increasing international tourism and providing a greater

LEARNING OUTCOME

* Understand that Caribbean economies are facing challenges associated with globalisation, new technologies, changing markets and the desire for sustainable development.

DID YOU KNOW?

The Sea Island Cotton revival was handicapped as seeds were taken from Barbados and cultivated in China, producing a fibre that is only slightly shorter. The quantity of this new cotton made it competitive and the price of Sea Island Cotton on the Japanese market fell.

2.22 (continued)

Figure 2.22.1 Construction of the National Academy for the Performing Arts in Port of Spain with Chinese finance and labour

range of goods and services from all over the world, there have been some disadvantages. Is the distinctive character of the Caribbean being eroded as it becomes more international? Some say that the Caribbean is becoming more Americanised, with basketball taking over from cricket, burgers taking over from traditional cooking and rap taking over from reggae.

Exploring for new resources

In Trinidad and Tobago new gas fields are being discovered offshore which will maintain production levels until 2050, but perhaps not beyond that date. New exploration techniques, though expensive, mean that resources previously seen as unrealistic could be workable and profitable.

Technology

Technology has improved dramatically in recent years, with the advent of the internet and the use of satellites. Communications and information systems have been improved throughout the Caribbean.

Improvements in technology have provided new opportunities for the Caribbean economy and many industries have benefited.

- Technology and increased mechanisation have led to improvements in efficiency in agriculture. Many industries, such as garments and food processing, benefit from modern equipment.
- The internet has provided instant access to information about tourist opportunities in the Caribbean. Many companies rely upon the internet for bookings.

Many Caribbean countries are advertising products to appeal to consumers in new and expanding markets, such as:

- ecotourism
- adventure tourism
- community tourism
- wildlife trips
- marriage on a Caribbean beach
- singles holidays.

Figure 2.22.2 A bauxite processing plant in Jamaica

Trading groups

Individual countries tend to have more bargaining power in trading when they belong to larger groups called **trading blocs**. For example, many European countries belong to the European Union and trade with the rest of the world as a single bloc.

CARICOM was set up to represent the interests of the Caribbean region. Its main aims are to:

- increase trade between individual members
- encourage the development of agricultural and industrial businesses
- increase the range of goods and services being produced and traded (some countries have become over-dependent on a single commodity, e.g. bauxite in Jamaica and bananas in the Windward Islands)
- remove tariffs (taxes) and quotas (limits) on goods traded within CARICOM and to establish the CARICOM Single Market Economy (CSME) to develop free trade within the region. Workers and companies would be able to set up in any country in the region and there would be no taxes or quotas.

The majority of trade takes place with NAFTA (the North American Free Trade Association – USA, Mexico and Canada) and the South American trading blocs, LAIA (the Latin American Integration Association) and Mercosur.

With the current trend of Chinese investment, China is becoming an important trading partner, with a lot of the clothing, household goods and electronic equipment in the Caribbean being made in China.

Sustainable development

Sustainable development is important for the Caribbean's future economic development. It aims to:

- meet the needs of the present without compromising those of the future – that is, manage resources efficiently without waste, which is especially important in the smaller Caribbean countries with limited natural resources
- improve quality of life and standard of living
- allow economic development without countries getting into debt
- improve technology levels and train people in the skills to use them.

DID YOU KNOW?

In 1996, McDonald's opened its first restaurant in Bridgetown, Barbados. After just six months the restaurant closed down owing to lack of business, with locals preferring the taste of Bajan fish, chicken and pork to the 'bland' burgers produced by the restaurant chain. Today, the restaurant building is home to Consolidated Finance.

Environmental degradation in the Caribbean as a result of economic activities

Deforestation

Damage to Caribbean forests began in earnest when Europeans settled. Over time, the amount of damage has been **exponential** (it has been more serious as time has passed). Brazil lost 17.5 million hectares of quality rainforest annually between 2000 and 2005 (the same area as Jamaica and Haiti combined).

Some Caribbean islands have lost very little forest – the Bahamas, Belize, Dominica and Guyana, in particular. Haiti doesn't have a lot of forested land (see Figure 2.23.1).

The main causes of Caribbean deforestation are:

• Large-scale agriculture – much forest was cleared for plantations (coffee, cotton, sugar) or for large-scale cattle grazing. This was mostly on the coast since the produce had to be exported.

• Subsistence farming – clearance for this had happened over centuries, but more recently population increase and demand for food increased the rate of deforestation. Much of Jamaica's Blue Mountains have experienced this, though globally the worst affected place is Brazil where vast areas of forest have been cleared.

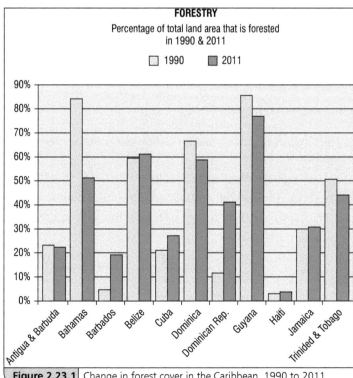

Figure 2.23.1 Change in forest cover in the Caribbean, 1990 to 2011

- Use of fuelwood and charcoal – all over the world poorer people collect wood for fuel. This is especially true in Haiti (one of the poorest countries globally), Martinique, Guadeloupe and the Dominican Republic.

- Logging for export – Guyana and Belize export high-grade timber and gain important foreign currency as a result. Secondary forest develops afterwards. Large-scale businesses tend to cause most damage.

- Mining – not only must forest be cleared to access minerals, but roads and airstrips are built to serve these activities. Gold-mining has caused damage in Guyana (see Figure 2.23.2) and bauxite production has contributed to more destruction of forest in Jamaica than any other economic activity.

- New building – forest close to towns has suffered as population grows and demand for houses and services increases. Tourism expansion leads to new hotels and other facilities plus infrastructure such as roads and airports. Tourists may come to see the lush forests but they indirectly cause forest and wildlife destruction – the Puerto Rican parrot is threatened by inland deforestation and coastal forest destruction in Guadeloupe means fewer Hawksbill turtles.

Figure 2.23.2 Destruction of rainforest caused by gold mining, Guyana

Other results of Caribbean deforestation

Forests act as a water store in the water (hydrological) cycle. The canopy limits the impact of heavy rain on soil and tree roots hold soil together. Deforestation therefore leads to soil erosion and to flooding. Results of natural disasters such as hurricanes are made worse. Unprotected slopes suffer from landslides sufficient to wash villages away as in Haiti in 2004 (Hurricane Jeanne) and 2010 (Hurricane Tomas). Eroded soil is washed offshore, silting up coral reefs and mangroves – again, these are key tourist attractions as well as important wildlife sites.

Trees retain carbon (they are referred to as 'carbon sinks') so their destruction changes the oxygen/carbon dioxide balance in the global atmosphere, the consequence being global warming. Warmer seas around the Caribbean will likely increase the frequency and severity of hurricanes.

Air pollution in the Caribbean

Compared with other parts of the world, the Caribbean region's air pollution is not too severe, though particular problems do exist. Outputs from industry and vehicles produce the main air pollutants – carbon dioxide, carbon monoxide, nitrogen oxides, sulphur compounds

DID YOU KNOW?

Outputs of CFCs (chloro-fluoro-carbons), or aerosol gases, can reduce the upper atmosphere ozone layer, allowing more ultra-violet rays through and threatening more people with skin cancer. A European Commission Report of 2013 also found that coral growth in panama and Belize was limited by aerosol emissions. Note that these aerosol emissions do not come from just the Caribbean nations – this is a global issue.

Figure 2.23.3 Trees killed by acid rain and other pollution

and solid particulates such as soot. Power stations based on fossil fuels (oil and natural gas) can emit some harmful gases. Trinidad and Tobago is heavily dependent on its fossil fuel resources, making it the second highest global producer of greenhouse gases per head of population.

Acid rain is the product of chemical pollutants dissolving in atmospheric moisture. Landscape damage from acid rain is serious (see Figure 2.23.3):

- Forest and other plant growth is limited.
- Rivers and lakes become acidic, killing wildlife.
- Soil acidity increases.
- Some building materials suffer from chemical weathering, causing pitting of the stone.

A natural cause of air pollution is volcanic eruptions emitting gases, dust and ash. The Soufrière Hills volcano in Montserrat caused problems across the Caribbean between 1995 and 1997. Being a stratovolcano, it emitted huge amounts of ash.

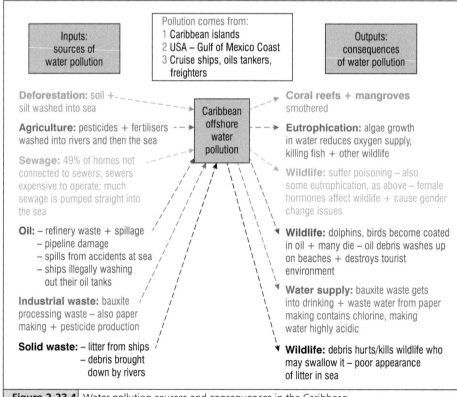

Figure 2.23.4 Water pollution sources and consequences in the Caribbean

Offshore water pollution

Caribbean countries need their surrounding seas to be clean. Pollution hurts people's standard of living, landscapes and wildlife. Tourism is an important aspect of Caribbean income, so damage to these environments could cost future income and economic prosperity.

Much sea pollution drifts southwards from the USA. The BP oil spill disaster in the Gulf of Mexico in 2010 caused damage in Caribbean waters. American freight and tourist ships spill oil waste and drop litter, as do cruise ships from elsewhere.

Figure 2.23.4 summarises water pollution in the Caribbean.

CASE STUDY	Measures to ensure the sustainable management of resources: Guyana

Guyana has progressed further than many Caribbean countries in terms of protecting ecosystems, and therefore the economy, from pollution.

1 Tackling deforestation in Guyana

Guyana has several projects aiming to protect and regenerate its rainforest.

Forest Stewardship (simply, looking after forest resources) promotes logging for profit without destruction, while providing 1,500 jobs in Guyana. The Forest Stewardship Council (FSC) accredits businesses who conserve the environment while utilising it. To replace lost forest WWF (Worldwide Fund for Nature, originally a UK charity) and the World Conservation Union replant local trees to replace those lost in previous clearances. Indigenous people are often involved, as in Barima, Guyana.

2 Sustainable mangrove swamp management

New resorts, marinas and coastal residential areas linked to tourism are one reason why the mangrove ecosystem is disappearing faster than other forest environments despite its immense economic value. Tourists are attracted by mangroves and their wildlife. Moreover, this environment is an important breeding ground for both commercial and game fish. Tourist

Figure 2.23.5 New saplings growing in a mangrove nursery as part of Guyana's Mangrove Action Plan

boats often cause damage to mangrove roots with anchors and propellers. Like rainforests, mangroves are an important carbon sink (a storage for carbon dioxide, limiting global warming).

Guyana has a Mangrove Action Plan:

- New saplings (young trees) can be planted to regenerate mangrove swamps. This helps renew the ecosystem and protect coastlines from coastal erosion (see Figure 2.23.5).

- Mangrove reserves allow people to visit and understand the importance of mangroves.

- Educational awareness programmes are run for schools and colleges.

UNIT 2: Human systems

1 a Study the maps of St Vincent (Figures 1 and 2) showing roads, physical features, and rainfall distribution.

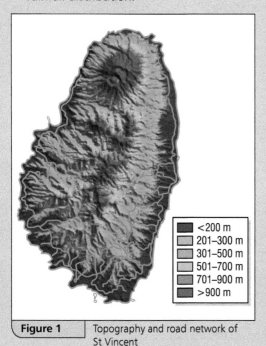

| **Figure 1** | Topography and road network of St Vincent |

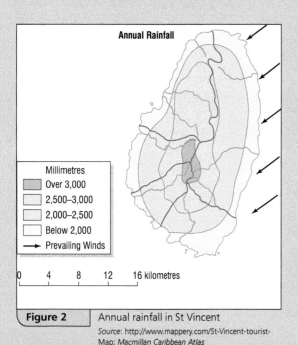

| **Figure 2** | Annual rainfall in St Vincent |

Source: http://www.mappery.com/St-Vincent-tourist-Map; Macmillan Caribbean Atlas

i Describe the pattern of the roadways on the island. (2)

ii State two reasons why fewer persons would live in the interior of the island. (2)

b Define the following terms:

   i population density

   ii population distribution. (4)

c Describe how one historical factor has influenced population distribution in a named country. (3)

d Compare the population growth in the Caribbean with either of Australia, China or Nigeria using the headings:

   i birth rate

   ii life expectancy

   iii government policies. (9)

2 a Study the population pyramid for Haiti (Figure 3) and answer the following questions:

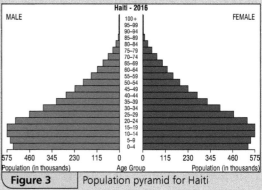

| **Figure 3** | Population pyramid for Haiti |

Source: US Census Bureau, 2016

i Did Haiti have a high birth rate in 2016? Justify your answer. (2)

ii What evidence on the population pyramid indicates a reduction in the rate of natural increase? (2)

b For the growth of urban population in a Caribbean country that you have studied,

   i explain two causes of the population growth (4)

   ii explain two benefits of the population growth. (4)

c   For a Caribbean country that you have studied,

   i   explain two reasons for immigration   *(4)*

   ii   explain two consequences of emigration.   *(4)*

3 a   Draw a graph or a chart using the information provided in Figure 4.   *(4)*

	Percentage contribution to GDP
Sector	**Year: 2015**
Agriculture	6.2
Industry	14.3
Services	79.5

Figure 4   Importance of each economic sector in Grenada in 2015

Source: The CIA World Factbook 2016 and other sources

b   Define the term 'primary economic activities'.   *(2)*

c   Define the term 'secondary economic activities'.   *(2)*

d   Describe two characteristics of tertiary economic activities.   *(4)*

e   Explain how each of the following factors has influenced the location of fishing or natural gas or food processing within CARICOM and Singapore:

   i   energy

   ii   capital

   iii markets

   iv   the role of government.   *(8)*

4 a   Draw a sketch map of a Caribbean country and indicate two areas where tourism is the major economic activity.   *(5)*

b   Explain why tourism facilities have developed at the two sites shown in the map in the named country above.   *(5)*

c   What are two benefits of tourism in the Caribbean?   *(2)*

d   What are two problems caused by tourism in the Caribbean?   *(2)*

e   Explain three ways in which ecotourism may cause environmental degradation.   *(6)*

5 a   Define the term 'subsistence farming'.   *(2)*

b   Describe how the following factors have influenced the development of agriculture in the Caribbean:

   i   historical

   ii   physical

   iii human.   *(9)*

c   For a country that you have studied,

   i   draw a sketch map and locate areas of large-scale and small-scale commercial farming.   *(5)*

   ii   compare the characteristics of large-scale and small-scale commercial farming that is practised in the country drawn in **(c) (i)** above under the headings:

      a   farm size

      b   Downership

      c   markets.   *(9)*

6 a   Draw a sketch map of a Caribbean territory and insert the major sugar cane growing areas.   *(4)*

b   Describe changes in sugar cane farming practices in Guyana in the last 20 years under the headings:

   i   government policy

   ii   value-added products

   iii new markets.   *(6)*

7 a   Describe two ways in which tourism in the Caribbean has caused…

   i   positive environmental development

   ii   negative environmental effects.   *(4)*

b   Explain two measures that can be taken to ensure sustainable management of tourism resources at each of the following levels:

   i   regional

   ii   national

   iii personal.   *(6)*

Index

Index

Index